D1226691

ENCOUNTER:

*Group
Sensitivity
Training
Experience*

ENCOUNTER:
Group
Sensitivity
Training
Experience

Carl Goldberg, Ph.D.

SCIENCE HOUSE, INC.
NEW YORK

For my wife, Merle

Acknowledgments

My understanding of groups in depth, as the reader might suspect, has profited from the seminal ideas of other social scientists. I attempt to trace my intellectual indebtedness to these original thinkers in Chapter 6.

Of more personal importance to me are those whose encouragement and counsel helped nurture my development as a social scientist. I wish to express my deepest appreciation to Alfred F. Glixman, now of Menninger Foundation, and Muzafer Sherif, now of Pennsylvania State University, for their exemplary role-models as rigorous, provocative, and resourceful social scientists, in addition to their personal kindness.

My wife, Merle Cantor Goldberg, who conducted many sensitivity training groups with me, gently prodded my ideas, while firmly curbing their extravagances. Her sensitivity and insight into group process have blended with my own thinking, and our separate contributions to the study of groups are no longer distinguishable. Notwithstanding, I, alone, take responsibility for the articulation of the theory and practice of group sensitivity training as described in this book.

Finally, I wish to express my indebtedness to the many participants from all walks of life who were members of training groups I conducted or who comprised groups in which I participated as a group member. Without the opportunity to work with and participate in these groups, this book would not have been written.

Table of Contents

Present Behavior . . . The Summary Period . . . The Self-actualizing Aim . . . Process Compared with Therapy Group Training . . . Confronting Frustration . . . Using Psychodrama . . . Changing Roles . . . Group Behavior and the Outside World . . . The Consultant's Technique . . . Warmup Exercises . . . Shortcomings of Process Group Training . . . Application Groups

Preface

The current profusion of group sensitivity training experiences is, as yet, too recent, too complex, and too controversial to investigate conveniently under controlled, experimental conditions. There are few, if any, adequate studies of what happens in sensitivity groups. As no one knows exactly what the results of sensitivity training are, it is impossible to make a rigorous evaluation of the field at this time.

My original intention in writing this book was a personal one—by putting my ideas down on paper, I hoped to systematize and make more cognizant my own thinking about the groups with which I work. Several years ago, as a research psychologist, I was involved in training residential child-care workers in group work. The methods employed were thought, at the time, to be the best available. The results of these group training methods, despite their theoretical justification, proved rather unsatisfactory. More recently, group sensitivity training, as I have come to understand it and employ it in training and supervising mental health workers and other professionals, has proven a unique vehicle for combining group therapy techniques—where direct group therapy treatment is ethically unfeasible—with the promise of a self-ameliorative approach that transcends the procrastinating endeavors of historically oriented treatment. Without the fetters of a genetic bias, sensitivity training focuses on group members' future-oriented strivings as enacted in their interpersonal encounters in the here-and-now. I have employed theoretical and experiential material to convey what it is consultants do in sensitivity training groups and their reasons for doing so.

My second reason was that a book that canvasses the entire field of group training, or at least attempts to do so, is currently needed. Most of the information presently available has been written by those of the T-group persuasion—primarily associates of the National Training Laboratory in Washington, D.C. A second large source of information germinates from the sensation-sensual variety of group training—the widely publicized Esalen type of experience. Thus laymen, and even many professionals, who speak of sensitivity training are usually referring either to the T-group or the Esalen variety. But it is important to realize that the T-group and Esalen approaches are not the only group training experiences available, nor are they necessarily the final word in group training.

If comprehensive studies of group process were available, I would have been content merely to formulate my own notions about the study of groups. However, seminal work, such as that of Bion (1961), Rice (1965), Ezriel (1950, 1952), and Whitaker and Lieberman (1964), is primarily concerned with group therapy or is correspondingly highly selective in its subject material. As a result, most of the substantial sources for the in-depth investigation of groups are concerned with group therapy rather than group training. An in-depth study of new approaches to group training is unavailable at the present time. There is need for an integrated text that makes a serious attempt to evaluate the various sensitivity training approaches. Also of service would be a comprehensive cross section of readings on the different approaches to group training. In the interim, I have attempted to lay bare the social and personal conditions that have created the need for group training and to explain the ways in which group training seeks to correct these conditions. This book is addressed to those who wish to consider the merits and limitations of sensitivity training.

Throughout the book attention is directed to the rationale or theoretical underpinnings of this method. As a consequence, I have attempted to trace the theoretical foundations of my thinking as a consultant. I have also included a chapter on the origins of group sensitivity training. It seems to me impossible to overstress the importance of a well defined theory of group process. Unfortunately, many consultants who work with sensitivity training groups avoid adherence to an explicit and coherent psychological theory, considering it unimportant at best, misleading and stultifying at worse. To be sure, rigid adherence to a single theory has dangers, especially in an area where little has been put to empirical verification and not much more has been agreed upon by the "authorities" in the field. It has been pointed out that while "those without much theory have a harder time organizing and comprehending what they see, those with a more systematic theory have a harder time noticing and interpreting important events that are not taken into account by the concepts of their theory" (Lippitt, 1958). My own approach to groups is, I think, 13 theoretically specifiable, but it is rather eclectic in nature, in order to deal with a diverse field of complex data. It is theoretically specifiable because advocates of psychological theory make a cogent point that cannot be readily dismissed: We must know what we are looking for before we find it. Theory must, therefore, precede group process methods. Without theory, our methods can be successful only fortuitously. With partially successful methods, we get at best partially successful results.

At first glance, the situation that confronts the sensitivity training consultant resembles the world of the infant as William James describes it: a big, buzzing, booming confusion. The participants interact, speak on innumerable, diverse topics, appear angry, insulted, flattered, and elated for no apparent reason—thus providing the consultant with a welter of raw data which must be explained and made meaningful. The consultant must then seek to create, improvise, or discover some meaningful pattern from the profusion of perceptual-cognitive and kinesthetic-affective sensations with which he, as a group observer, is impressed. In short, the consultant must make some interpretive sense of what is transpiring in the group of which he is a participant-observer.

Although the validity of this point of view should be obvious to those in the group training field, it often is not. It must be emphasized again that theory is essential and inescapable in any ameliorative endeavor. At best, a consultant working with groups without a sound and well defined theory is operating by means of a pragmatic hodgepodge; he is only concerned with whatever "works" in one situation and is unable to apply successful methods from one event or group session to another. Lacking a frame of reference to contain and study patterns of behavior, he can neither accurately generalize about human

14

behavior nor effectively generate productive research. If a group training method does not have a clear and well defined theory, its aim and the rationale that justifies its employment are very likely to become obscured and equivocal.

In summary, these statements indicate the need for conscious employment of psychological theory in conducting groups. Theory in any field of endeavor is nothing more than a systematic explanation of events useful to the purpose the observer or practitioner has in mind. Once a theory is formulated, it enables the observer or practitioner to collect useful information progressively and precisely. Having a theory, he understands the meaning of the data he is collecting. The consultant or practitioner can then apply this information to new situations whenever appropriate, discarding both information that is irrelevant to the purpose he has in mind and those parts of his theory that are demonstrated to be inaccurate.

Having expressed the need for theory, my own theoretical bias in studying sensitivity training groups should be discussed. My conceptual framework centers on Bion's postulate concerning the existence of a *group mentality*. Bion defines a group mentality as the "unanimous expression of the will of the group, an expression of will to which individuals contribute anonymously" (Bion, 1961). The group mentality is opposed to the manifest and avowed aims of the group members. It is the unconscious, subtly expressed nature of this mentality that makes the in-depth investigation of groups elusive and complex.

Frankly, however, to speak of a group mentality goes against the grain of my empirically imbued training as a psychologist and scientist. My training was with psychologists who took a hard-nosed, experimental attitude to the study of groups. In their minds, the stimulus impetus for the behavior of 15 persons in groups was to be specified in terms of normative learning within a circumscribed culture, and to a lesser extent by physiological drives. To explain social behavior in terms of motives shared by all men, regardless of their social history, was heresy, particularly if these motives were attributed to unconscious processes and therefore incapable of being experimentally demonstrated. As a student, I had the feeling that the hard-nosed, empirical, conceptual frameworks provided by my esteemed professors were valuable for research exploration and the delineation and manipulation of social situations on a broad systems level, but that these frameworks lacked much in the way of insight about the "real" world—the world as it is experienced (phenomenologically) by people. These scientific formulations seemed to have little relevance to the highly charged, dynamic experience of people in stress and conflict.

This attitude agrees with the humanistic position that social scientific formulations about human behavior often tend to *conceal* rather than reveal what is experientially going on in a person. If this is the case, then such formulations are not very efficacious models for understanding people in distress and do not lead to insights in inducing therapeutic modification. In the development of a science, particularly of a science concerned with amelioration, there is a need for a strategy of discovery, as well as a strategy for precision experimentation. As each individual must constantly risk giving up habitual and stultifying behavior in his own self-exploration, so the clinician or the group training consultant cannot afford to suppress intuitions and ideas that he feels are productive merely because his insights are speculative and not yet empirically confirmed.

What Foulkes and Anthony have said about the sensitivity of the group therapist speaks as loudly to the group training consultant: Too much science will deplete group therapy; too little will relegate it to the status of faith-healing. The consultant "must steer an uneasy course between the two, trusting to his scientific training and experience to keep him off the rocks" (Foulkes and Anthony, 1957). Hopefully, the consultant will couch his terms—if not in his statements to the group members, at least in his communication with colleagues and in his own thinking about his work—in such a way that they can be put to empirical test. It is not, however, necessary for each consultant to be an experimentalist. The practitioner need only concern himself with the validity of his method insofar as it ensures the soundness of his ameliorative work. This is his professional responsibility; beyond this there is avocation.

The purpose of this book is not to establish beyond a reasonable doubt additional general laws and principles concerning groups in depth, but to indicate how insight accrued from my own work with sensitivity training groups may begin to pull together and make meaningful the highly fragmented knowledge already available about groups and human behavior.

We are the hollow men
We are the stuffed men
Leaning together
Headpiece filled with straw. Alas!
Our dried voices, when
We whisper together
Are quiet and meaningless
As wind in dry grass
Or rats' feet over broken glass
In our dry cellar.

Shape without form, shade without colour,
Paralysed force, gesture without motion;

Those who have crossed
With direct eyes, to death's other Kingdom
Remember us—if at all—not as lost
Violent souls, but only
As the hollow men
The stuffed men.

—T. S. Eliot, *The Hollow Men* (1925)

Why Group Sensitivity Training?　1

We are the hollow men
We are the stuffed men . . .
Shape without form, shade without colour,
Paralysed force, gesture without motion;

Eliot points to the central tragedy of our times: the individual's lack of an internalized identity and his want of a sense of inner direction in a world where man's technological and intellectual brilliance has been developed to the extent that famine, disease, impediment to interstellar travel, and all other environmental impositions could be virtually obsolete if man would devote his full emotional energies to the resolution of these problems.

Man has been cast adrift from the traditional anchoring institutions of his social system. In the past, venerable ethical, social, and occupational concepts and beliefs engendered by institutions served to define the role and function of each societal member. 21

A sense of identity and value as a member of society was gained by the individual who was able to internalize these societal concepts. However, the foundations of these institutions have long been eroding. The stability of public and private life, certainly as seen in America prior to World War I, no longer exists. In less than half a century there have been at least four catastrophic wars—including, ironically, a war to end all wars and a war to make the world safe for democracy.

The individual can no longer ask public leaders and professional experts to define his place with other men in society. He must find his own place in an ever-changing world.

Societal Guidelines To an increasingly precipitous extent, "individuals today have called into question the whole process by which men are mobilized and used in our society for purposes and in ways that deny their essential humanity. War, even limited war, is such a denial, and therefore, a contradiction of all the goals involved to justify it" (Casteel, 1968). In light of this realization, traditional societal institutions seem to be in a state of collapse, no longer able to absorb the emotional and intellectual energies of the denizen. Public and private commitments are no longer absolutely binding as they were within the more ordered and less questioned societal institutions. Morality is now regarded as situational, tentative, undetermined, and open to revision. Individuals are expected to question for themselves the meaning of life: Who am I? How did I get this way? Where shall I go? The attempts at solutions to these questions are disturbing, both to those who have attempted to answer them situationally and to those who have attempted to maintain traditional solutions despite the collapse of societal guidelines.

The more an individual must rely upon his inner resources for solving personal difficulties, the less time, experience, and energy will be available to develop skills in anticipating and relating to common needs and desires of other persons in his interpersonal encounters (Fried, 1964). Under conditions where the individual lacks social skills, interpersonal accommodation (or the matching of his personal needs and the resources that satisfy these needs) becomes rather difficult to induce. This situation results in what Marc Fried has referred to as *social deprivation*. Social deprivation may range from highly intelligible material and economic commodities to more elusive psychological reinforcements and interpersonal gratifications. "The deprivation may begin in the family in the form of inadequate status-roles; they may be compounded by living experiences as the individual grows and develops" (Fried, 1964). Under conditions of social deprivation the ever-present situational crisis is compounded by inadequate internal or psychodynamic resources, and behavioral pathology results.

Social deprivation also evokes a ravenous craving for social contact, a hunger that may be experienced as unappeasable. Consider the current American scene: We have become such an other-directed society that we cannot lose weight alone; we must report our progress or our impasse to a group of other fatties on a regular basis, in order to shame ourselves into doing what we insist is for our best interest. Alcoholics Anonymous, with little or no professional help, has been able to do by employment of shame, self-confession, and fear, activated and nurtured by a

Social Deprivation

23

group of similarly wretched souls, what psychoanalysis and other traditional methods of psychotherapy have failed miserably to do—wean the alcoholic from his imbibing. Blum and Blum (1967) report more alcoholics helped by Alcoholics Anonymous than any other type of treatment, including intensive psychotherapy. Impressive results have been reported by Synanon, Neurotics Anonymous, Divorcees Anonymous, and similar self-help groups.

This is not entirely surprising. Large, impersonal institutions have lowered the individual to the status of a perforated punch card. To keep records on a massive human society, there is need to reduce all that constitutes a man to the few salient elementary characteristics he shares with all other men. Unfortunately, because of the preponderance of adverse interpersonal experience (which results in a lack of exchanged information on how others think and feel, to say nothing of our need to get on with the business of living), we have begun to believe that the coded information on punch cards is all there is to a man. We strip him of his uniqueness and wholeness and by so doing dehumanize him (Casteel, 1964). The individual feels like a fleeting shadow amid the pale cast by giant machines. "Automation has become the symbol of the disenfranchisement of men from the world of meaningful work, and a sign pointing toward the possible enslavement of human beings to a self-determined technological process which threatens to take over every aspect of our existence, from the production of goods to the manipulation of genetic inheritance" (Casteel, 1964).

Now that the machinery has been activated, the individual questions if he, as the frail, labile, vulnerable being he takes himself to be, is necessary. One person described his experience as follows: "I was at the

New York University looking around one morning, and the sheer hopelessness of breaking through to any of those front office people really struck me. It just seemed so useless and pointless, being referred from one building to another by people too bored by the routine of their work to help out. Around registration time, when 44,000 students come back to school, nobody pays any attention to one's personal grievances" (Eisenhower, 1969).

The result is mass alienation, which has brought into bold relief, as perhaps in no other age of human history, the central human quest: a search for interpersonal encounters. Perhaps "the most pressing existential crisis of our age," writes the humanistic psychotherapist G. V. Haigh (1967), "is the pervasive sense of aloneness, which so many of us feel so much of the time."

Self-help groups have attempted to help the hollow, stuffed individual buttress himself against the devastation of alienation and social deprivation through small groups of peers who share, support, and reinforce the individual's own strivings, ambition, and quest for a viable and acceptable sense of identity. Unfortunately, these self-help groups are for the most part repressive, inspirational approaches to human misery. Because they are unable or unwilling to probe the deeper underlying recess of the individual's precipitation, they have not been able to quiet his perturbance.

The individual's inability to develop the self-reliance and autonomy he expects of himself has resulted in feelings of denigration, frustration, and anguish. He feels that he is ailing, possessed by a

Inter-Personal Encounter

25

sickness neither physical nor psychiatric, but a malaise of spirit; a sickness of alienation no less epidemic and socially contagious than one of organic etiology.

The Desire For Help

From the earliest awakenings of consciousness, men have tried to analyze and work out their own problems by themselves. The flourishing business psychotherapy currently enjoys is no small testimony to the feelings of people in conflict that they are not as successful as they would like to be in dealing with their own difficulties. In recent years, however, there has been considerable criticism and dissatisfaction directed against traditional forms of psychotherapy. "We have found," said J. L. Moreno (1953), a social theorist and pioneer of psychodrama, "that the analytic and the activistic forms of group psychotherapy are not applicable to the deepest disturbances of the individual and the group. They are applicable to social problems . . . in a setting in which the group is artificially cut off from the community during the treatment as if the rest of the community were nonexistent and as if the influence coming from it could be disregarded."

Individual psychotherapy, particularly of the more psychoanalytic methods, is seen as artificial because it it has very little semblance to the patient's life experiences in his everyday world. Never before or ever again can a patient expect to be enveloped in a fully accepting, tolerant, and perpetually analytic vacuum where he need not make decisions or censor his intrapsychic ruminations. Individual therapy, many people feel, takes too long, is too slow for what currently ails them, and is often unexciting. In traditional psychotherapy, many patients feel that there is

26 | not enough give-and-take between patient and

therapist to stimulate the patient out of his characterological rut.

Group psychotherapy, on the other hand, induces
interaction among the patients, making it more
difficult to avoid getting involved (Wolf and Schwartz,
1962). Group therapy for hollow, stuffed people is
more palatable, but nevertheless not fully acceptable,
because it is contained within a sickness model. As
such, it is too often concerned with reconstructing
and working through past situations, so that the
pursuit of new growth and self-actualization, that is,
attention to the healthier parts of the personality, is
neglected.

That criticisms of psychotherapy are heavily stereotyped and, consequently, frequently inaccurate is
somewhat beside the point. These perceptions of
traditional psychotherapy have persuaded a considerable number of people, dissatisfied with their
current modes of functioning, to seek other forms of
care and attention.

Therapy Seen As Learning

At the same time, the concept of education has always
had a positive flavor in American life. We believe we
can solve our problems. It is impressed on us from
our earliest youth that knowledge is power. If one
studies diligently or works arduously enough, one
can avoid difficulties whether they be physical, social,
or emotional. The essence of the American dream is
that despite one's humble beginnings, by work and
effort, particularly through the medium of education
and by assuming responsibility, one can rise to any
heights he desires.

Thus, each of us cherishes, however dimly, a longing
for the promise of youth—the exalted heights of
personal attainment, which we hope to realize

without feeling we are dependent upon others. Group sensitivity training experience, being cast more in an educational framework than in a treatment model, has made the experience more palatable to the person anxious to emphasize that his problems are not such that he needs others to care for him. Indeed, he attempts to verify this contention by gravitating toward groups, who by their educational orientation convey a self-reliant, active, and "healthy" pursuit of self-improvement. The enthusiasm and popularity of the new forms of group experience seem to be an attempt to implement the promise of our unfulfilled youth.

Society's Need

The present methods of group training have grown out of dissatisfaction with prevailing methods of dealing with personal and interpersonal tensions and conflicts. The fervor and enthusiasm for these new kinds of group experience parallel the quest by other types of social reform, known as *social movements,* for alleviation of intolerable social conditions. Group sensitivity training, like other social movements, has its "inception in a condition of unrest, and derives [its] motive power on the one hand from dissatisfaction with the current form of life, and on the other hand, from wishes and hopes for a new scheme or system of living" (Blumer, 1951). Accordingly, group training is perceived as a consequence of social ferment attributed to the failure of the existing social order to meet adequately the needs and desires of a segment of the population (Elridge, 1950).

The effect that sensitivity training as a social movement has on our alienated, hollow man in relation to his customary stance in the traditional societal

28

institutions deserves some comment. We need to ask ourselves why a particular social movement comes to be regarded as a solution by a very large number of malcontent people (Cantril, 1963). The existing societal institutions offer opportunities for success to the individual in terms of self-advancement. This requires the individual to be introspective and to scrutinize his own personal resources. This process concomitantly evokes considerable self-consciousness about aspects of his self which he would prefer to ignore. A social movement, on the other hand, "particularly in its active, revolutionary phase [the period in which group sensitivity training is currently], appeals not to those intent on bolstering and advancing a cherished self, but to those who crave to be rid of an unwanted self" (Hoffer, 1951). The old order has failed to define the individual's identity in such a manner as to match his ego-ideal, the self he wishes to be, and has instead accentuated a self he wishes to negate and forget. He seizes upon sensitivity training, without fully realizing why, as a means to resist the demands of the old order.

An 2
Overview

A sensitivity training group is composed of six to fifteen people, who meet together for the expressed purpose of self-exploration and personal growth (eight to twelve participants are usually preferable). The task of these dynamic groups—whether they are called sensitivity groups, T-groups, Encounter, basic encounter, self-analytic, human relations, study, or interpersonal groups—is *to study behavior in the immediate group situation,* commonly referred to as the here-and-now. Every group member has the opportunity to observe his own and the other participants' behavior, the implementation of diverse personal and interpersonal strategies, sentiments, and attitudes in relating to others, and the effects these interchanges have on the task of the group. Each participant can potentially gain a greater appreciation of himself from the feedback of other group members with regard to how he performs within the group. In most sensitivity approaches, emphasis is on how participants 31 *function as group members* rather than on personality problems or speculation about childhood traumas. This is a controversial issue, however, as there is much disagreement among the philosophies of the diverse forms of sensitivity groups as to group objectives. In the Encounter, basic encounter, self-analytic, and T-groups the objective of the professional person in the group is often to influence therapeutic changes in the individual group members rather than for the group to concern itself with group functioning.

**A
Situation
without
Structure**

Generally, a sensitivity group has no pre-set agenda or formalized structure. It is an unstructured, leaderless situation in the sense that none of the usual parliamentary work procedures contained automatically in task groups in western society are present in the training group. The participants are generally not told what should be discussed by the group beyond some initial instructions to the effect that "we are here to study how we function as a group." "Since the group has no topic nor any formal way for finding an 'appropriate' one, it has to 'move' to find out where it wants to go before it can get where it wants to be" (Blake, 1957).

The absence of an agenda and rules for procedure is intended to mitigate the stereotyped roles and role relationships that frequently serve as defenses against recognizing underlying group processes. When habitual, stereotyped roles from the everyday world are stripped away, the feelings and interaction of group members become the focus of the group's attention. "The process of achieving personal growth begins with the exploration of feelings within the group and proceeds to wherever the group members take it. A strong effort is made to create an atmosphere

32

of openness and honesty in communicating with each other" (Schutz, 1967).

The person who participates in group training may be anyone from Maine to California; anyone from the scholarly university president with his numerous degrees to the youthful, inquisitive college freshman or the dissident, rebellious student hippie; from the energetic captain of industry to the shy, reticent housewife. Participants who have come to community groups I have conducted have been college students and recent graduates, professors and teachers, businessmen, government workers, high echelon officials, scientists from the physical and social sciences, female lawyers and engineers, hippies and mod-dressed artists, newspaper reporters, and housewives with children. The American scene appears caught up with the idea and promise of group experience.

Perhaps the most significant development in American education in recent years has been the shift of emphasis from the individual student to the small group as the focus of educational experience. No longer is the situation of the educator-expert preaching *ex cathedra* considered the most effective method of education (Powell, 1949). Reconsideration of our understanding of human communication and social interaction, particularly as popularized by Marshall McLuhan, presents a new perspective on the overall process of education. McLuhan has contended that until recently society has been confined by the "linear" sequence of the printed page. Casteel (1964) states: "The consequence of this linear style has been to give dominance to the rational, logical ordering of concepts and to put a premium upon the detached, noninvolved

Group Training Philosophy

attitude of a reader and upon the basic ways of carrying on interpersonal relationships—electronic communication, especially as instrumented through television, is changing all of that. Encounters become instantaneous, inclusive, and involving of the whole person."

This emphasis, then, relies on a new concept—education as an interpersonal, dynamic experience in which one rethinks and reconsiders the goals and meanings of human ideals and action. No longer are decisions for the priority of our actions left in the hands of professional experts. In view of the current perspective on the learning process, the hallmark of the sensitivity training group is the shared approach to problems and conflicts emanating from the clash and interchange of the different perspectives of group members (Powell, 1949). This does not imply that sensitivity training groups are designed to level personality by submerging the participant's individuality beneath the pressures and demands of the group. Rather, laboratory training in groups helps the participants develop more flexible and realistic strategies on the basis of their discerning assessment of their effectiveness in implementing personal and interpersonal goals in the dynamic interactive situation that confronts them. Realistic goals can be developed only when the participants come to appreciate the effect group norms, values, and process have upon the reception and interchange of group members' sentiments and actions. Simply knowing about human behavior and group process does not automatically enable us to function as well as we would like in the existential everyday world. Learning to apply our knowledge about people to real life requires direct experience (Rice, 1966). Often, we wish that we had time and the release from pressures of immediate decision-making to experiment with new modes of relating to others and to explore our inner potentialities. Group training is designed to provide participants with this opportunity. The group, however, must learn how to function as an integrated unit if it is to employ effectively the resources of its membership to this end.

Group Processes and Dynamics

The concept of *common group tension* is essential for the understanding of what transpires in the group. Common group tension refers to the covert, shared aspects of the group process. The manifest content of the group discussion may, and often does, embrace any conceivable topic, but regardless of the manifest content, there always rapidly develops an underlying group tension or emotion of which the participants are not aware, but which significantly influences their behavior (Ezriel, 1950, 1952).

The Consultant

Each sensitivity group has a consultant (or trainer, as he is called in T-groups). The consultant is the professional person in the group. It is he who organizes or is assigned a group because he, the people who assign him, and/or group members think that he is qualified to take a group. (A perhaps facetious but nevertheless generally factual way of distinguishing the consultant from the participants is that he does not pay to be in the group while the group members generally do.) His task is to help the group understand its behavior as a group. His major task is to point out group tensions and delineate their meaning to the work of the group.

Ideally, the consultant is a person with considerable academic training in the social sciences, who has had and continues to have special training and supervision in the particular group sensitivity training approach he employs as well as training and experience in group therapy. Depending upon his personality and philosophy, the consultant may be silent, supportive, provocative, didactic, or whatever (Schutz, 1967). In line with his particular philosophy of group training and with the role he assumes, the consultant does whatever he thinks is required to maximize the experience by helping the participants understand what is transpiring in the group and how each member influences and is influenced in this process.

Varieties | 3

In one sense there are as many varieties of sensitivity training groups as there are group leaders who conduct sensitivity training. Each group leader, consultant, or trainer has his own notions about human growth and group training. To say this is not only to pose a problem for categorizing sensitivity groups, but also to present a statement of the impossibility of trying to investigate the entire group training movement. Nevertheless, what Corsini has said about the various forms of group therapy holds true for sensitivity training in groups as well. To say that there are as many different forms of group training as there are consultants and trainers who run groups is inaccurate because "it is necessary to distinguish between methods and different styles of conducting similar methods" (Corsini, 1964). If we allow some leeway in the practitioner's conversion of a theory to meet his own personality prerequisites, it becomes possible to classify sensitivity training groups into a number of 37 distinct, although certainly not discreet, categories. People associated with the same institution, influenced by the same mentor or those loyal to a school of thought, may be assumed to hold and operate by similar beliefs and techniques. Institutions, academic or professional, seduce and indoctrinate colleagues in their own persuasions. Another reason for similarity in working with groups is that private and public funds are available to those who operate within a philosophical framework that is in vogue or that has caught the fancy of the public.

Regardless of the precise reasons there do appear to be some similarities among certain training groups as contrasted with others. It is possible to systematize the sensitivity training movement into twelve different groupings: Bion, psychodrama, marathon, Gestalt, Encounter, basic encounter, T-group, Esalen and human potentials, interpersonal skills, discussion, self-analytic, and process group.

The Bion Method

The Bion form of group training is referred to by various names. It is best known by its association with W. R. Bion, an English psychoanalyst who first developed the method during World War II. Bion did much of his work at Tavistock Clinic in England, and the clinic has continued to promote the method, so that the approach is also referred to as the *Tavistock Conference*.

The Conference attempts to provide a setting in which experience can be studied and at least partially understood as it occurs. The emphasis in the conference is upon learning which is felt as an experience and which is translatable into action in work and community settings. Special attention is paid to covert processes which operate in and among groups and to the way in which such processes further or hinder task performance. The function of leadership and attitudes toward authority are emphasized. Phenomena related to the existence or non-existence of "defined boundaries" and control of transactions across them are studied and, when possible, explicated. In these matters, as in all others which are under scrutiny, the conference leadership itself is an object of study. Concentration is upon the functioning of groups as wholes rather than upon individual personality (Tavistock Institute, 1968).

In some of the varieties of group training, the prime objective of the group experience is for the consultant to increase or decrease participants' effect which, hopefully, will enable them to modify their own psychodynamics in some beneficial way. The consultant in the Bion group, on the other hand, is essentially concerned with alerting the participants to the ongoing group process and encouraging them to study and explore the effect the group experience has on them *as members of a social unit*. Mindful of the studious climate of the Bion group, this form of group training has also often been referred to as the *study group* approach. The consultant's interpretation of what he sees happening in the group is not necessarily intended to be a statement of what is happening most importantly at that moment, but a statement of what he is interested in studying at that moment. In a word, the consultant's behavior in the group is intended to generate an atmosphere of study. He is generally interested in investigating the maximum level of anxiety (and the kind of anxiety) that permits learning in a group, as opposed to the amount and type of group tension that retards learning (Shapiro, 1968).

Consistent with its more academic endeavors the study group method has formulated the best developed and most clearly articulated theory of group functioning of any of the group training approaches. This theory is derived from the work of Bion and his successor at Tavistock, A. K. Rice. (Bion's ideas are discussed in some detail in Chapter 6.) When the study group is used as part of a larger conference concerned with group relations, the entire conference is called the *group relations* method.

The various forms of group training do not differ greatly in regard to the wide spectrum of participants who are selected or drawn to a particular kind of group conference or workshop. The participants found in any one type of group training workshop are probably no more homogeneous as a group than are the kinds of people drawn to the whole spectrum of group training approaches. If this is the case, it is reasonable to assume that the kinds of behaviors participants *bring* to the various sensitivity groups are rather similar across the board. However, reports from the different kinds of groups suggest that marked differences in behaviors are evinced by the participants, even where similar sounding techniques are employed by the group leaders. To what then do we attribute these differences in behavior? Perhaps the *modeling* behavior personified by the consultant, that is, the role the consultant takes with a group and more or less directly suggests that participants emulate, is largely accountable for differences in group training "results."

In sharp contrast are the study group and the T-group approaches. The T-group trainer acts "like the best group member should behave (he 'shows off')," states Sam Culbert, the director of training at the National Training Laboratories (NTL). On the other hand, if the study group consultant acts as if he is speaking to any participant individually, he will generate tremendous feelings and power into the relationship (Culbert, 1968). As a result, the consultant speaks only to the participant as a social unit, and not directly as an individual. The individual participant in the Bion group is regarded by the consultant as a *role* within a group structure, rather than in terms of his unique psychodynamics.

Psychodrama

The psychodramatic method of training groups and individuals has a long past. Its roots originate at least as far back as ancient Greece. Its recent and recorded history has been almost entirely dominated by one man. To speak of psychodrama as a training technique is to speak of J. L. Moreno, a part-time psychiatrist and full-time promoter. Psychodrama is not exclusively a method of group training as are some of the other sensitivity group experiences, particularly the Bion approach. Moreno has attempted to utilize his method in a greater number of ways: from individual psychotherapy with one therapist and one patient to situations called *sociodramas*, in which Moreno has tried to induce a nation to resolve its guilt over the assassination of John F. Kennedy and the Soviet Union to repudiate the crimes of Nikita Khrushchev. Perhaps to a greater extent than in any of the other approaches, the leader in psychodrama, who is called a *director*, does precisely what his title implies. He directly guides the participants in enacting their behavior (generally, in front of an audience which is called to participate in the proceedings). The director suggests at various junctures in the psychological representation that the protagonist (the participant with whom the drama is primarily concerned) and other participants "playing" themselves or other significant figures in the protagonist's life reverse roles with one another. He may also ask people from the audience to incorporate themselves in one of the actor's roles so that the community (the audience) and its representatives (the actors) come together to enact a social drama that has *meaning* for the participants *beyond* the specific *situation* initially evoked by the protagonist. The director uses a wide variety of techniques, as varied as guided fantasy and dream analysis, as well as a myriad of psychodramatic situations and various forms of nonverbal exercises. The use of nonverbal techniques is emphasized, for psychodramatists hold that knowledge of body language is an appreciation which modern man has largely ignored. "Because language frequently engenders tensions which reinforce and perpetuate symptoms, the [consultant] must teach a new language, one which more adequately fits the actual sensation and observations of the [participant]" (Luchins, 1967).

It has been pointed out that despite the image of sexual frankness and the liberalized morality of a swinging, uninhibited generation, contemporary speech still conceals its meaning by euphemistic expression—pleasant and safe words for feelings and thoughts that are neither pleasant nor necessarily innocent.

Whether or not one regards psychodrama as having merit as a technique in goal training, it is important to point out that psychodrama has, in part or whole, been incorporated into most of the other group training approaches—T-group, Gestalt group, marathon groups, Encounter groups, and so forth. In the field of group training Evergreen Institute in Colorado, which is operated by Moreno-trained staff, appears at the present time to be the center, independent of Moreno, that utilizes psychodrama on the largest scale as the basis of its training.

In summary, it should be recognized that psychodrama used auspiciously by a well trained professional

is a valuable auxiliary technique for both psychotherapy

and group training. "Psychodrama," states Michael Miller, a psychiatrist who has used the technique for many years, is an "ideal technique for releasing the repressed, pent-up emotions and conflicts of the psycho-neurotic and for liberating him from his inner turmoil and destructive tensions" (Miller, 1968). Unfortunately a large number of people who employ psychodrama are not well trained, if professionally trained at all, and they do much to discredit the technique. Miller warns that employing the method with psychotics offers the least value and holds the greatest hazards. "The powerful emotions and conflicts whipped up in the psychodrama often disturb such patients even more since they were already highly disturbed and aggravated" (Miller, 1968). The danger of a technique often resides in its popularity and uncritical usage among the lay public. In addition to the mental health field, other professions have employed psychodrama in various ways: for example, in the form of theater games as part of training in a professional acting curriculum.

In a few short years, groups referred to as marathons have become popular. Different marathon groups are not so much related to one another by techniques or even by the group leader's theoretical orientation, as they are by the concentrated period of time the participants spend together as a group, isolated from their normal, everyday experiences and activities. Marathons may consist of a single session of twelve or more hours without a rest break in which food is brought in or even disregarded. They may also be run for two, three, or more days, with participants allowed short periods away from the group for sleep and food. The majority of marathon groups are run

The Marathon Group

by experienced group therapists. Groups generally have a clearly stated personal change or growth goal for the participants. Because the time the group spends together is so concentrated, marathons are viewed as an opportunity for intensive emotional experience in a group setting. Leon Lurie of Washington, D.C., one of the more innovative therapists, employs marathon groups to commence his therapy groups because in one marathon, a group can reach a point of interrelationship that might otherwise take six months to achieve (Lurie, 1968).

In that the goal of the marathon is personal change rather than group training, there is some question whether marathons are actually a form of sensitivity training or a more concentrated form of group therapy. It is possible that they may be either or both. The orientations of the leaders are diverse enough to defy clear description.

The Gestalt Group

Like the marathon group, the Gestalt group is most concerned with finding ways and means for creating changes in individuals in a group setting. Similar to Moreno, the Gestalt group's founder, Fritz Perls, is a part-time therapist and full-time promoter. More than any of the other sensitivity training methods, the Gestalt approach is to disregard the group as an entity and to concentrate on each individual in the group in rotation. The leader devotes full attention to each participant alone, using a host of exploratory techniques which are aimed at getting quickly at the participant's feelings and fantasies. The goal is to help the participant develop a new life style. Perls places little value on interpretation—explanations of why the participant acts as he does. Instead he offers descriptions of the individual's emerging gestalts—the individual's awareness of how he organizes his perceptions, thoughts, and emotions. Perls claims that "confrontation through description permits increased self-awareness and opportunity to modify behaviors—through personal experimentation" (Fine, 1969).

There is more divergence of group training orientation among Encounter groups than perhaps any other of the new group experiences. Nevertheless, all those who conduct Encounter groups seem agreed on one matter: Therapy and personal change are more important than the study of group process or anything else that smacks of theory rather than deeply felt experience.

The difference between marathon and Encounter groups may be minimal. If any distinction clearly emerges, it is that marathons are always run for a concentrated and protracted duration, whereas Encounter groups may be time-concentrated experiences but frequently are not. Marathons meet for a single period of time and then cease to be, or, at least, cease to be marathon groups. Like Lurie's group, they may function thereafter as therapy groups, meeting regularly with no stated termination. Encounter groups frequently meet on a regular basis, e.g., weekly. The group as an entity is not expected to make a transition into a therapy group; but many of the leaders who conduct Encounter groups view them as extensions or introductions to individual and group psychotherapy, rather than as substitute or unrelated experiences. Lawrence Tirnauer, a psychologist in the Washington, D.C., area, seems to express the view of many such

The Encounter Group

Encounter leaders in regarding Encounter groups as having value in the following ways: 1. Getting new people from the general population into therapy via Encounter experience; 2. Continuing the intense emotional experience stimulated in the participant's previous personal or group therapy; 3. Providing continual growth for professional psychotherapists.

For people with considerable therapy experience Tirnauer suggests "leaderless" Encounter groups, frequently theme-centered. Recently, he offered the following workshops:

> *The Challenge of Change, Danger and Fulfillment.* Participants will explore in the immediate and intimate setting of an interactional workshop the personal meaning of change for them. Change may involve leaving the comfortable, giving up the familiar, risking rejection. Some challenges to change come from within, others come from other people or events.

Offered for psychotherapists and other interested people, such as social workers, educators, clergy, counselors, etc.:

> *Directions: Old and New.* Life at its fullest consists of finding new direction, new experience, new ways of relating to others and of being with oneself. It also consists of rediscovering old capacities that may not have been sufficiently valued in the past. The workshop will focus on the direction that may be emerging for each of us.

> *The Tides of Marriage.* In this encounter workshop participants will face such marital issues as freedom vs. discipline, intensity vs. indifference, marital impasse, the quality of commitment, and others.

These theme-centered workshops are designed especially for the professional psychotherapist and others in closely related "helping" fields because, in

Tirnauer's words, "the psychotherapist's personal growth and increased understanding is the *sine qua non* of his being professionally useful to others." Other interested individuals "for whom increased freedom to understand and relate to others is part of their work, or who simply want to increase their capacity to live life more fully and with more satisfaction [who would this exclude?] are welcome" (Tirnauer, 1968).

According to Tirnauer, the interaction centers about what is going on in the group rather than on any particular technique. Techniques are useful nevertheless to stimulate impasse. Tirnauer believes that prior personal therapy experience of a participant enables him to tolerate anxiety that is induced by getting involved with others. The locus of behavior change need not take place in the group, according to this advocate of the Encounter group. Hopefully in the thralls of group experience new behavioral alternatives to areas in which the participants feel "uptight" and "hung-up" come into awareness. The specifics of these new behaviors are to be worked out in the situations outside the session in which the participant has been experiencing difficulties. Advocates of Encounter groups contend that groups such as theirs, which are short-lived but intense, are the most effective modality for personal change. People who come together without expecting to see one another again are often more open and self-disclosing to one another.

Encounter groups have expanded from the professional offices downtown and from their seashore and mountain resort hideaways into the suburbs (apparently to give the "uptight" establishment a chance to unwind on its home ground). Aureon Institute, a center within the human potentials movement with offices in Manhattan, now is located in Tarrytown, New York, where it holds frequent Encounter groups.

The Basic Encounter Group

Carl Rogers refers to the sensitivity training approach he employs on the west coast as a "Basic Encounter Group." It is difficult to distinguish it from Encounter groups. Nevertheless, it may be useful to regard it separately from the Encounter group, because Rogers' philosophy in working with people comes from many years as a nondirective therapist in a one-to-one relationship with clients, and is somewhat different from the training in depth-reconstruction therapy the leaders of many of the Encounter groups have had. Rogers reports that his group is addressed to those of us who live in "a precarious balance. We have learned to get along with ourselves and our world in some way, and the possibility that this balance might be upset is always a frightening one. Almost invariably in groups, every person finds the balance is disturbed, or possibly upset, but finds that in a climate of trust he is enormously supported in being *more* himself" (Hall, 1967).

For this individual and group potential to be activated "a proper psychological climate" needs to be created. Rogers believes that if the therapist, as a role-model, can come through to each of the members of the group with whom he is intensively involved "as a person who cares about him and understands what he is struggling to express, he [the participant] gradually will begin to choose healthier directions for himself. Instead of focusing on the diagnostic or causative elements of behavior . . . [the group leader is] more concerned with the dynamics of interaction. Not about how a person became what he is, but about how does

48

he change from what he is" (Hall, 1967). Rogers has stressed that a major impediment to satisfactory interpersonal communication is the tendency to judge, evaluate, approve of, or reject another person on the basis of the manifest content of his statements. He feels that we need instead to tune into the other's feelings by accepting his frame of reference and sharing his experiences with him.

In an intensive group with much freedom and little structure, the individual will gradually feel safe enough to drop some of his defense and façades; he will relate more directly on a feeling basis [come into a basic encounter] with the other members of the group; he will understand himself and his relationship to others more accurately; he will change in his personal attitudes and behaviors; and he will subsequently relate more effectively to others in his everyday life situation (Rogers, 1967).

It is not clear from Rogers' description what techniques he employs to create the permissive atmosphere that results in personal change. It is evident, however, that Rogers' concern is not with the group as a phenomenon, and his approach, as much as it is legitimate therapeutically, has minimal value for group training. He offers nothing in regard to sensitivity training that is not already contained in his treatises on individual psychotherapy relationships.

The T-group is the best known of the sensitivity training movements. It has the longest history of any of the existing approaches to group training technique, dating back at least to the first Human Relations Conference at Bethel, Maine (1946). To their credit the T-group advocates have been most diligent in

The T-Group

reviewing their work and attempting to verify experimentally their methods and subsequently to revise them. This endeavor has been largely spawned by the Institute of Applied Behavioral Research, formerly known as the National Training Laboratories. Unfortunately, the research that the T-group school has generated has been pockmarked by inordinately poor research designs and confounding and contaminatory factors induced by bias.

The T-group may stand for a single sensitivity training group experience of at least ten hours, or it may be part of a larger laboratory conference consisting of techniques such as role-playing, case studies, theory presentation, and intergroup exercises, running forty hours or more. The T-group approach may vary from a solid block of time such as a marathon, to two to six hours a session over an extended period of time. The T-group approach therefore refers to a number of different groups including those oriented more toward organizational dynamics. "In addition to having the characteristics described for the Encounter group, the T-group often includes attempts to understand the dynamics of group norms, roles, communication distortion, and the effects of authority on a number of behavior patterns, personality and coping mechanisms" (Schutz, 1967).

Basically, it is a group experience designed to provide maximum possible opportunity for the individuals to expose their behavior, give and receive feedback, experiment with new behaviors, and develop every lasting awareness and acceptance of self and others. The T-group also provides such possibilities to learn the nature of effective group functioning. Individuals are able to learn how to develop a group that achieves specific goals with minimal possible human cost. The T-group becomes a learning experience that most closely approximates the values of the laboratory regarding the use of leadership, rewards, penalties, and information in the development of effective groups. It is in the T-group that one finds the emphasis on the participants creating and diagnosing their own behavior, developing distributive-making norms to protect the deviants, and finally, showing as much as possible all the information that is created within and as a result of, the T-group experience (Argyris, 1962).

In the T-group there is stress on learning concepts and specific techniques for a number of interpersonal conflict situations. Frequently, these situations are simulated by techniques such as role-playing, guided group fantasies, and so forth to insure that these situations and strategies for their resolution are experienced by the participants. The trainer takes considerable responsibility for the success or failure of the learning experience. As a result, he usually takes it upon himself to start the group.

The NTL Institute gives an example of how a trainer, their term for the staff member in a typical T-group, might open the group:

> This group will meet for many hours and will serve as a kind of laboratory where each individual can increase his understanding of the forces which influence individual behavior and the performance of groups and organizations. The data for learning will be our own behavior, feelings, and reactions. We begin with no definite structure or organization, no agreed-upon procedures, and no specific agenda. It will be up to us to fill the vacuum created by the lack of these familiar elements and to study our group as we evolve. My role will be to help the group to learn from its own experience, but not to act as a traditional chairman nor to suggest how we should organize, what our procedures should be,

51

or exactly what our agenda will include. With these few comments, I think we are ready to begin in whatever way you feel will be most helpful (NTL Institute, 1968).

The members of the group then respond to the ambiguous situation. Some may try to get the trainer to explain more, even to tell them what to do. Others may propose to elect a chairman or vote on topics for discussion. Often some individuals withdraw and wait in silence. Whatever behavior is elicited from a member, it is the outcome of his observations and reactions to the behavior and reactions to the behavior of other members, and it is these perceptions and reactions that are the data for learning.

The NTL Institute has listed the following assumptions about the nature of the learning process which distinguish T-group training from more traditional models of learning:

1. Learning responsibility. Each participant is responsible for his own learning. What a person learns depends upon his own style, readiness, and the relationships he develops with other members of the group.

2. Staff role. The staff person's role is to facilitate the examination and understanding of the experiences in the group. He helps participants to focus on the way the group is working, the style of an individual's participation, or the issues that are facing the group.

3. Experience and conceptualization. Most learning is a combination of experience and conceptualization. A major T-group aim is to provide a setting in which individuals are encouraged to examine their experiences together in enough detail so that valid generalizations can be drawn.

4. Authentic relationships and learning. A person is most free to learn when he establishes authentic relationships with other people and thereby increases his sense of self-esteem and

decreases his defensiveness. In authentic relationships persons can be open, honest, and direct with one another so that they are communicating what they are actually feeling rather than masking their feelings.

5. Skill acquisition and values. The development of new skills in working with people is maximized as a person examines the basic values underlying his behavior and obtains feedback on the degree to which his behavior produces the intended impact (NTL Institute, 1968).

In present-day approaches to personal change, there appear to be two widely variant philosophies: the traditional dynamic psychotherapies, such as psychoanalysis, exemplified in the group training movement by the Tavistock group, and the process group (to be discussed later), which insists that emotional disturbance has its root in early developmental relationships. The roots are deep and require considerable probing and continual working through once the precursors of dysfunctional behavior are discovered. The human potentials movement—exemplified by the Esalen approaches, the Gestalt group, and some of the Encounter and T-groups—on the other hand shears the flower from the stem and root and exclaims that short, intensive emotional nourishment, largely through the release of inhibitions, "gets out all the old air and some of these held-in feelings" (Glaser, 1969). It also leads to instant human pleasures and all those promises forgotten from childhood: "You can learn to know an orange, squeeze a rock, and get back in tune with your senses" (Glaser, 1969).

According to Gibb, "The growth potential movement is controversial, seductive, outrageous in aspiration, and exciting in attainment. It is disrespectful

The Esalen and Human Potentials Movement

53

of the protective boundaries among professional disciplines and crafts. It breaks new ground, far outstrips whatever research is available, takes from many diverse fields, and enriches these fields with . . . little concern for paternity of ideas or method" (Gibb, 1969). If the movement could be categorized by any one theoretical system—and its advocates would angrily claim it can't—Schutz's work is perhaps the most well considered and theoretically grounded. Furthermore, Schutz appears to be gaining the status of patron saint of the movement, with Perls as second consul. "Schutz develops the theme that joy, which is the feeling that comes from the fulfillment of one's potential, comes from the development of the body, the person, one's interpersonal relationships, and the effectiveness of one's organization. . . . Schutz uses 'The Impossible Dream' from *Man of La Mancha* as a recurring theme. He does not deal with the disquieting thought, shared by many clinicians, that persistent efforts to reach the unreachable is an invitation to neurosis, rather than a prescription for either fulfillment of potential or attainment of elation or delight" (Gibb, 1969).

The Esalen Institute at Big Sur, California, is named for an Indian tribe that once roamed the area. It is staffed by such diverse sorts as dancers, theologians, businessmen, gurus, weightlifters, and masseurs, in addition to all sorts of academic and practicing psychologists, social workers, and medically trained persons. The techniques employed at Esalen are varied. They range from the intensive Encounter group experiences to sensory mediation, micromediation, touch, smell, and nude bathing—with or without group therapy and massage thrown in. The aims of the techniques are reflected by the titles of the books coming out of Esalens: "Joy," "Sense Relaxation," "Structural Integration," and "Keeping in

Touch with Massage." In filling their bag, they have borrowed from Moreno, Perls, Schutz, Maslow, Don Quixote, Norman O. Brown, Zen Buddhism, Buber, existentialism, and what-have-you. A considerable number of their techniques are nonverbal. At the beginning of 1969 Esalen had inspired at least thirty-seven centers. One institute in Washington, D.C., Orizon, seems to reflect the broad human potentials movement in stating its reason for being:

> Compared with what we ought to be, we are only half awake. Our fires are damped, our drafts are checked. We are making use of only a small part of our possible mental and physical resources . . . [Orizon provides] the opportunity to take a sufficient leave from your daily self. . . . The potentialities for deeper experiencing of life are within each of us (Orizon Institute, 1969).

Orizon asks if you are willing to explore them.

The Inter-Personal Skills Group

The interpersonal skills approach to group training is the approach least concerned with therapeutic experience and most interested in the study of group functioning and dynamics. These groups are frequently instituted as part of an academic course in the study of groups, organizations, or leadership skills. Dr. Jane S. Mouton, of the University of Texas, was one of the first social scientists to employ the approach as a regular part of teaching technique. Students in her classes participated in training groups in order to experience problems of decision-making in groups. Lecture material was correlated to relate to salient events occurring in the group in order to maintain a direct relationship between theory and experience. This consideration is also salient in the process group approach to be discussed in detail presently.

The Discussion Group

The discussion group has been a rising phenomenon in American education in the last few decades. It was originally conceived of as a means of solving deficiencies in the formal education of adults and to keep the citizen up-to-date on current ideas in science, literature, and philosophy. Many high schools, colleges, public libraries, and community service agencies formed "great book" discussion groups. One community college offers the following program:

> Do you want the stimulation and understanding that comes with college study, but not the full responsibility of a credit course? Do you want a knowledge of human endeavor in far-flung fields outside your own speciality? Do you want to meet with new friends who have common interests? . . . A study-discussion course may answer your needs . . . [it brings] together congenial, alert minds in united inquiry . . . (Bulletin of the University of Virginia Extension School [Northern Virginia Center], Fall, 1969).

The last statement suggests that the popularity of these groups may be due more to expressive and social gratifications than to information obtained from discussions.

The Self-Analytic Group

The leaderless, or self-analytic, group has had a long history. Religious orders have employed it for centuries. The Quaker meeting is a well known example of the leaderless group. It consists of silent meditation until some member of the group is moved to express ideas or feelings he feels cannot be contained and must be communicated to his fellow participants.

In more recent times, leaderless groups have attempted to enact the same kinds of objectives as have the Encounter groups, but with no assigned

56

leader present. Most recently a lucrative enterprise called "Personal Growth Group Through Encounter Tapes" has been developed by Betty Berzon and Jerome Reisel at the Western Behavioral Science Institute at La Jolla, California.

> [Personal Growth Group is] a program of interpersonal exercises for small self-directed groups. The purpose of the program is the personal growth of the individual participant. There are one and one-half hour sessions in the program. In each session there is a different kind of interpersonal experience. Instructions for each session are presented on a set of audio-tape recordings. At the beginning of each session, group members listen to the taped instructions. They then turn off the tape recorder and proceed with the activity described. The same group meets for the entire set of ten sessions. The tapes can be reused indefinitely for any number of separate groups. The focusing activity at the beginning of each session is designed to bring the group members into confrontation with each other. And to help them learn as much as possible from that encounter. The focusing activities establish the norms for the group.
>
> For instance, one focus is on the *expression of feelings*. Group members are encouraged to be aware of how they feel during each activity. Afterward they are asked to talk openly about their feelings. As a result, they can develop new emotional resources, and they can find new choices in their relationships with other people. . . . Encounter tapes also focus on the participant's *strength* rather than on his weakness—on what is right with him, not what is wrong. He is encouraged to believe in his potential as an effective human being (Encounter Tapes, 1968).

The cost is $300 per kit of ten sessions.

Group experience as fun and games hasn't stopped here. A series of parlor games (you remember the old ones—Monopoly and Parcheesi!) recently were put on the market. One of these is called Group Therapy. Packaged like the now-passé parlor games, with board, cards, and token, very little of the action appears to occur on the board. According to an advertisement in the New York *Village Voice*,

> The object is for each player to progress from the "Hung Up" segment to the space marked "Free." The player draws from three sets of cards, each set giving increasingly difficult instructions. His card might read, "Demonstrate your most vain private habit," or "Hold someone in your lap. Rock and sing to him personally." "Show the part of your body you are most proud of," or "Sit on top of the person here who makes you most nervous. Tell him why." The other members of the group will then judge how honestly the player has performed, by holding up cards reading either "cop out" or "with it." Accordingly the player will move back or advance toward "free."

The Process Group

The process group is the special kind of sensitivity group I myself conduct. It is discussed in considerable detail later.

The various kinds of sensitivity training groups have been outlined; it may be helpful now to breathe life back into this discussion of group training by quoting an account of a sensitivity group participated in by freshman and sophomore classmen in the medical school at the University of Maryland. According to one of the participants, students for these groups responded to a call for those who were "interested in improving their interpersonal relations."

> The events of the group, however, were neither immediately personal nor entirely amenable to description. The experience may be best discussed in terms of process. At the first session

58

participants introduced themselves and explained what they expected to gain from the experience. Topics were easily exhausted and uneasy silences ensued. Participants often sat and stared at each other, grinned embarrassed grins or even giggled. When someone spoke, the topics were generally safe areas of common interest such as medical school. Occasionally the moderator would refocus the group's attention on itself with a question such as "I wonder what this discussion has to do with what is going on in the group?" Usually this question was followed by a dead silence. People became restless and embarrassed by the silent periods which came frequently with the elimination of external topics.

After several meetings, attempts were made to reprimand those who missed sessions. Other attempts were made to insure the participants' freedom to do as they pleased. There were attempts to say "we" and urge group action while others said "I" and resisted regimentation.

One of the people who was concerned over attendance missed a session right before an exam. Upon returning he brought up a relatively neutral subject for discussion immediately after the start of the session. Someone suggested that this may have been a subconscious ploy to avoid the embarrassing situation of the spider who is caught in his own web. The suggestion was promptly denied and the suggester was even more promptly upbraided for considering such a thing.

A person who had had previous experience with such groups began attending the sessions. The original participants seemed to resent his apparent self-assurance in the group and some direct hostility was expressed. Someone made the observation that people in the group were anxious because they didn't know what to say or do. The comment did not decrease the anxiety.

There were appeals to be more friendly and talk about personal things. There was the continued feeling among some participants that the group was not moving fast enough, that the group wasn't going any place. Someone inquired as to whether anyone knew just where the group was supposed to be going. He suggested that everyone had his own reasons for being there and that there was no single "direction" the group could take.

After a couple of months the sessions continued to start out superficially with little reference to previous events in the group. If this superficial period became prolonged, the moderator would refocus the attention of the group on itself. However, the discussions were becoming more personal toward the end of the hour sessions. Often personal conflict developed when one person acted contrary to what someone else deemed appropriate.

There was an attempt from some quarters to have planned discussion topics on a formal schedule to help the group become spontaneous. This was rejected and someone suggested that the lack of organization in the group seemed to be bothering some people.

The moderator's apparent right to intervene and direct the group defined for him a specific role which the other participants did not have. The contrast became sharper until one of the moderator's "I wonder-how-you-feel-about-it?" questions were countered with the same question. The moderator was challenged, asked to define his position, blamed for the alleged failure of the group, and urged to take more direct part over a period of about four sessions. There was a strong counter-protest against attacking the group's only authority reference. Someone suggested that the group was using the moderator with his defined position as a scapegoat for the participants' own frustrations which grew from the anxiety-producing situations in the group. The comment generated little interest. Scapegoats were more comfortable bedfellows than the burden of introspection, although this attitude began to change.

There was continued resentment that some

participants were violating what others believed to be the "raison d'etre" of the group. Furthermore, the individuals concerned began to show a feeling that the mysterious direction that the group was supposed to take was a more intensive consideration of themselves. The inability of many in the group to accommodate themselves to an unstructured situation seemed to lead them to focus on what they perceived themselves to be. In the absence of external behavioral guidelines a person must depend on his internal guidelines. One must know what he is if he wishes to know what behavior is appropriate for him. That is, the group moved toward a consideration of the identities of the participants.

As the group moved into the identity-fixation stage the session became increasingly more fascinating. Psychological and social processes left the shroud of academic vagaries and became an integral part of the world which I generally acknowledge as being real. The experience was rewarding. Maybe I even improved my interpersonal relations (McCann, 1968).

Applications | 4

To enumerate the ways that sensitivity training can be employed is, in a sense, to delimit its potential prematurely, as the rising star of group training has as yet to reach its zenith. It may be wiser to indicate some of the areas in which it has already been employed. Basically, there are five purposes: personal growth, training for professional workers, resolving intragroup and intergroup tensions, community education, and as a research tool.

Personal Growth The essence of this book is a search for the means (as well as a description and explanation of ways) to combat the social deprivation and alienation discussed in the first chapter. I will return to this area in Chapter 9.

Training The discussion of the philosophy of sensitivity training in Chapter 2 suggests that traditional methods for training people to work with others need to be recast. The new emphasis should be on learning through dynamic interaction—learning by participation both as a follower and as a leader. One cannot properly attend to another's needs unless he is able to attune himself experientially to the feelings and thoughts of others. In the past, professional workers often were told to enter individual psychotherapy, particularly psychoanalytic therapy, to work out their own "hangups" and countertransferences. This kind of therapy (see Chapter 1) is too lengthy, too expensive, and often, although personally beneficial, not translatable to specific problems and the development of necessary skills in working with others. These facts have become increasingly more evident as professional workers have shifted the major portion of their work from one-to-one confrontations to groups.

Furthermore, take the situation of the experienced psychotherapist who has had hundreds of hours of therapy and years of professional work. How much more can he be expected to gain from continued psychotherapy? To whom can he turn for treatment? Encounter group advocates view intensive group experiences as a means of meeting the professional's

continual need for growth and restimulation rather

than treatment. Those who train professional workers have begun to realize that "by enlarging the therapist's awareness of the processes taking place in the therapeutic system in which he participates, we may make possible an increased measure of responsiveness and control on his part" (Lennard and Bernstein, 1960). But when a therapist is trying to perform a service—look at what his patients are doing—it is often difficult for him simultaneously to pay attention to all of the group problems taking place, such as how his own behavior influences the patients in the group. Despite this difficulty it is a task which the group therapist *must* perform. Sensitivity training provides an opportunity to study problems which are usually ignored because of attention to other matters.

Let me describe how one such professional training program was organized. Due to general dissatisfaction with the existing program for group work training, I was asked to supervise and train the social work staff in the psychiatric service of a large federal hospital. After the first year, personnel from other disciplines and services in the hospital negotiated for and were admitted into the group work program.

During the course of this program the hospital social workers received three hours per week of formal supervision. In addition to their work as group therapists, they met together in a sensitivity group for an additional hour and one-half weekly. The goal of this supervision was to teach the social workers about group work in four ways:

Through being in a group experience themselves as members rather than as leaders. For an hour and one-half a week social workers met together in a process

Process Group Experience

group. In these sessions each of the social workers had the opportunity to experience her own reactions and those of the other group members under conditions where she was not certain what was expected of her. She had to negotiate with the other group members to develop viable means of coping with a highly unstructured and uncomfortable situation. This climate showed the importance of group contact, the setting of clear and definable goals, the effectiveness of various kinds of negotiation in a group, and the impact of underlying group tensions. The social workers were already intellectually familiar with these phenomena, although they reported that these tensions were disguised or otherwise elusive in the groups they worked with as therapists.

To a greater and greater extent, in summarizing a process group session, the social workers paralleled their experience as participants with similar situations in the groups where they were therapists. Situations experienced as anxious and uncomfortable in the process group inevitably were the situations that these young social workers had the greatest difficulty working out in their own groups. The realization of what they were doing and where they had been getting stuck was enhanced, perhaps maximized, by the process group experience. This is not unusual. Simply knowing about human behavior and group process does not automatically enable professional workers to appreciate what their own patients experience in groups and in other interpersonal situations.

Thus from the feedback of other group members, each social worker was able to gain a greater appreciation of the phenomenological world of the patient, as well as clearer insight into her own transactions with others.

The consultant's task was to help the group members understand their behavior. The last part of the session was devoted to summarizing and systematizing what transpired within the session, its connection with what the workers had been reading about in the group literature, and its relation to difficulties they had been experiencing in the groups they were conducting.

Supervision of their own and other social workers' groups. Once a week for an hour and one-half session the social workers presented reports of their own groups. Wherever possible attention was directed toward similar processes or difficulties in the process groups. In addition, the consultant presented from time to time a formal rationale for group work strategies to meet difficulties the workers were encountering in their own groups.

Systematic readings. Each week the social workers were assigned a number of readings, which ranged from the history of group psychotherapy to surveys of group therapy methods, social process from sociological and social psychology literature, group dynamics and group processes, theories of personality that relate most cogently to group therapy practice, and readings on specific situations and problems in group therapy (selecting patients for a group, establishing a group contact, resistance, transference, dream interpretation, and so forth).

Conducting therapy groups. In running their own groups the social workers attempted to integrate the three other learning experiences in such a way as to plan, implement, and conduct the kind of therapy that best served their hospital assignments while at the same time meeting their own present skills and personal attributes.

67

Frequently, I have been asked to train professional staffs that did not have the time to meet on a regular basis. In training these staffs I have devised a Group Sensitivity Training Conference. This approach is a direct modification of the Tavistock Group Relations Conference. It differs in that the small group experience, called a *process group,* is conducted like the process groups that meet on a regular basis.

A period of group sensitivity training may run from a single group experience of one and one-half to two hours, called a *demonstration,* to a week or more of intensive training, called a *conference.*

For purposes of staff training the period of G.S.T. should be no less than *three* full days (or parts of several days that constitute at least three full days). This is because group sensitivity experience for the purposes of staff training is conceived of as an intensive experience made up of at least eight subparts. Each component part of the experience is precisely scheduled to help modulate the ongoing experiential and *proactive* (future strivings and orientation) development of the participants *as a group.* Some of the component parts are scheduled more frequently than others, other group techniques logically proceed others, and still other techniques necessitate some period of group development to maximize the learning experience.

The following is a *brief* description of the component parts of a G.S.T. Conference.

1. *The process group* is the crux of the conference. The purpose of a process group is to study its behavior in the here-and-now situation. Each participant has the opportunity to observe his own and other

participants' behavior, the implementation of diverse personal and interpersonal strategies, sentiments, and attitudes in relating to others, and the effects these interchanges have on the task of the group. Each participant can gain a greater appreciation of himself from the feedback of other group members as to how he performs within the group. A *consultant*, or *trainer* as he is sometimes called, serves the group. His task is to help the group understand its own behavior. It is the job of the consultant to point out *underlying group tensions* which the participants may not be aware of but which significantly influence their behavior and delineate its meaning to the work of the group.

2. *The large group* consists of the entire conference membership together with all the consultants. Its task is to study behavior in sessions that comprise more persons than can form a face-to-face group. It provides opportunities for the participants to experience and to learn to cope with situations, for example, when rivals for leadership emerge and existing subgroups adhere or split. Here the participant experiences a sudden lack of support, "sides" are taken spontaneously, and actions are performed for apparently irrational reasons. The stresses and conflicts activated in the large group are more congruent with those of the larger society in which we live than are the stresses and conflicts of the process group (Tavistock Institute, 1968).

3. *Intergroup events* provide participants with opportunities to study relationships between and among groups as they occur. Conference participants form their own groups for this purpose (Tavistock Institute, 1968).

4. *Application groups.* A group experience that focuses entirely on analytic "understanding" of one's

participation in interpersonal situations may fail to bridge group sensitivity training experience and the participants' job situation. The application group experience makes this connection. In the application group the consultant takes an active leadership role. He helps the group locate common core work-situation problems shared by the participants. By using experiences gained during the conference, the consultant helps the group formulate a treatment rationale for attending dysfunctional interpersonal situations on the job. (This type of group is described in detail in Chapter 9.)

5. *Lecture and discussion sessions* help participants to systematize cognitively what they experience in groups. In such a context, participants can develop hunches and make predictions about their own behavior and that of others in groups, which can be put to test. These lectures and discussions take up research findings, theoretical knowledge, and skills related to some major aspects of group functioning.

6. *Demonstration* consists of role-playing, socio-drama, group dynamics, and related methods. The entire conference meets together to try out new ways of behaving in structured situations and to increase its understanding of intergroup relations. Inter-personal dynamics, concepts, principles, and ex-periences frequently become more lucid when they are isolated and dramatically enacted.

7. *Psychodrama* is one of the most effective methods of demonstrating interpersonal phenomena. It uses a number of dramatic techniques from the theater, which have many centuries of proven effectiveness.

8. *Readings* are made available to the participants prior to the conference to help orient them to the conference. Readings subsequent to the conference help integrate the experience.

We live in an era of raging racial and social tensions, indeed, of open combat in the streets of our cities and on the campuses of our universities. The old order has collapsed, rendering the traditional societal guidelines for human conduct suspect if not impotent. New ways of bringing dissident factions together are constantly being sought. Encounter groups and T-groups have been employed so that the factions can meet to "reason together." In so doing, it is hoped, they can attend the issues the old order has failed to treat adequately.

Tom Cottle, a young Harvard psychologist, for example, has experimented with what he calls "self-analytic groups" (described in Chapter 3 as a type of Encounter group), in which black and white high school students met immediately prior to racial integration of their schools. Cottle's intention was "to transport integration to a laboratory setting modeled after the real and often frightening world of contemporary high school students. Our participants were lower and middle class Negro and white boys and girls, and their difficult task was to meet together and to speak directly upon the issue of race and social relations." In these sessions, "an experienced leader 'trains' group members to pursue the personal expressions and interpersonal processes which arise 'spontaneously.' Group members are encouraged to analyze their feelings and verbalize their attitudes, actions, and even fantasies. The emphasis in self-analytic group rests on the meaning of group interactions, as well as private revelations" (Cottle, 1967).

Unlike most other kinds of Encounter groups, a specific structure for interaction (a set of instructions) is imposed on the group: "Anything can be said by anyone at any time, but the inferred rule is that expression and analysis must run contiguously."

Cottle is rather vague about his rationale for such a rule, which appears to be based on the assumption that freedom of expression may be evasively subverted unless critical regard is given to explanations of feelings and expressions. Consequently, by assuming responsibility for his own thoughts, feelings, and actions, a person develops the self-critical ability to discern realistically his personal and interpersonal strategies. This sounds reasonable in theory, but the actual effectiveness of such group techniques in the very indigenous area of resolving intergroup tensions is still far from being conclusive.

Cottle is not alone in seeing merit in employing group training in an attempt to mitigate misunderstanding among the races. Pontiac, Michigan, has been the victim of some of the fiercest and most violent race riots in recent years. Many concerned persons, both black and white, consider the social tensions there "an open keg of gunpowder with people smoking around it." To divert the explosion they have urged the city's school system to appropriate $25,000 for the first system-wide school sensitivity training program in the nation, the purpose of which is to enable the white and minority groups to understand each other better and by so doing to reduce mistrust and hostility.

Community Education

The tensions and dissatisfactions grating the heterogeneous factions within our society have revealed an eroding commitment among homogeneous units in the community. Dissatisfaction and strife characterize not only universities but also secondary and primary schools. 'God is dead' or retreating among most of the religious denominations. Strife and regimented slowdown to a precipitous extent are crippling the traditional double backbone of the establishment, the teaching profession, and the police force—a situation inconceivable less than a generation ago.

Shortly after moving into the Washington, D.C., area, I was asked to deliver a talk at the Young Adults' Coffee House at the local Jewish Community Center. Although the topic was somewhat provocative —responsibility and "hangups" in young adult heterosexual relationships—I was surprised by the unusually large audience, over 300 people for a coffee house program. Although my talk was well received, the question and answer period—a dialogue among audience members, moderated by the speaker and focusing on issues raised by the talk—stimulated far more emotion. I had a feeling then, accentuated by subsequent visits to the coffee house, that these young people were desperately struggling for a voice. It was distressing to see inability of many of these young adults to articulate what they wanted of themselves and of others. What was apparent nevertheless was the struggle of many of these people to cast off inhibiting shackles and restraints that were perceived as externally and unwillingly imposed upon them, and a contradictory need to remain in a hopeless entrenchment through force of habit and fear. The struggle and protest at the turn their lives had taken, struck and reverberated in a common chord in us, and I silently vowed to find a means for these young adults to deal with their feelings.

Earlier that month I had employed group sensitivity techniques as part of a staff-training conference for management interns of the Department of Health, Education, and Welfare. The ability of these bright, young management interns to obtain insight into their personal and interpersonal struggles and to develop skills for dealing satisfactorily with these struggles suggested the possibility of employing 73 group sensitivity experience with adults in the community.

The coordinator for young adult programs at the Jewish Community Center had been struggling for some time with the problem of alienation of the young adults in the community. Washington, D.C., is a transient city that attracts young, ambitious people and at the same time leaves them in a psycho-social whirlwind, without the support of family ties or intimate friendships. Often friendships are nipped in the bud as newly made friends find employment in other parts of the country. These are fertile conditions for social deprivation and the resulting alienations. Frequently, it is the young people who cannot fit into the social system of their home communities who are lured by more promising prospects in Washington. But they find that here even more than at home they lack a social identity. They have only an occupational role, frequently as a minor cog in a massive bureaucratic machine, which fails to recognize individuals unless they are in upper echelons of government. This role further serves to threaten and undermine the young adult's sense of autonomy and intrinsic self-worth.

Taking these thoughts into consideration, the program coordinator, a female psychodramatist, and I decided to initiate weekly sensitivity training groups at the Jewish Community Center.

Group training seems appropriate to the community educational needs of a community center. Many of the people who find their way to the community center in Washington, for whatever explicit reason, also feel a strong dissatisfaction with their existing life style. In this way they differ little from their counterparts in other parts of the country. A fair number of them are in serious distress. The community center has a number of programs that answer the educational and recreational prerequisites of its clients. It nevertheless lacks the resources to attend to the personality needs of a considerable number of these clients. Limited counseling, generally providing referral to available community resources, may be offered, as well as some repressive-inspirational support through "Y" courses in personal effectiveness or psychology of adjustment. These are a far cry from meeting the community center's needs. Many centers wash their hands of the problem, claiming that the correction of emotional distress is not their province. Intensive and dynamic psychotherapy—in fact, the very aura of "treatment"—is seen as alien to the expressed purposes of many centers, which is to provide "clean" fun and public education, as well as a strengthening of religious life.

As a result, the only activities which are sanctioned are primarily social, pleasant, relaxing, informative, and recreational; those that don't get people too emotionally stimulated, because "there are other classes being held in rooms down the hall." Individual and group psychotherapy, which are restorative rather than proactive, require considerable time to be effected. The community center is, at present, unwilling and unable to support long-term therapy programs. Moreover, in restorative therapy, regressive reactions frequently occur and, indeed, are sometimes encouraged in modifying feelings about early life experiences. The community center cannot tolerate "disturbed" behavior because of its professed responsibilities to the sensitivities of the other clients it serves. Because it does not see correction of emotional experience as one of the center's functions, adequately trained staff are not hired for this specialized purpose.

But what of the distressed client of the center who cannot afford private treatment, who may be frightened away because of the "sickness" implications of a clinic or private psychiatric referral? Because the center attracts these marginally adjusted people, who may feel incapable or unwilling to accept treatment until their difficulty becomes seriously exacerbated, it seems that group experience with an educational and self-help orientation might be well suited to the needs of the community center. Furthermore, community center staff, by participating in training groups, can supplement their interpersonal skills. After sufficient training and supervision, they may conduct their own training groups.

Research Tool

Because group sensitivity training is so recent and largely devoid of high-powered theoretical assumptions, it is relatively free of bias. It was Bion's original intention to use his groups for unbiased observation and study of group processes. It is also the hope of many in the field that a better understanding of how groups function and personality develops may be obtained from the study and comparison of the diverse forms of training group experiences.

Public 5
and
Professional
Reaction

To say that sensitivity training as a social movement
has had an enthusiastic reception is a gross under-
statement. Group training, without the benefit of
Madison Avenue promotion, has developed into a
million-dollar venture for many of the institutes
that have promoted it. People of all walks of life are
functioning (critics claim "carrying on") both as
"professionals" and as participants. Not only has
sensitivity training found a market in those searching
for sensation and rebirth, but according to one report
(Reid, 1968) about 50 percent of the churches in New
England indicate that they provide some type of small-
group experience.

In spite of this spectacular reception, or perhaps
because of it, a good number of laymen and professionals have seriously questioned this group training phenomenon. They are curious about what
actually happens in group experiences. They ask: Are
these new group experiences distinctly unlike tra- 77

ditional methods? How? What are the dangers involved? How can these dangers be averted? Are these experiences indicated for everyone? If not, for whom are they indicated? Contraindicated? Who should lead the group? What experience, training, and personal qualifications are required? Should these group experiences be regulated by the traditional watchguards of therapeutic endeavors (the American Medical Association, the American Psychiatric Association, the American Psychological Association, etc.) or left unfettered? Should standards be created? These are some of the questions any intelligent participant or outside observer of training groups might pose in a rational consideration of the group training movement. There are many negative reactions to the new group experiences among professionals. Mental health workers in a number of fields differ greatly in education, training, and personal skills. Many paraprofessionals (and nonprofessionals) who are involved in ameliorative endeavors are poorly trained and educated. Many have been prevented by the more established professions from engaging directly or at least working freely in traditional therapeutic endeavors, such as individual psychotherapy. Individual therapy was first seen as the private domain of the medically trained person. More recently, as the training of the latter two professions came to be recognized as being relevant to psychotherapeutic endeavors, psychiatry has reluctantly shared individual therapy with clinical psychology and psychiatric social work.

Group therapy has created different problems. It was initially used for patients who could not be handled in individual therapy due to unsuitability (particularly for analytic therapy) or due to the unavailability of medically trained therapists. Subordinate staff were permitted to conduct group sessions. With the increased recognition of the efficacy of therapy in groups and of the need of training to effectively conduct groups, more stringent requirements have been propagated for group therapists—again limiting the permissible functioning domain of the paraprofessional. Paraprofessionals who have not the skill, training, or education recognized as sufficient by the established professionals have been continuously in search of a technique and approach they can call their own.

Where the individual or profession is discriminated against because of extrapersonal qualifications—education, training, etc.—the attempt has been made to seize upon a technique where *personal* characteristics rather than extrapersonal attributes are the most vital fact in effective functioning. Consequently, the search has been for methods which assume that ameliorative progress is engendered through the interaction of change agent and patient as existential beings. This rationale contends moreover that too much training and education hamper rather aid the therapist, for he becomes technique-oriented rather than person-centered.

The new group experiences, with their emphasis on existential, "gut" confrontations, seem admirably suited to the search by these paraprofessionals. Parenthetically, the nonprofessional competing with the professional often seeks an approach which is more interesting and exciting than the traditional approach. The nonprofessional may contend that proof of the efficacy of his approach is that he runs interesting groups. An untrained person may have an interesting group, however wasteful he is of the opportunity to systematically and informatively work out group objectives. Moreover, a group where fragile participants are exploited by those in quest of sadistic fun may, depending upon where one sits, be an interesting group.

To maintain his identity as person-centered rather than technique-oriented, the untrained worker resists putting his notions about group training to test. As one group training leader (who according to his biography teaches industrial management) claims: "Sensitivity training is indeed a religious enterprise. I am even more surprised to find myself thinking it is the *most* religious enterprise of which I know . . ." (Clark, 1967). Religious experiences are generally supposed to be accepted on the basis of faith, and require no (scientific) proof.

All these attitudes and expectations have resulted in criticism directed at the new group movement. Some charges have been specifically directed at a particular group training approach, while others are directed at the entire movement. Professionals and laymen alike have been critical. In this chapter criticism has been placed in a number of general areas, linked whenever possible to the particular sensitivity training approach for which it seems most relevant. I agree in whole or part with much of the criticism leveled at sensitivity training. Nevertheless, I feel that there is a more balanced exposition of group training if the criticism is answered as the advocates of sensitivity training might answer the charges, based upon how they have answered other criticism. Critics and advocates will speak for themselves.

Sensitivity Training Is a Form of Therapy

It is important in answering this kind of statement that "therapy" be clearly defined. Does "therapy" mean some highly formalized arrangement of two or more people where one is designated "doctor," "therapist," or "healer" because of his training, experience, license, and expertise, and the other as the "client" or "patient" because he claims to be (or is declared to be) "ill" or "disabled"? Does "therapy" mean some beneficial effect that results from any of the infinite number of life experiences or relationships that most human organisms are exposed to? Or is something quite different meant by "therapy"? If the former definition of therapy is used, usually referred to as psychotherapy, group training advocates would likely deny that sensitivity training is another form of therapy. If therapy refers to the beneficial effects of interpersonal experience, then no advocate of group training would deny that therapy can and does take place in training groups. The important difference, however, is that few sensitivity training advocates see their task as deliberately encouraging and influencing psychodynamically "beneficial" effects in their groups. Most group leaders encourage beneficial experiences in terms of learning what it means to be a member of a group—what forces bear on a member of a group—and the development of increased perceptual acuity gained from feedback of how the participant functions in an interpersonal situation. Unlike psychotherapy, minimal if any attention is directed toward interpreting and explaining present and past behavior. (But this greatly varies from group to group.) On the other hand there is considerable emphasis on exploring and trying out new behavior *in the group*, instead of just talking about it and waiting until the participants return home to try it out, as usually typifies psychotherapy. Whether the consultant or group member takes an interpretive function as exemplified by the Tavistock group or foregoes explanation of behavior as in the Gestalt group, interest is centered on the group's or the participant's immediate, here-and-now experience. If from these learning experiences participants are able to make modifications in their personal functioning, which makes their life more fulfilling, so much the better. This is not, however, the overriding intention, and the group experience should not be regarded as worthless or ineffective if specifiable personality changes cannot be discerned.

A. *An Ineffective Form of Therapy.* To evaluate sensitivity training one cannot legitimately use some universal standard. Each group training approach poses certain objectives which it claims proper sensitivity training should fulfill. It is only within the framework of these criteria that the method can be judiciously evaluated. For example, the Tavistock consultant maintains that he is interested in the participant developing a greater appreciation of the effect group emotionality has on the group. He cannot therefore be faulted if as a result of the administration of a battery of psychological tests before and after the group experience there is no discernable difference in ego-strength or other psychodynamics of the participants. He can, however, be admonished if more effective interpersonal understanding and greater leadership skills cannot be ascertained. Likewise in the T-group, where claims are made for specific benefits, such as greater interpersonal competence, demonstration of these effects can be asked for.

B. *Subtly Designed Therapy.* According to some in the field this appears to be one of the most serious and valid charges leveled against certain of the sensitivity training approaches. T-group trainers have on occasion criticized fellow trainers who have misled participants into assuming that the training experience is concerned with learning new techniques, theories, and concepts about groups, and that it does not concern itself with rather intense and critical feedback. The repartee has been: How can one learn about groups without experiencing what goes on in groups? How can one lead groups without experiencing what effect one's leadership endeavors have on others in a group? This is further fuel for the argument many sensitivity training group leaders pose, that people who gravitate toward group training, even those groups with educational orientation, are asking for some kind of therapeutic experience. Their argument is supported by their opinion that direct request for traditional psychotherapy is too threatening for persons who gravitate toward group training. Consequently, those advocates who intentionally design their groups to gain psychodynamic benefits insist that they are merely responding to the hidden pleas of the healthier parts of the participants' egos.

C. *Potentially Dangerous Form of Therapy.* This becomes a serious charge when taken with the previous claim that therapy in group training may take a subtle form in contradiction to the participants' manifestly espoused wishes. Sensitivity training advocates generally claim that there are certain built-in safety precautions in their approach: A trained consultant or trainer won't permit group members being scapegoated, exploited, or inordinately upset from the experience. There are in all groups healthy mechanisms at work which prevent exacerbation of pathology. Furthermore, advocates of the human potentials movement claim that it is the more traditional approaches to personal change (traditional psychotherapy despite its trained psychotherapists) which actually exacerbate disturbed behavior in group members. These traditional approaches, they claim, insist on emphasizing "sickness" and "protecting" participants. Sensitivity training with its focus on self-actualization all but eliminates this possibility. However, it is interesting to note that group trainers who have had the least experience working with seriously disturbed persons are also the least concerned with the charge of being involved in a potentially dangerous method. The converse seems true of those who have had clinical experience.

Lack of Research on Effects of Sensitivity Training

Many group training advocates refuse to even respond; others claim that the lack of research proof should not hold them back from benefiting people. They say that if others are interested in doing research they would welcome the information but it isn't their interest. They are too occupied *doing* to spend time researching. Still others point to the complexities of group training research and indicate that group therapy, with a much longer history, is still virtually as "unproved" as is sensitivity training.

There have been a number of recent studies conducted in sensitivity training, many the result of doctoral dissertations. Doctoral dissertations being what they generally are, we are left where we began. The bulk of the other research has been generated by the National Training Laboratory, which has a heavy financial interest in verifying its method.

Sensitivity Group Trainers Are Poorly Trained

Those group leaders who have been classified as poorly trained have answered back by saying that until there is some well established theory and empirical evidence indicating which skills and which kind of leadership training is best, no one can be properly regarded as better trained than anyone else. Moreover, the more experience one has in running groups the better equipped one is likely to become. Since there are no experts or established theories in group training, a trainer can best become expert by being in groups and by leading groups.

Better-trained group advocates point to their

84

training and experience in traditional groups and clinical settings. Furthermore, they point to their own continuous growth and restimulation and claim that they parry countertransference by participating in other trainers' groups.

A. *Group training has no clear theory.* Some group training advocates point out with impatience that group therapists no more than twenty or thirty years ago were in the same boat—they either proceeded "by ear" with little or no explicit theory or borrowed a conceptual frame of reference from their work with individuals. Other advocates of the new group movement contend that a well defined theoretical system is not necessary to insure good group work. They claim that some of the great psychological theorists, notably Freud, were not renowned as skillful practitioners; on the other hand they claim many skillful therapists do not have well formulated conceptual frames of reference. The sensitivity training advocates of this persuasion contend that beneficial therapy, or group training for that matter, accrues to participants who have leaders with desirable personality variables rather than many logged hours of training and didactic knowledge. Even were this not the case, it is the contention of many group training advocates, especially those of the human potentials movement, that a well developed theory of sensitivity training is premature at the present time.

B. *Leaders of sensitivity training groups do not know how to proceed.* This charge is similar to the previous one. Those with experience in traditional approaches claim that there is much overlap from the traditional groups to the new group training approaches. Almost all group training advocates insist nevertheless that group training is a new and experimental technique and that the leader must at this stage of the development of group training be flexible and innovative.

C. *Group leaders have personal problems of their own.* "Who doesn't!" the advocates retort. They contend, moreover, that the criteria for traditional psychotherapists should not and does not apply here. They contend that those who currently raise this charge are psychoanalysts who believe that no one but analysts know anything about working with people. Moreover, analysts, they claim, know less about the new group methods than perhaps any other professional group. Not to evade the charge, advocates of group training contend that they best prevent their own problems from impeding their effectiveness by intermittently becoming participants in others' groups.

D. *Group training is at best disorganized, at worst dangerous and ineffectual because it is nondirective.* All advocates of group training claim that this is a misleading, confusing, and false criticism. Several of the sensitivity training approaches, they point out, are far more directive than are most traditional psychotherapies. Moreover, even where the approach is "nondirective," a distinction should be made between nondirective and chaotic. The effectiveness of group training in these approaches is in large part a result of the relatively unstructured nature of the groups, which permits the participants to contact and develop interpersonal skills that they already possess to some degree. The liberating atmosphere of the group permits exploration of personal and interpersonal resources by deemphasizing success, at least in time-limited ways. Furthermore, most group training leaders don't permit their group to flounder endlessly. Group leaders allow their group to flounder ideally to the point at which the participants experience their failures and frustrations without rationalizing or dismissing them by externalization. Once the group comes to grips with its frustration, the leader helps guide the participants in more or less direct ways, depending upon his training philosophy. This criticism is left over from the critics of the beginning of the sensitivity training movement. "It's probably true that the early leaders in the group dynamics field did place somewhat excessive emphasis on democratic permissiveness as a panacea; but few workers in this field [today] cling to [this] simple belief," that sensitivity training should aim solely at bringing about effective interpersonal relations and egalitarian cooperation. "Rather, the view now is that laboratory training [in groups] can help to increase the participants' capacity to select more flexible and more realistic modes of behavior on the basis of discerning assessment of their own goals and needs and the interpersonal and task situation that confronts them" (Greening, 1964).

A. *Group training is an excuse for regression.* This is a criticism directed mainly at the human potentials movement. The human potentials people claim that most adults have lost their sense of spontaneity and love of sensation. We have become a nation of walking zombies, we are told. In order to refurbish that lost promise of youth, some regression is necessary to get in touch with that which we once possessed but have since forgotten. They borrow from Ernest Kries: regression in the service of the ego. Recently it was reported that "two dozen men and women took off their shoes and played 'nursery school' for an hour yesterday in the Fountain Room of the Fairmont Hotel [San Francisco]. Several of them were professors of psychology. They joined hands in childish dances. They finger painted, both on paper and on one another. They leaped wildly on a big-truck inner

Group Sensitivity Training Is Dangerous

tube. They played Indian—two of the men enjoyed kicking down a castle built of blocks by two women" (San Francisco *Chronicle*, 1968). This took place at the American Humanistic Psychology's 1968 convention. Such carryings-on were tame compared to their 1969 meetings, where nude groups were reportedly held. Other group training approaches such as Tavistock and process groups insist that people in groups are always regressing in that they are adversely influenced by the primitive and contagious emotions perpetrated in groups. In order to work maturely in a cooperative endeavor these emotions must be laid bare and made conscious.

B. *There is a lack of responsibility in sensitivity training.* In the existential world people act irresponsibly because they rarely question their societally induced roles and the sanctions that reinforce these roles. In group training, however, the emphasis is on the here-and-now and the effect that the participants' sentiments and attitudes have on their interchange in the group, which becomes the focus of study. A sensitivity training group will rarely accept "that's the way I have always acted or behaved" as an excuse for dysfunctional behavior by a participant. This, claim group training advocates, leads to responsible behavior rather than social conformity and unquestioned behavior outside the group. "The purpose of sensitivity training groups is to provide an existential setting in which participants can intensively review and possibly revise their basic views about man's nature, group behavior, and the roles and processes necessary for accomplishing tasks with others."

"In such an existential setting the people who feel that they cannot benefit from a further confrontation of themselves and others may be those whose views of man are so unrealistic that they cannot endure the threat of having them revised; or, at the other extreme, those whose views are so satisfying to them that they see no need to revise them. . . . Most people however probably fall somewhere between these two groups, and it is for them that sensitivity training is designed" (Greening, 1964).

C. *Sensitivity training makes one feel sorry for oneself.* This is regarded as a totally false and misleading charge. It evidently results from the layman's misunderstanding of psychotherapy, and his identifying sensitivity training with psychotherapy. In group training the "whys" of behavior are not really emphasized but rather the "what" and "hows": What are you experiencing, and what are you going to do about it?

D. *Group training is too people-oriented rather than responsibility-oriented.* This seems to be a charge stemming from business management's mistrust of the entire human relations movement that preceded the recent group training movement. It appears based on some irrational philosophy that one can be committed and responsible to ideals and beliefs without relating them to people. It undoubtedly helped to suppress the human sentimentality of some business executives as they climbed over other people on the way to the top. It implies that feelings need not be considered. If someone has a job to do he plows ahead regardless of the human toil. The tragic absurdity of the Vietnam situation is a reflection of this odd thinking.

E. *Group training sets up a stress situation.* This charge is based on the likewise odd thinking that unpleasantness can be avoided and must be avoided at all costs. Realistically, however, one learns by experience. If a person learns efficient strategies to handle stress in group training these stress situations won't have the deleterious effect upon him outside one group they would have had if he were not prepared. | 89

F. *Sensitivity training is an invasion of privacy.* In that most sensitivity training groups are concerned with here-and-now behavior of participants, such a criticism seems unwarranted (Perls and Moreno, who are more concerned with past behavior, are excepted here). At the core of this charge is undoubtedly the fear that feelings are private matters and these dark secrets should not be brought into the open.

G. *Group training takes away one's defenses.* This charge is directed essentially at the human potentials movement. Group leaders with clinical experiences generally know better. Human potentials advocates on the other hand contend that people have the necessary social skills and spontaneity to enrich their existence, but their defenses have impeded them from achieving "joy," "love," "intimacy," etc. In a sense they don't want people to learn anything new as they wish them to unlearn self-defeating defenses.

H. *Permissiveness is a panacea created by sensitivity training.* This is a charge leveled against the T-group and human relations movements. The T-group advocates may have been guilty of this charge twenty years ago. Lewinian philosophy, elevating democratic practices as a social utopia, may have overemphasized permissiveness. This shortcoming has been corrected as T-group training practices have become more sophisticated.

Group Training Is Ineffective

In that research investigation is lacking this charge can only be bandied about verbally without leading to any satisfactory conclusions. The specific ideas critics often point to in indicating the ineffectiveness of group training reveal, however, the pessimism in back of these charges:

A. *Human nature cannot be changed;*

B. *People know themselves better than anyone else;*

C. *People already know how to deal with others.*

These charges are representative of the antipathy to self-introspection of any type, as well as being criticisms of sensitivity training. They are based on self-fulfilling and closed premises. And as such there is little point in trying to contest them.

D. *The real world won't accept the things that go on in group training.* It is often difficult to discern just who it is that comprises the real world. I suppose the participants in group training are a few of these real people. As they learn to become more effective in understanding their own needs and those of others and how to accommodate others in mutually gratifying ways, change is made in their world. Accordingly, the NTL school claims to be trying to change the world. I also suppose that the people who make the above charge are also people who comprise the real world. It appears that it is they who won't accept the changes emanating from sensitivity training, but they prefer to make it the group participants' problem rather than their own.

E. *Sensitivity training is anti-intellectual.* This criticism is mostly directed at the human potentials movement, which emphasizes nonverbal, emotional encounters. They answer that we have lost contact with our feelings, so that words and thoughts are employed to hide what we actually feel, desire, and fear about ourselves and others. Rather than promote even more sophisticated intellectual defenses, we need to regain feelings.

A. *Sensitivity training is a brain-washing technique;*

B. *Sensitivity training groups are run by Communists and anarchists.*

Paranoid Charges

Although I had heard from time to time some vague mention of paranoid-sounding charges against sensitivity training, I dismissed them as "put-on" and not something anyone but the kind of crank found on a Joe Pyne television show might insinuate or believe. To my shock, I recently came across a story in the *Washington Post* about a California couple who publish a right-wing periodical, who in claiming that sensitivity training is a secret weapon of communism, along with sex education, designed to destroy the morale of the nation, were taken seriously enough to warrant the use of the United States House of Representatives office building auditorium and an audience of congressmen and their wives.

Sensitivity Training Is a Cult Game

A. *The effect is only temporary;*
B. *Sensitivity training enables participants to act as "hit-and-run" cowards;*
C. *Veterans of group training cannot do more than just express anger;*
D. *Sensitivity training breeds narcissism.*

Advocates of all the approaches to group training would agree that the criticisms cited above are often valid. They would point out in their own behalf that it is not group training that produces these aversive behaviors. Sensitivity training experiences bring to the surface dysfunctional behavior to be scrutinized and modified. If participants leave the sensitivity training experience with these adverse behaviors intact, the particular group leader they were working with may not have been doing his job properly (perhaps there wasn't sufficient time). Advocates of group training would deny that this demeans the usefulness of sensitivity training any more than it does group therapy, where the same behaviors occur.

It is a fact of life that powerful people try to take over in all the life situations we find ourselves in; that is why we refer to them as powerful people. Would a sensitivity training experience be a meaningful one without their obtrusive presence? Certainly not! What do the participants as a group intend to do about the behavior of these obtrusive social agents? The participants' attempts to cope with difficult social conditions form an integral part of sensitivity training.

Powerful People Take Over Sensitivity Training Groups

People don't enter sensitivity training groups because they are seriously emotionally disturbed, or because they are devoid of social skills. They want to increase skills they already possess. For many people in our culture this represents a vicious threat to their present adjustment. Many of us live in precarious balance. "We have learned to get along with ourselves and our world in some way and the possibility that this balance might be upset is always a frightening one. Almost invariably in groups, every person finds the balance is disturbed or possibly upset" (Rogers, 1967).

"These persons view unstructured group situations as nothing but a stress situation—nothing more than an experiment to test your tolerance for frustration . . . the small group efforts of Lewin [are seen] . . . as having been perverted by the sensitivity training cult into a sort of personal therapy" (Odiorne, 1963).

"There are many people in our culture who also feel that a person should be contained, disciplined, preferably unaware of his feelings, and should live in terms of discipline that was handed down by some authority" (Rogers, 1967).

Those who cling to the "rugged individualist"

Conclusion

school claim that "too much emphasis on human relations encourages people to feel sorry for themselves, makes it easier for them to slough off responsibility, to find excuses for failure, to act like children. When somebody falls down on the job or does not behave in accordance with accepted codes, we look into his psychological background for factors that may be used as excuses. In these respects the cult of human relations is but part and parcel of the sloppy sentimentalism characterizing the world today" (McNair, 1957).

Many of these criticisms are valid and telling. Nevertheless, I will describe in the following chapters what group sensitivity training, as I practice it, can and has accomplished.

Origins | 6

No doubt sensitivity training began when the first band of men came together to resolve their differences through verbal confrontation rather than through combat with war clubs. Dr. T. R. Van Dellen tells us that "witch doctors and native healers knew a few psychiatric principles a thousand years before Sigmund Freud was born. Their savvy center[ed] about abre-actions . . . a technique that creates an intense state of excitement . . . [and] a release of powerful emotions," resulting in a feeling of serenity and temporary relief of nervous symptoms (Van Dellen, 1967). Further-more, primitive healing released repressed emotions by letting people "act out" and sublimate these feelings in tribal ritualistic ceremony. In a sense this is the beginning of psychodrama, one of the major tech-niques in the sensitivity training movement. In *acting-out* behavior a person unwittingly acts upon impulses which have been festering inside him but which he 95 has been unable to acknowledge due to their forbidden and threatening nature in terms of the person he wishes to believe he is. Instead of remembering upsetting experiences from the past in a way that enables him to deal with the painful feelings these events have produced, he relieves his tension by motor activity that is harmful to himself and others. One of the ways in which destructive consequences of acting-out behavior can be mitigated is by enabling the protagonist to relieve his tensions in more controlled and socially acceptable motor activity, for example, by means of psychodrama training.

Group abreaction and controlled ceremonial acting-out proved effective in religious conversion and faith healing. Some religious leaders, although unlettered, were skillful therapists. Every interpersonal technique that has ever evolved has been impressed and modified by the prevailing *zeitgeist* to answer the interpersonal needs of that period in time. This is especially true of ceremonial therapies, for they have evolved into present-day forms of psychotherapy and methods of group training.

Education Theory

More recently, impetus for group training has come from new emphasis in education. With encouragement from John Dewey, William James, and other leaders of progressive education, learning has shifted from the expert-student situation to free discussion and give-and-take of ideas and opinions within small groups. In recent years education has come to be regarded as a dynamic interpersonal experience. By exchanging ideas with his colleagues, the student has been encouraged to think about and reconsider the goals and meanings of human ideals and action. The result has been the development of discussion groups concerned with all areas, from the great books to existing social problems.

> The chief characteristic of this approach to group behavior was its emphasis upon the *thinking* function of the group process. Although emotion was recognized as an accompaniment of group behavior, it was regarded more as an infrequent interruption into the process than as a constant, central, and inescapable aspect of it. Problem-solving was the goal of the group process and made it indispensable to the democratic way of life (Casteel, 1968).

Turning peer-oriented discussion groups into a training technique came with the development of the Human Relations Management training program of the 1920's, from the pioneering work of Elton Mayo and his associates. During this period consultation services to business, industry, education, and social and religious organizations were developed. They attempted to improve the services of these organizations through greater awareness, appreciation, and employment of human relations principles. These services were based largely on an atheoretical, liberal, and pragmatic philosophy, until the impact of Kurt Lewin and his students' work became prominent in the 1930's and 1940's. From their pioneering studies emerged the group dynamics movement.

Lewin and those associated with him were of a practical bent, never content to leave their theories to lie fallow as academic principles. Lewin's research was an attempt to answer some of the important social needs of the day. Once research findings seemed promising they were quickly applied to existing social problems. Lewin's famous study of the comparison of lecture method and small group discussion was utilized to persuade American housewives to use less "choice" meats to aid the Allied war effort during World War II. His studies with Lippitt and White on leadership styles were evolved from his own personal experiences in Germany and his deep concern about the effects of totalitarian governments. He hoped to develop methods to improve democratic leadership, so that totalitarian government would never rise again.

National Training Labs

In 1947 several of Lewin's students, Bradford, Benne, Lippitt, and others held the first Human Relations Leadership Conference at Bethel, Maine. They had three concerns: 1. Study of leadership style and methods of group control is insufficient for understanding the dynamic and complex process that underlies group discussion and decision-making. A study of the skills and responsibilities required of group members is also necessary; 2. The study of leadership has to be approached in terms of group functions rather than purely from the personality study of individuals; 3. Methods need to be developed for group members to "discover, analyze, and cure their own group illnesses. Efficiency as a group member or leader is based not so much on a set of skills as on a sensitivity to group interaction problems and group needs and the ability to carry out the needs of the group" (Bradford, 1948). The success of the Bethel group in employing group dynamics, psychodrama, and group therapeutic techniques in training leaders quickly stimulated a large following and the establishment of the National Training Laboratories in Washington, D.C. Summer workshops were continued at Bethel. For the most part the group leaders, or trainers as they are called in T-groups, tend to come from academic rather than clinical settings.

Another mainstream of sensitivity training comes from Tavistock, a British psychiatric clinic located near London. At Tavistock, W. R. Bion and his successor, A. K. Rice, developed a group method to help large groups deal with their intragroup tensions. Bion was a senior psychiatrist during World War II. He was placed in charge of a large military psychiatric hospital. Apparently "the Brass" were distressed by the acting-out of the patients (quite out of keeping with the British army's tradition of disciplined behavior). Bion promoted daily leaderless study groups to permit the patients to deal with their interpersonal difficulties. Bion used several guiding principles to organize these study groups: 1. The objective was to study group tensions in an attempt to discover how neurotic behavior resulted in the men's waste of energy, discontent, and frustration; 2. There were to be no attempts to find "answers" for these group tensions until the majority of the unit were able to acknowledge and understand that such tensions existed; 3. The solution to a unit problem would not be administratively resolved but would result from the work of the men as a functioning unit; 4. Group tensions were to be explored whenever they occurred, regardless of the time of day or night, and not, as in many hospital settings, held in abeyance until the next ward meeting; 5. The study and acknowledgment of the problem was more important than temporary relief of the tension; 6. The study group would concern itself with real life situations, not hypothetical ones.

Returning to Tavistock after the war Bion incorporated his innovative and apparently successful study group method into his psychoanalytic group therapy practice. Although an admirer of Freud and a disciple of Melanie Klein, Bion was dissatisfied with the prevailing psychoanalytic conception and understanding of groups.

Although Bion has denied it, there appears nevertheless to be much resemblance between his group technique for studying intragroup tensions and the British army's leaderless group situation employed to select army officers. According to Hans Ansbacher (1951) the leaderless group method was originated by B. Rieffert, who directed the German Military Psychology Corps from 1920 to 1931. Around 1935 another military psychologist modified the method. Before that time the psychology corps employed the leaderless group situation as a personality assessment of officers in the following way. A small group of fellow officers were asked to discuss a topic of common interest. They were individually rated by observers for salient personality attributes on the basis of intellectual and interpersonal capacities revealed during the discussion. Eventually the technique made its way to England where it may have influenced Bion.

The study group technique, heavily informed by psychoanalytic thinking and developed as a method to study men under stress, is at variance with, perhaps even opposed to, the T-group approach. The T-group method is based on group dynamics principles. Pragmatic and liberal, the aim of T-groups is for men to work more cooperatively and democratically with one another (and in my opinion often at the cost of their understanding why the tensions were generated in the first place). At the core of the study and T-group differences are philosophies of change which are especially at variance with one another. (See Chapter 8 regarding concepts of change.)

A third important influence on group training is **Psychodrama** *psychodrama*. It is one of many techniques employed by mental health workers to aid more traditional therapeutic interviews. According to psychodrama's founder, Jacob Levy Moreno, M.D., the technique provides for direct expression of the patient's emotional disturbance, for he is encouraged to act out various life situations related to his difficulties. The theater-like atmosphere of psychodrama enables the individual to face his problems with less emotional tension than in real life.

Moreno is fond of suggesting psychodrama's origins in the ancient world. "Drama is a transliteration of the Greek word which means *action*, or a thing done. Psychodrama can be defined, therefore, as the science which explores the *Truth* by dramatic methods" (Moreno, 1946). Truth is here given an ontological rather than a factual meaning. The search for the truth was the highest virtue according to Greek philosophy. Aristotle saw the search as having a therapeutic function in addition to its moral aim. Man, he claimed, being human, is by the nature of his being less than perfect. Fallible to iniquities of the flesh, mind, and spirit, man is impeded in his pursuit of the good life. Let us remember, however, that impediments were experienced as feelings of *public shame* and *disgrace,* not as internalized guilt and pangs of conscience, which inflict modern man and find their most appropriate source of remedy in the therapy of the Victorian Sigmund Freud. Guilt is a Judeo-Christian concept, totally alien, and, one would imagine, puzzling to the Greeks and to their noble concept of *arete*—moral and heroic courage in the face of predestined fate. According to Aristotle, as a spokesman for the *zeitgeist* of his period, immorality, being a public wrongdoing, could only be rectified within the throes and witness of the entire community.

It is said that at the climactic point in Aristophanes' play *The Clouds* which was being performed in Athens, a play which had as its purpose the ridicule and humiliation of Socrates, Socrates strode down the main aisle and cried out to the audience, "He is an imposter—it is false. I am the true Socrates." This illustrates the dramatic power of conscience as expressed in a monologue. In psychodrama the protagonist has the opportunity to speak for himself. At the point of the greatest intensity of feeling the climactic "affective movement" occurs, which ushers in the moment of truth (Miller, 1968).

Within the Greek social structure's provision for moral rectification is found the earliest recognition of the need for group therapy.

This early group therapy is literally milieu therapy. The French word *milieu* means environment or social community. Aristotle noted, in one of the world's first books on psychotherapy, *The Art of Poetry*, that the drama "is representation of an action that is serious, complete . . . with incidents arousing pity and fear in such a way to accomplish a purgation of such emotions." The Greeks used the word *catharsis* to refer to the process by which the citizens of the community could rid themselves of shame and immorality by sharing their deep emotional concerns with one another. "The audience could identify to varying degrees with the feelings, personalities, and events portrayed in the drama. Thereby, they could attain not only a release for cumulative pent-up emotion, but also achieve insight into themselves and others to whom they relate. The more real the impact of the drama, the more the audience could relate what was occurring on the stage to their own real experiences" (Miller, 1968).

The cathartic method did not completely lose its power nor its usefulness after the classic period. Public confession has been a familiar form of punishment and redemption throughout western civilization. The passion, morality, and mystery plays were common dramatic devices with cathartic purpose. Private confessions introduced by the Roman Catholic Church to redeem iniquity represent an attempt to take the curative powers out of the community of men and reserve it for the clergy. Various churches did, however, recognize the need for redemption through communion with one's fellows. With this more or less implicit aim they set up religious retreats, where the participants discussed their social, personal, and religious concerns with a greater degree of freedom than they could in the open community. Generally, however, clergy oversaw the discussion, keeping it within prevailing church-sanctioned limits. The Quakers were early users of groups with no formal leader present.

Moreno, a visionary of no less than cosmic dimensions, recognized the unsound practice of keeping disturbed feelings private. Unable to share feelings about oneself and others because we fear criticism from our fellows, we do not compare these feelings with those of others and appropriately modify or justify them. It remained for psychodrama, Moreno | 103 tells us, to rediscover and treat the idea of catharsis in its relation to psychotherapy.

Psychodrama and Group Training

Early sensitivity training designs made extensive use of sociodramatic procedures, including role-playing, role reversal, soliloquy, and so forth, as originally described by Moreno. Human relations difficulties, as experienced by *ordinary* people, were according to Ronald Lippitt identified through discussion and sociodramatic methods used for diagnosing action aspects of situations. They were used for practicing the skills necessary for avoiding, handling, or resolving such difficulties.

During this early period in the evolution of group training, action was halted on occasion in order for members themselves to assess their effectiveness as an operating group. Under such conditions attention was drawn to problems of functioning as a group, as well as to individual difficulties in adjusting to the group situation. In the present form of the training group the latter aspect, involving feedback evaluation of problems of operating effectively as a decision-making group, has become more prominent. Dramatic methods have receded in importance. Now problems of functioning as a group constitute the primary material of analysis and evaluation, with emphasis placed on certain aspects of the problem-solving process.

The significance of the dramatic procedures in the genesis of the training group and then use as a basis for diagnosis of problems, for practicing social skills, for dealing with them, and of interruption techniques for stopping "work" to evaluate psychological properties of situations, indicates that the training group method owes a substantial debt to the rationale on which classical dramatic action is based (Blake, 1957).

The theory underlying my own work with sensitivity training has numerous roots. Certain theorists, however, have been central.

When I began working with training groups, early in 1968, my method was formed of my own experience plus a blend of social psychological concepts. Particularly important were group dynamics, attitude change, reference group theory, Kelly's work on personal constructs, role theory, and cognitive dissonance theory. Like most eclectic theoretical positions my approach to group training often seemed inconsistent. The inconsistency was perhaps less a lack of understanding of the events transpiring in the group than an inconsistent rationale for promoting effective group behavior. My training in analytic group therapy denied social events and concerned itself with the individual in the group as he manifested his intrapsychic conflicts. In any dyadic encounter my orientation was to disregard the participants as equals who were trying to promote an interpersonal transaction with the resultant explicit and implicit rules, rewards, sanctions, and so forth. My approach was to view the dyadic encounter as consisting of a protagonist and a social object. The protagonist acted out unresolved intrapsychic conflicts by treating the social object *as if* he were a significant figure from his own past. My trained inclination was to confront first one of the participants as the protagonist, next the other, and call for some reality-testing in regard to the inappropriateness of the protagonist with the social object. Such an approach suggested psychotherapy, which was not acceptable in the context of group training. Nor did such an approach do justice to the rich survey of social psychological knowledge I gained as a social scientist in graduate school. Social psychological concepts, while important for understanding group phenomena, did not appear to offer a good method for group training. My earlier experience working with knowledgeable social scientists in training cottage care workers in a residential treatment school had demonstrated to my mind that social scientific approaches to group training, without clinical intuition and skills, were rather shallow and ineffective. This impression was reinforced by what I considered then to be the naïveté of social scientific approaches to sensitivity training that I saw demonstrated by some of the NTL trainers. With my introduction to Bion's ideas began a consistent and workable model, ideally suited for training persons who claimed to be more concerned with learning about their participation in groups than with personal change and amelioration.

Influences on Bion

Bion's work is heavily influenced by the analytic thinking of Freud and Klein. Sigmund Freud has shown that social groups activate within each of their members unresolved wishes, hopes, and fears originally stimulated within the primary group (the family). Each group member projects onto the other group members and, most particularly the group leader, these unconscious and unresolved primary group feelings. In so doing he acts as if these motives were being elicited by another member of the group rather than festering within himself. In this manner the individual attempts to deny thoughts and feelings with which he is unable to cope. Klein's theories of projective identification and the interplay among the paranoid-schizoid and depressive positions were of central importance to Bion in formulating an explanation of why participants treat one another as they do in groups. According to Bion, Klein has theorized "that at the start of life itself the individual is in contact with the breast and, by rapid extension of primitive awareness, with the family group; furthermore she has shown that the nature of this contact displays qualities peculiar to itself, which are of profound significance both in the development of the individual and for a fuller understanding of the mechanisms already demonstrated by the intuition genius of Freud" (Bion, 1961).

In his contact with the complexities of life in a group the adult resorts, in what may be a massive regression, to mechanism . . . typical of the earliest phases of mental life. The adult must establish contact with the emotional life of the group in which he lives. This task would appear to be as formidable to the adult as the relationship with the breast appears to be to the infant. The belief that a group exists, as distinct from an aggregate of individuals, is an essential part of this regression, as are also the characteristics with which the supposed group is endowed by the individual. Substance is given to the phantasy that the group exists by the fact that regression involves the individual in a loss of his "individual distinctiveness" indistinguishable from depersonalization, and therefore obscures observation that the aggregation is of individuals (Bion, 1961).

According to Bion's interpolation of Kleinian theory the group members' identification with the leader is the result not simply of *introjection*, taking on the characteristics of the leader as desirable qualities of one's self, but simultaneously of *projective identification*, the group members attributing the leader with qualities (thoughts, feelings, and actions) which are actually being experienced by group members without their acknowledging these behaviors as their own.

**Dependency
Pairing,
Fight-
Flight**

With the above rationale as his theoretical premise Bion contends that successful, rational, and sophisticated work in a group is generally impeded, sometimes abetted, by a number of unconscious, basic assumptions (emotions) to which groups fall prey. Bion arrives at this contention by assuming that the foremost condition for being a member of a group is to insure that the group will survive. Having made this assumption, Bion suggests that groups employ two different levels of group process to accomplish basic aims of survival. The first level is that of sophisticated, rational work. Every group of individuals who meet together to perform a task show work group activities, that is, mental functioning designed to further the task at hand. The second level consists of three emotional assumptions. Bion refers to these basic assumptions as dependency, pairing, and fight–flight.

Dependency occurs when a group behaves as if the members have come together in order to obtain security from one individual, usually the leader, who is able to supply all the needs of the group. When the group is dependent the members relate to the leader as dependent children to a parent. On the basis of studies of a large number of training groups Stock and Thelen (1958) formulated a number of illustrations of Bion's assumptions. Dependency is exhibited when participants agree to go along with the dominant mood of the group; when group members prefer to proceed along established lines; when members are annoyed when the actions of the leader are not what they expected.

Pairing is present when two members of the group are involved in a conversation. Other members sit in attentive silence. The basic assumption of the group is that the two participants are engaged in a sexual relationship, regardless of the gender of the people involved. There is an air of hopeful expectation in the group that a "messiah" might arise as a product of this union, unite the group by means of their allegiance to his mission, and in so doing avert the other group members' thoughts from their own inner turmoil. Stock and Thelen's examples of the pairing phenomena include instances of participants extending group friendships outside the group, group members keeping the group discussion on a personal level, and participants bringing intimate material to the group.

Fight–flight operates on the assumption that the group has come together for purposes of preserving the group. The group's self-preservation is seen as achieved by only two techniques—fight or flight. Such a group views the survival of the group to be of paramount concern, with the welfare of the individuals in the group secondary. The group often feels that absent members are a danger to the coherence of the group. It deals with neurosis by fighting with it or running away from its owner. The group seeks a leader who will either mobilize the group for attack or lead it in flight. The ideal leader is, therefore, one with marked paranoid tendencies. Stock and Thelen's examples show group members ready to take sides in an argument, exposing their annoyance to other participants, and becoming sarcastic when annoyed. The dependency, pairing, and fight-flight emotional proclivities are regarded by Bion as displacing one another ". . . as if in response to some unexplained impulse. They appear, furthermore, to have some common link, or, perhaps even to be different aspects of each other. . . . Each basic assumption contains features that correspond so closely with extremely primitive past objects that sooner or later psychotic anxiety, appertaining to these primitive relationships, is released" (Bion, 1961).

Bion has written his seminal volume, *Experience in Groups* (1961), in such a way as to reflect the development of his own thinking about groups—from naïve phenomenological observations of how people treat one another in groups in which he participated to sophisticated theoretical assumptions about the dynamics of groups in general. It may be helpful to present Bion's thinking by summarizing his book chapter by chapter.*

Chapter 1

Bion began his work with groups at the Tavistock Clinic in 1948. He comments initially that his previous experience in groups has been with patients, trying to persuade these patients to make the study of their internal group tensions the group's task. Bion finds it disconcerting that the professional committee of the Tavistock Clinic seemed to believe that patients could be cured in such groups. Bion claims no such optimism. The groups he works with have eight to nine members on an average.

This chapter is devoted largely to a description of what events take place during an initial group session with group members who are not patients.

At first Bion sits silently as members gather and proceed to engage each other in superficial conversation. Then silence falls again on the group, followed by further disconnected conversation. Then silence falls again. Finally Bion, who has become aware that he is the focus of group attention and that he is expected to "do something" confided his anxieties about this to the group. The group reacts with indignation, expressing their firm belief that they are entitled to expect something from Bion. This typifies group activity—Bion's interpretations generally reflect to the group the unfounded assumptions they have

* This material on Bion was developed by Dr. David Irwin, Senior Resident Psychiatrist, Walter Reed Army Hospital, Washington, D.C.

made about what should take place in the group and how Bion should conduct himself, e.g., "it is evident that the group has certain good expectations and beliefs about me, and that you are sadly disappointed to find they are not true."

Bion finds his contributions to be generally ignored, denied, or minimized. He notes the development of powerful affective forces in the group, chiefly anger directed toward himself, and anxiety. The group then spends considerable time dealing with its doubts and misgivings about Bion's personality, apparently convinced that his behavior is deliberately frustrating and provocative. Bion asserts that the group is unable to face its emotional tensions without believing that it has some type of god who is fully responsible for everything that takes place.

Bion chooses to emphasize two features of this initial group session: The group performance is almost devoid of intellectual content; and critical judgment is almost entirely absent, as judged by the fact that assumptions are fully accepted as statements of fact.

Chapter 2

Bion's interpretations of group behavior are generally made in terms of the group's attitude toward him, less frequently in terms of their attitude toward another member. He believes this is relevant because individuals are always either consciously or unconsciously assessing the attitude of the group toward themselves and behaving accordingly. To illustrate, if a member feels his contributions are not valued by others in the group he will tend to avoid expressing them.

The author asserts that absent members can be extremely important in a group, even to the point of taking the role of group leader. That is to say, the absence of group members brings the group to act 111 in such a way as to suggest that it may be more sensible not to come to the group.

Bion postulates the existence of a group mentality, which he defines as the "unanimous expression of the will of the group to which individuals contribute anonymously." The group mentality is opposed to the avowed aims of the group members. In the group mentality the individual finds the means for expressing contributions which he would prefer to make anonymously, yet in the group mentality he finds a major obstacle to the achievement of the goals for which he has joined the group. The group mentality will often be reflected in the impatience of the group with anyone who expresses a neurotic symptom.

The author postulates that the frustration a group member commonly experiences relates to his awareness that he has gratified certain of his impulses anonymously through the group mentality and by so doing has threatened his individuality. Thus, group mentality challenges the capacity of the group to fulfill individual needs. To meet this challenge, the group elaborates a particular group *culture*. This refers to the structure or organization of the group at any given time. Bion states that the group can be thought of as the interplay among three forces: 1. individual needs; 2. group mentality; 3. group culture.

The author claims that a valid group interpretation may be based on the behavior of one or two individuals in the group, since he feels that "silence gives consent," and that unless the group actively repudiates its leader, it is in fact following him (the principle of collective responsibility).

Chapter 3

Interpretations should be phrased simply and precisely. Concrete illustrations should always be given, if possible; and the therapist should avoid the use of technical terms such as "group mentality." Furthermore, he should not mention the theoretical concepts upon which his interpretations are based.

Bion finds that group reactions to interpretations based on the concepts of group mentality, group culture, and the individual are erratic and unpredictable. He concludes that these theories are inadequate. He replaces these theories with new theories of group dynamics based upon the existence of certain *basic assumptions* (ba), having a powerful influence upon the activity of group members. (In a later chapter he develops the Work Group concept.)

Three basic assumptions: 1. Pairing (baP)
         2. Fight-flight (baF)
         3. Dependency (baD)

Chapter 4

Bion states that as soon as the group becomes aware that the leader is neither proposing rules nor a formal agenda, it sets out to correct these omissions with marked intensity. He suggests that the reason for this behavior is that the group is attempting to structure itself in such a way that the three basic assumption groups cannot emerge.

Bion further explains the dependency group. Members feel that benefit comes only from the leader and that they can learn nothing from each other. They believe they are receiving "treatment" only when talking to the group leader. However, the group matches this belief in the omniscience and omnipotence of the leader with an equally strong feeling of disappointment in whatever the leader does. The group becomes increasingly frustrated. The dependency group shows marked hostility toward the scientific method and instead behaves as if it places the greatest value upon the efficacy of magic. It takes on a distinctly religious quality, and in fact references to religion are frequent. Members will often react to interpretations by the leader with a period of silent awe.

Bion then discusses the strong aversion which all group members have when under the influence of the basic assumptions for the process of development or learning by experience. This process is, according to Bion, necessary to achieve personal growth, but in the basic assumption groups it seems possible to achieve the fantasied goal of being instantaneously and effortlessly equipped for group life.

Chapter 5

Basic assumptions are tacit. The group members do not overtly express the assumption, yet they behave as if they were fully aware of the assumption. Interpretation of the basic assumption gives meaning to the behavior of the group as a whole according to Bion. Interpretations, when accepted, represent the behavior of the sophisticated group, or Work Group. All Work Group interpretations have in common one feature—they express the recognition of the need to develop rather than rely upon magic.

The Work Group, or sophisticated group, has the following characteristics:
  a. meets for a specific task;
  b. has a high degree of cooperation;
  c. values the scientific approach to problems;
  d. emphasizes development, or learning by experience.

The distress felt by members of a group arises from the conflict between the basic assumption group and the Work Group. There is no conflict among basic assumption groups, only a transition from one to another. Members are constantly facing simultaneous pulls toward the polar opposites of the Work Group and the basic assumption group.

114   Bion postulates the existence of a Proto-mental

System, which contains prototypes of each of the three basic assumptions. This system is viewed as a matrix in which physical and mental events are undifferentiated, and from which flow the emotions associated with the basic assumption groups. While any one basic assumption is in operation at the observable level of group behavior, the two remaining basic assumptions are confined within the Protomental System.

Henry Ezriel, a fellow Briton, extended Bion's work in his own psychoanalytic practice with groups. Ezriel has maintained that the most important advantage of group therapy over individual sessions is that groups can provide an arena for observing patients' transactions with one another and the therapist. Events that occur outside the therapy session cannot be directly observed and scrutinized. In his work with groups Ezriel focused increasingly greater attention on the immediate, ongoing group activities, referred to as the here-and-now, in order to contrast them with behaviors and events that transpire beyond the session, which are referred to as the there-and-then.

Trained as an analyst, Ezriel probably showed reluctance in making such rules as "from now on we will only speak about what is presently concerning us in the *immediate* group situation instead of what was bothering us prior to the session." Indeed, the patients might wonder what has taken possession of the good doctor if he makes such a curious statement. The patients would point out with considerable indignation that they came to Ezriel's group not to be study group dynamics but to address difficulties they experience in their everyday world. It is perhaps fortunate that

Common Group Tension

Ezriel was reluctant to insist on here-and-now discussion. He permitted the patients to freely discuss what they will, but at the same time observed its immediate group impact. In so doing Ezriel observed that despite how trivial and disconnected the manifest content of the group discussion may have appeared at first glance, closer attention disclosed that each of these manifest topics had as well a covert component consisting of common (shared) group tension, which affected the course of the manifest discussion. Ezriel found, like Bion, that each of the patients contributed and participated in this common group tension. Changes in the group discussion reflected fluctuation in the group emotion or mood, which varied from moment to moment or sometimes persisted for a session or more.

System Balance

Whitaker and Lieberman, clinical psychologists with strong backgrounds in group dynamics, took hold of Ezriel's conception of a common group tension and connected it with their elaboration of Thomas French's concept of a focal problem in individual psychotherapy sessions. The result of this amalgamation was an interesting group analytic technique for studying the behavior of a group as an entity. According to Whitaker and Lieberman's rationale, the common group tension consists of three components: a forbidden motive (the wish); a reactive motive (the fear); and the resulting attempt to resolve the antagonism between the wish and the fear. The forbidden wish is a desire that the group as an entity or a majority of the group share about some relationship or event they would like their participation in the group to bring about. The reactive motive is the fear of what might occur if the forbidden wish were satisfied. The *solution* is an attempt at compromise—satisfying the wish without inducing the catastrophic reactive situation which patients fear might occur if the wish were to be fulfilled. Solutions may either be *restrictive*, which serve primarily to alleviate fears but do not deal with the disturbing motive; or *enabling*, which alleviate the reactive motive while at the same time permitting some expression of the disturbing motive. The enabling solution, which results from a successful mediation between the satisfaction of the wish and countering the reactive motive, must be accepted at some level of awareness by all members of the group. If any group member "refuses" to go along with the compromise there is no group solution. A group's culture, its log of past behavior, is structured by the group in terms of a normative system of enabling solutions, which have been found to meet the group's problem and conflictual contingencies in the past.

The authors view the group as always in a continuous state of flux. The reactive motive, the disturbing wish, and the solution are all in equilibrium with each other. A change in one causes changes in the others. Whatever happens in the group in the next moment will affect the equilibrium of the moment before. The authors observe that there is a definite continuity in sessions. If the equilibrium at the close of a session is marked by emphasis on one of the disturbing motives, the patients are likely to mobilize defenses against this disturbing motive in the next session. The next session will be marked by more restrictive solutions and/or greater emphasis on reactive fears. If the equilibrium at the close of a session deals primarily with the reactive motive, the interval will yield defenses against that fear and the next session will be marked by a reduction in anxiety level and the establishment of solutions that can successfully deal with the reactive fear.

The motivational dynamics for this perpetual group adjustment are conceived within a homostatic model that is akin to cognitive dissonance theory in terms of personality system. They are best explained by Heider's concept of balancing mechanism on an interpersonal level. According to cognitive dissonance-balance concepts, it is a psychological given that the integrity or organization of a personality system as well as the functional quality of a social system must be kept intact. When new information is processed (received and taken in) by a system of disturbing the existing equilibrium of the system, the system resists change (attempts to maintain equilibrium). The system does this by either distorting the new information or denying either the value or the existence of this information. If the information is too impressive to distort or deny, the system must undergo change so that the present system and the new informational input agree with each other. This change results in a systemic balance or unity. Change is resisted because it deprives the system of its habitual strategies of handling threats to the system. Habitual strategies for group problems (a system of enabling solutions in Whitaker and Lieberman's terms) provide the system with reliable resources. However, after having undergone change these solutions may no longer be appropriate for handling group problems. The ability of the system to handle threats after change is unpredictable. This uncertainty generates high degrees of tension in the system. When the tensions reach too high a level the system stops carrying out its normal functions and catastrophic measures to reduce tension are attempted. If these fail to meet the internal threat to the system, it collapses like an exhausted animal which cannot escape its adversary.

Parsons and Bale's social system theory is useful in understanding training groups as systems. Their conceptual scheme assesses the system's role behavior in terms of instrumental and expressive dimensions in relation to both the surrounding social environment and the system's external objectives, both within its own internal structure as a social matrix and in an intrapsychic perspective.

The sources mentioned above have influenced my own group training approach, which I refer to as "process group." The techniques and rationale of group psychotherapy—both of the psychoanalytic and the interpersonal schools—have supplied a theoretical framework. This framework is supplemented with the findings of small group research and the writings of social philosophy, particularly philosophers of the pragmatic and existential bents. To this we add game theory and interpersonal strategizing, for interpersonal games people transact because they feel this is the only means of securing the gratifications they seek.

Structural Aspects | 7

I will refer to sensitivity training in the groups I conduct as an experience under unstructured conditions. Such a statement is accurate only when the unclear role expectations and demands in a sensitivity training group are contrasted with the highly explicit demands of other situations we participate in every day of our lives. To speak of the conditions in a training group as being unstructured is, of course, an overstatement. There are a host of behavioral cues and limiting conditions to the group training experience, which make the situation less than totally unstructured. One important limiting condition is the group consultant. The consultant may influence the structure of a sensitivity training group to maximize the training experience in a number of ways he deems desirable.

Eight to twelve group members participate in a continuous group, that is, a group that meets regularly. The ideal group is one in which there are a sufficient number of participants. Each participant then feels that he does not have to speak more than he wishes, to prevent "dead silence" or to keep the group moving in a session. Correspondingly, in a group that is too large participants have to wait their turns in order to address themselves to the group; and when they do speak, the issue they are relating to is no longer of concern to the other participants. (This is not to discredit experience in large groups, which was briefly discussed in Chapter 4.) A process group is of such size that interaction can be free and spontaneous. Process groups should consist of heterogeneous membership. Having a variety of different personality styles in a group activates and maximizes differences in personal goals, attitudes, sentiments, and defensive stratagems. The clash and interchange of these interpersonal differences are the grist from which groups generate excitement, challenge, and growth. While heterogeneous composition is favored, process group training is not a melting pot for homogenizing group members' individual differences. These differences need to be explored and more fully developed, not dissipated. There is a procedural consideration involved as well. The participants' varied backgrounds serve to insure exploration of present group tensions. Participants with similar vocational experience and personal interests spend much of their time and energy conventionally and wastefully chatting about their similarities outside the group. This reinforces already existing behavior patterns and prevents the participants from exploring and relating to covert issues influencing the present group situation. In a group composed of heterogeneous membership the participants will not put up with the few participants who pursue issues that fall beyond the pale of the present group situation, for these issues are generally of concern to only a minority of the membership. Under these conditions the group is more amenable to exploration of present group tensions. It is the present group situation rather than extragroup concerns that the participants have in common. A group begins to work seriously together as an ensemble when it becomes aware of common feelings rather than common experiences and future goals (Mann, 1953).

Thelen clearly summarizes these points about group composition:

> Group growth, although not directly related to the growth of each individual, is, however, in the last analysis dependent upon the kinds of people in the group. The basic emotional dynamics of the group is a working-out of the changing strains in the network of relationships among the members and trainer. For example, if everyone in the group were thoroughly content to be forever dependent on the trainer for all decisions the trainer would find it very difficult to teach the group very much about the nature of dependency, its uses, forms, and causes. Training is much easier when some people in the group are satisfied with being dependent and others react against the feelings of dependency. Under these conditions the trainer can help the group see that some of its conflict centers around the finding of an appropriate balance between dependency and resistance to dependency (Thelen, 1954).

An exception to the need for heterogeneous membership is allowed for in-service staff training. "Staff training" refers to participants who work in some related way outside the training group. Generally they are employed by the same agency and usually have professional status. In this contingency the structure of the training experience needs to be more defined than it is for a group comprised of strangers. 123

A staff training group is concerned with members of the same natural group. The task of the training experience is not simply to explore how participants behave in groups but also to apply this knowledge of group functioning to existing agency problems, which they share as members of the same group. Application experience (described in Chapter 9) is added to the basic group experience to bridge experience in sensitivity groups to specific work situations. It is the least one can do for the agency, which frequently provides for the sensitivity experience of its employees.

Physical Setting

The physical setting does not generally matter, provided that it is relatively comfortable and free of distractions. Chairs, single chairs rather than couches, are preferable and are arranged in a circle with ashtrays available. Studies of small groups have demonstrated that the seating arrangements of the group members may influence the group process.* In general we know that variation in group process results not only from group configuration but also from the spatial distance of the participants. In an interpersonal encounter the closer two persons are to one another the more likely it is that aggressive and sexual feelings may be activated in the persons. However, in any encounter a certain degree of spatial closeness is necessary for the participants to experience contact and feel obliged to relate to one another. This threshold varies from culture to culture. In the Latin culture, for example, the threshold for interpersonal contact is probably higher and persons need to be spatially closer to experience a comfortable interpersonal

---

* The reader interested in this phenomenon is referred to the work of Thomas and Fink and the classical studies of Bavelas, Leavitt, and their students reported in the *Handbook of Small Group Research,* by A. P. Hare, (1962).

posture. It has been observed therefore when the "psychological space" between group members is disturbed during the course of group experience there will be accompanying adjustments of physical space, e.g., shifts in arrangements of chairs (Foulkes and Anthony, 1957). During periods of tension where it is difficult for the participants to widen spatial distance between one another, participants often make use of what Goffman (1959) has referred to as *involvement* shields, to keep the others at a distance. A participant may hide behind a newspaper or book. Others symbolically prevent involvement by drawing their legs close to their bodies or crossing their arms tightly across their body or pulling into themselves by mute withdrawal.

The physical location may also have some impact on the content of the group discussion as well as the group tensions being experienced by the participants. Still vivid in my memory is the lively discussion held by the participants of the first sensitivity group I conducted. The group was part of a week-long conference held on the grounds of a large psychiatric hospital. The evening before the session, the participants were taken on a tour of the back wards of the hospital. In the group session the next morning the participants discussed at length their impressions of the wards and their concern over whether the patients were getting proper care. The consultant was a clinical psychologist on the staff of the hospital. The group understandably, although unaware of its apprehension, was concerned with the limitations of psychology and psychiatry *in terms of themselves*. They were expressing the fear that something harmful might happen to one of them and they wondered if the consultant would take proper care if this unfortunate event should occur. The fear of not being taken 125 proper care of is an apprehension expressed in more or less direct form in every sensitivity group I have ever consulted. What is most interesting about this incident is not the fear being expressed but the influence the physical setting had on the manner of expressing the fear.

Frequency of Sessions

I have generally scheduled sensitivity groups in one of two ways. If it is a staff training group, as many sessions as possible are scheduled within a concentrated period of time called a *group sensitivity training conference* (see Chapter 4). If, on the other hand, the group is of heterogeneous composition, the sessions are scheduled for mutual convenience of consultant and participants, once a week on a regular basis—usually for a period of ten weeks. Participants drop out and other participants are added to the group every tenth session. In addition, I have conducted some training groups for mental health workers for over two years on a weekly basis. I have also conducted demonstration groups for only one or two sessions. There are dangers, however, involved in this last arrangement. I have serious questions about running demonstration groups on a one- or two-shot basis. Research is necessary to determine the kind of experience and the effectiveness gained in more concentrated (as opposed to more diffuse) sensitivity training scheduling. Parenthetically, in experimental psychology considerable investigation has been conducted on massed versus spaced learning. However, since the test material employed in these studies was didactic and frequently non-ego-involving, the results might not hold up for group training experience.

126

A single process group can last anywhere from one hour to two and one-quarter hours. A two-hour session seems to work best. The initial hour and one-half is given over to free discussion, and then the group is stopped for recapitulation. In groups which follow the summary with psychodrama, free discussion usually ends after an hour and ten minutes, with ten to fifteen minutes spent summarizing the session before moving into psychodrama. A session lasting one hour and one-half, with one hour devoted to free discussion seems adequate, but less than one and one-half hours is insufficient for a process group.

Duration of Session

I take no stand on this issue, in keeping with my conception of the consultant as a nonauthority figure in the group. Nevertheless, I perceive the task of both participants and consultant as relating to and inter-preting outside contacts of the members to what is going on in the present here-and-now group situation; that is, what is currently transpiring in the group that induces participants to bring up and discuss their outside activities with other participants, and, for that matter, what are the tensions that are generated in the group that induce the participants to engage in outside activities with one another.

Outside Contacts of Group Members

Dynamics 8

Process group training seeks to help people become aware and appreciative of attitudes and behaviors they normally experience as dysfunctional and unfulfilling. Process group training helps participants gain greater control over these attitudes and behaviors. To create an atmosphere conducive to a process of change an understanding of how modifications in behavior take place is necessary.

I recognize three basic, morally acceptable ways to change attitudes and behaviors.

1. The change agent directly modifies the client's situation; the client is therefore induced to change his own personal behavior because these environmental conditions enable him or force him to do so. The change agent may or may not explain to the client the need for change. Examples of this method range

from providing children or distressed adults in adverse living conditions with a healthier environment, to imposing "cold turkey" on drug addicts and "drying out" alcoholics. Under this concept of change, the client is perceived as incapable of or unwilling to modify his dysfunctional behavior on his own under the present environmental conditions. The client's environment is therefore altered for him, so that he must either modify the strategies he habitually employs when feeling anxious and upset or undergo the stress without relief.

2. The change agent may ask the client to give new behavior a trial to see if it is not more gratifying than the strategy habitually employed. Here again, explanations may or may not accompany the ameliorative attempts, or they may precede or follow the change in behavior. Where explanations are not given or are rendered after the new behavior has already been enacted the client is urged to proceed on the advice of the change agent. The change agent presents himself as an expert or authority in these matters. Firm, but generally nonoppressive pressure is asserted for change. Undesirable consequences if change is not induced are enumerated with more recalcitrant patients. In the process people may ge goaded, needled, cajoled, or tricked into making modifications in their behavior. The trial change procedure assumes that it is more amenable, functional, or perhaps more ethical for the change agent to suggest changes in behavior than to induce them. When new behavioral patterns are developed, it is assumed that new attitudes and values will become internalized in a consistent way with the new behavioral patterns (Festinger, 1954). This assumption is supported by considerable empirical data that suggests that where there is a disparity between a person's attitudes and the new behavioral patterns he has developed, and where the new ways of

responding have become gratifying, the person will change his attitudes so that they become more consistent with his new behavior. Psychodrama, Gestalt, human potentials training, and traditional education, counseling, and behavior modification are examples of this method.

3. The change agent attempts to modify the client's attitudes and values by bringing the emotional and functional purpose they serve onto a conscious level. Having laid bare the reasons "behind" his behavior the client can then deal with them. It is assumed that once the client understands what he is "really" seeking, he will come to realize that his present behavior will never achieve the goals he seeks. His present behaviors are inferior compromises. They are predicated on subjugated feelings about himself that he is neither capable nor deserving of the things he seeks. The change agent, by being sensitive to the needs and ideas of others, creates an atmosphere that enables the client to discover the advantages of change for himself. Sensitivity training groups, as well as all forms of intensive therapeutic endeavors concerned with both cognitive and emotional insight, are examples of this concept of change.

Advocates of each of the three approaches agree at least on one point: the need for social reinforcement or support for the client upon leaving the change experience. Without the continuation of a *powerfield* (Lewin, 1951), that is, an induced field which rewards the client for maintaining new and more risky behaviors, these new behaviors will be neither stable nor long maintained.

Ameliorative endeavors generally employ one of these concepts of change and do not seriously consider

Using Change Concepts

the other two until the concept initially attempted simply doesn't do the job. However, amelioration, like personality development, must be viewed sequentially. There are critical periods in which one change concept is required rather than another; therefore, an approach that combines concepts of change is preferable to one which relies exclusively on a single concept. (Mindful of this I enlisted a second consultant, a psychodramatist, in conducting my process groups.)

As a number of studies seem to verify, group leaders, regardless of their skills and the fact they were or were not successfully analyzed, tend to be more aware and responsive to either instrumental or expressive imperatives present in social situations. Combining psychodrama with group process interaction was thus conceptualized as providing the participants with two somewhat distinct but related means of modifying dysfunctional behavior and exploring new behavioral alternatives.

Why Training Groups Work

Process groups are effective in influencing change in interpersonal behavior because their simple structure (lack of an agenda) forces the participants to come to grips with their deep-seated reasons for coming together with other people in an interpersonal situation. In task situations or other highly structured situations the reason for being present is determined beforehand by the nature of the task. Usually in such situations the members gather together to discharge a community function, pioneer a cause, find expressions of common talent, advance a shared interest, solve a problem, accomplish a task or merely, for congenial social intercourse. Does our presence, for example, at a formal dinner party attended by people whom we regard as intellectually and personally inane enable us to recognize the frustration and loneliness we experience? Generally not! Indeed, the very purpose of most of our social functions is not to reveal but conceal our concern over not having accessible people whom we hold in warm regard and with whom we wish to exchange our ideas.

Adverse to laying bare our fears, we sustain (or even assail) the stated goals of the groups and organizations in which we find ourselves. We do not contact our deep-seated intentions about what we want of ourselves, and how we define ourselves in terms of our needs and ambitions, in these situations. For some who are actively concerned with how they present themselves to others, so much of their time and energy are spent resisting negative definitions of themselves that little opportunity exists for creating a prototype of the kind of person they might wish to be. They spend much of their time telling themselves and others that there is no one in the world who is going to tell them what to do. When they secure those precious moments of respite from the imposition of others, they find that they don't know what they want to do with themselves. "In the structured groups of everyday life, the specific roles and role relationships, the procedures, the recognized standards of behavior provide defenses against the recognition of underlying processes. . . ." (Rice, 1965).

Task-oriented groups, therefore, have value for people because they structure or consume an interval of time, much the way compulsive television watching serves our need to avoid responsibility for constructively employing our daily existence. In highly structured situations the individual can lose himself, emersed within the details of the task to be performed. He does not have to concern himself with the ongoing social process—particularly the impact it has on his own feelings and ambitions. Members of structured 133 groups pay a price for the groups' capacity for consuming time. They must "resign still more of their individual proclivities in favor of ensuring the survival of the group and its structure" (Berne, 1963).

The goals of a task-oriented group are generally externally determined. They come into being to resolve problems that exist in the community. Mothers against sex education in the schools may not have said a word to one another before forming a group. Once their task is completed they may disband and cease to meet as a group unless some other external "cause" is able to rally them together again.

The job of the task group is not to study difficulties, conflicts, tension, differences in ideology or effect among group members unless the group cannot avoid doing so in order to achieve its goals. As time is generally at a premium, there is not much desire or opportunity for the group members to concern themselves with what other members are feeling, unless it is the only way to settle some argument (more often to postpone it) and achieve consensus. The task group is concerned with finding appropriate standards and methods that *already exist* (this saves time), not with inventing its own solutions. The task group is not interested in what the participants personally think of these solutions.

The goal of the process group on the other hand is to study its own process. It has no explicit goal other than this. It is a continuous task, for process is continuously being generated, as the group's task is never totally achieved, time pressure in reaching the group's goal has no bearing. In the process group there is no escape by losing oneself in performing a task or being entertained. Should a group member not participate in the work of the group, he pays the price of being bored and frustrated. Boredom occurs because there is no inherent group structure or given agenda with which to preoccupy oneself. The group that does not involve itself in work, therefore, cannot satisfactorily structure its time. Each participant who does not involve himself in the task feels deep within him that some important part of himself as a fully functioning person is being denied by his passivity and dependence upon others. H. F. Thomas has expressed it aptly: ". . . If there is any answer to the problems of meaning in my life, it does not lie out there someplace, but within me. Life does not present me with meanings. Life merely *is*. The meaning, the true zest for living, comes from full involvement with life. In order for growth and the development of one's potential to occur, the individual needs to face himself as he is at each moment. [There must be a] willingness to use one's own experience as the final authority for truth" (Thomas, 1967).

The Here-and-Now

Participants in a sensitivity group come to a session with the day's frustrations and tensions. They seek to enlist the other group members in their behalf and receive their kindly support. They want the other participants to support their arguments and decisions that brought on upsets with their associates. They don't regard themselves as neurotic but expect instead to be congratulated for bearing their heavy burdens so well. They hope that the other participants will say, "Of course, you're right! You don't have to feel guilty, hurt, or denigrated." However, these troubled participants also sense that they contribute to their own upsets. They are not sure just how, or if they really care to face their hurt. The healthier part of their egos nevertheless pushes for remedial attention and understanding. Simultaneously their defenses mobilize to ward off the threat to their self-esteem that

135

comes from acknowledging their own contribution to their upsets. In this way ambivalance, the neurotic condition that each of us is prey to, ensues.

The way the ambivalent participant in a sensitivity group presents his problems to the group is precisely how he presents his situation to himself. The study of personality shows that *perceptual styles* are highly consistent in interpersonal and intrapersonal situations. Thus as the participant's perceptions of his plight, due to his ambivalence, results in an *insoluble problem* for him to resolve, in corresponding fashion, the presentation of his difficulties to the group presents the group members with an insoluble problem. Any suggestion or solution offered by the other participants violates implicit assumptions that the troubled participant has imposed. For instance, some member of the group suggests that perhaps the troubled participant received an angry reaction from his superior because he gave the impression that he was not listening and did not care. The helpful participant has in this instance violated the assumption that the group is intended to support group members and not criticize them. The troubled participant is likely to defend himself against the criticism by denial. He will likely retort, "It was not like that at all! You were not there so you cannot know!" On the other hand, another participant may support the troubled participant by suggesting that the troubled participant's antagonist may have been experiencing his own personal problems. This violates the assumption that the group is intended to help participants modify dysfunctional behavior. The troubled participant may counter therefore by bemoaning, "But why do I always get these kinds of reactions from people. If you knew what it was like you would understand!"

A process group, unlike a sophisticated therapy group, is not "trained" to deal with the covert, unconscious processes that induce participants to discuss extragroup events and thereby avoid facing themselves and the urgency of what they are *immediately* experiencing. The training group must therefore concern itself with overt perceptions of material presented to them. Since the participants are not privy to the participant's experiences outside the group, there-and-then events brought to the group present it with insoluble problems. It is only the perceptions, attitudes, and behaviors arising within the here-and-now that the group is party to and consequently is in a position to realistically evaluate.

When someone enters a group situation, he finds little room to negotiate how he wishes to be treated by others. This is because people generally react to the person's pre-situation role rather than to the individual who occupies the role. During a session with a group which had been meeting continuously for six or seven weeks, the consultant (myself) remained silent, permitting the group to carry on the discussion. In the course of the session one of the middle-aged civil service employees discussed a recent incident at work where he, as a supervisor, had to make a rather straightforward administrative decision. The group, composed of three middle-aged civil servants and seven participants in their mid-twenties to early thirties, quickly reacted to the role of supervision. Some criticism evoked from the younger participants bordered on the paranoic. The relationship this civil servant had built up with these group members seemed to be completely ignored. The group was oblique to him as a person and was reacting instead to his outside function as a supervisor. Having brought in his role from the outside he could no

Negotiation for Roles

longer negotiate how he wished to be treated as a person. The younger group members were reacting to him through the distorted optics of their anti-establishment perspective. The civil servant ceased to be a person for them. He was instead an abstraction, the supervisor as a stereotype. People find it difficult to express sympathetic feelings for an abstraction.

Another example of negotiation of roles occurred earlier that day. I had supervised a young psychotherapist who was working with an adolescent patient. Prior to going over her impressions of the last therapy session she mentioned that she had been experiencing her own personal problems recently. As she discussed what had taken place in the session she and I became aware that both she and her patient were relating in a more satisfactory manner during this session than they had been in the previous six months of therapy. It also became evident that the patient was relating to the therapist in a "healthier" way than he had before—he seemed less caught up with his own preoccupation and more aware of what the therapist was experiencing. The patient was picking up the therapist's preoccupation with her own difficulties. This caused a strain or unbalance in their transactional system. In the former therapeutic role relationship she was the therapist—the one who gives aid and comfort—and he, the patient—who acts "sick" so that he can receive aid and comfort. To maintain a comfortable relationship under this role arrangement the patient would have to maintain himself as "sick." During this session, however, the therapist could not appropriately play the giving, comforting role because of her own preoccupation. At the same time the patient could not secure the usual gain from being a patient. There is a healthy, assertive, autonomous striving in all of us; it was present in

this patient and he responded to the therapist's

distress as an opportunity to relate to her with under-standing and support. Hopefully, if the new role was gratifying for the patient he would continue to play it and the role would become more and more an integral part of his behavior.

Of course therapists should not approach their patients with their own personal difficulties and ask to be comforted, with the belief that such transactions would enable the patient to respond in a "healthy" manner. A regular diet of such behavior would more likely result in the patient feeling exploited. But the terms of the social (therapy) contract should be part and parcel of the continual ongoing transaction between patient and therapist, leaving their roles open enough for continued renegotiation. This process is equally relevant to group training. The consultant needs to be aware of which preconceived notions of demands and limitations of role behavior participants bring to the group. Having revealed the assumptions that the participants are operating by, more rational role negotiation is feasible.

Why do sensitivity training groups have such impact upon their participants? Why do the normative structures of training groups frequently appear to hold members so unswayingly within latitudes of permissible group behavior? Realistically considered, sensitivity groups are not primary groups from which the participant customarily derives satisfaction of his needs. The group member may spend no more than one and one-half hours a week in the session. He may even depart from each session with no discernible results for his efforts.

Observation of everyday life suggests that people are impelled to compare themselves with others. In

Social Comparison

139

groups this comparison joins with a desire for approval from others and becomes a more or less explicit standard for judging one's own performance within the group. Each group member tries to locate himself in relation to others in the group in terms of his task performance and his abilities and opinions (Festinger, 1954). If the individual tends to compare himself in all social situations which are available to him, why does this process have such a potent impact within a sensitivity group?

The process group is concerned with the here-and-now. The members of a sensitivity group are usually not interested in or impressed by a participant's past performance or standings in other groups. The process group is concerned essentially with the participant's ongoing performance in the immediate group situation—what he brings to the group and the effect it has on the group. This is probably unlike any other social situation the participant finds himself in. In the business world he can rationalize his failings to achieve desired positions—his competitor is married to the boss's daughter; went to the right school; is comfortable with devious practices, etc. His difficulties within the family are viewed as resulting from his wife's hysterical personality or his son's incorrigibility (which is a product of the rebellious younger generation). This kind of rationalizing distorts his social comparative perceptions and masks how he influences and contributes to what happens to him.

In the process group such rationalizations are not easily tolerated. The group is generally committed to have no rocks upright in its quest for honesty in terms of not allowing participants to excuse themselves for not measuring up to others. Participants use group feedback of their behavior to discern what it is that they contribute to their own failings. Participants who attempt to ignore these feedbacks do not get away easily.

Man is born into a prefabricated world not of his own making. Man is born into a culture which defines to the smallest degree the acceptable and rejected behavior of his existence. If man were a simple organism whose function were to maintain himself in a hedonistic yet energetically conservative fashion these strictures would not invite his regard, if indeed they would exist at all. Man is, however, not a creature whose enduring pleasure can be met simply. He is a complex being who at times risks the simple pleasures and security he has gained in quest of more substantial joys and personal enrichment. Man then is not a creature whose destiny is to fulfill his culturally prefabricated dictates, but is a being whose quest is perpetual self-exploration and whose nature is never final and resolute unless he recants from the ordeal and gives in to the cultural strictures. The nature of man, if unfettered, is seen as continuously emerging and being redefined in terms of his new experiences—new perceptions, ideas, feelings, and relationships.

Nevertheless, in the culture in which he dwells his intrapsychic and interpersonal explorations are transacted. He can never escape grappling with the terms of this human condition. The fully functioning individual, consequently, can no more disregard the demands of society than he can deny the promptings of his emergent being. To avoid the dilemma of embracing one set of demands at the unrealistic exploitation of the other, the individual must avoid the dilemma of regarding his human condition as a question that demands an answer. If his human

Social Conflict

condition is a problem then it is a problem without an answer (Watts, 1961).

Man's emerging nature is never finally perfected nor are cultural demands ever absolutely set. His own nature and the demands of others are in perpetual struggle. He may opt out and surrender his autonomy. In so doing he becomes an object for others to manipulate; for example, a hospitalized patient who is pushed back and forth in a stereotype role. He becomes an object for others to project their own torments and demands upon; he will not protest or assert who he is and what he strives to be.

Sensitivity training stands neither for the demands of the culture nor for the separation of the individual from his context. We need to view the struggle as authentic and optimistic, yet never resolved.

Conducting 9
a
Process
Group

The room is not very large. A circle of chairs occupies most of the space. Seven or eight participants have arrived; they sit, dispersed, around the circle. Two or three more participants will arrive shortly. An attractive woman of perhaps thirty-five laughs uncomfortably as she straightens her short skirt and leans over to whisper to a middle-aged man sitting stiffly in his chair, fidgeting with his tie. A tall, lanky youth pushes the window up and down, finally reaching a satisfactory level, coaxed by the staccato of smiles and grimaces he receives from the circle of occupants. He slides into a seat next to a slim girl, devoid of cosmetics, seated slightly back from the circle. A heavy, bosomy woman with a painted smile furtively studies the others in the group. It is now 7 P.M. I enter the room and seat myself facing the door. I light a cigar as the apprehensive eyes of the participants attempt to engage mine. The tension in their countenances concedes a plead for me to lead 143 them, to tell them *why* they have come to the group. They are asking me what they *should* do to abate their anxieties about what is expected of them. As I examine their faces, one thought from among many takes hold: "Even if I should choose to lead them and try to resolve their dilemma, I would be certain to disappoint them. No one can really resolve another's dilemma, for who can tell another how to live and what he need not fear!" Casting aside these reflections, I say in an even voice, intentionally devoid of affect, "I am Dr. Goldberg. We are here to study groups . . . that is, we are here to study *how we behave as a group*." Again, my eyes canvass the group, resting for a moment on each of the participants in turn. The group is already in process; but to the participants, perhaps without exception, my definition of the group's task is perceived as insufficient direction and preparation for a task, which the participants are beginning to wonder if they wish to engage themselves in.

The Group Task

Let us examine at this point the consultant's initial statement to the process group for cues which the participants may use to proceed with their task. "We are here to study how we behave as a group," defines the group's task as learning about what happens in a group by studying how the assembled participants operate as a social unit. Furthermore, the consultant's statement structures the role relationship of the consultant vis-à-vis the participants. The task of studying group activity is a joint project of the consultant and the participants (implied by the pronoun "we"), but the consultant, by using his professional title, intimates that he will not participate simply as another group member. The consultant has implied moreover by saying "how we behave," rather than "how we have behaved" or "how we should behave," that the task is not a prepared one or a retrospective or purely intellectual activity. The participants should be attending to how they behave as a group in the here-and-now, which is an ongoing, continuous process. Undoubtedly, more information is also implicit in the consultant's opening statement, although for our purposes this is sufficient.

It is important for the consultant to refer back to the task at hand throughout the course of the session. When the consultant feels that the group is attempting to avoid involvement with the goal for which they have convened—a study of what is going on in the immediate group situation—he needs to point this out to the participants.* In so doing the consultant attempts to delineate how untested, preconceived, irrational, and dysfunctional implicit assumptions, which the members brought with them to the group, have been operating in the group from the onset. These preconceived assumptions have prevented the group from getting on with its task, and have prevented the participants from understanding and making use of the consultant's assessment of how the group is proceeding at its task.

Resistance in the participants to working as a group can best be understood by appreciating the influence on their behavior as a group of the participants' preconceived notions and assumptions about what it means to be a member of a group. *Preconceived notions*, referred to as fantasy in psychological literature, are

---

* Tobi Klein, a colleague who has participated in several of my workshop demonstrations of process groups, has pointed out that repeated statement of the group's task early in the development of the group reduces the participants' resistance to the task more than interpretation of underlying group emotions does. This contention needs investigation.

the fairy tales we tell ourselves about what the world is all about. These notions may have little external validity. Preconceived notions are based upon what we would like the world to be instead of what we have actually found to be the case. Due to their self-reinforcing or self-fulfilling nature, these notions are resistant to critical judgment.

Self-Fulfilling Events

Self-fulfilling prophecies occur when we set up situations that make a particular event we have predicted inevitably occur. Moreover, we forge the event as an unquestioned natural law by denying to ourselves our own participation and responsibility in the event. An example may be illustrative. Tony is a waiter in an expensive restaurant. He has been a waiter most of his life, never having made much money as he often gets into arguments with customers and fellow workers, resulting in frequent changes of employment. Tony has some difficulty explaining these arguments to himself, for in his mind he is an authority on social behavior. Closest to his heart of course are the tips of his customers. He claims with much conviction to anyone who cares to listen that he can distinguish a good tipper from a cheapskate the very instant the customer enters the restaurant. Let us observe Tony as he seats a middle-aged man who has entered the restaurant. Tony looks at the man, who isn't particularly well dressed. "Mama mia, another cheapskate!" he bemoans to himself. Indeed, Tony trusts his hunch. His service is inadequate; he keeps the customer waiting and fills his water glass only after repeated requests. The customer leaves thinking to himself, "What a crummy waiter! I will leave him no more than the nickel tip he deserves." Tony sees the nickel tip and declares, with no small satisfaction, of which he is apparently unaware, "See, I was right! He was nothing but a cheapskate."

There are three important features in the above illustration, which are found in all self-fulfilling events: 1. Tony's behavior is *dysfunctional* to his better interests. The kind of service he rendered resulted in a smaller tip than he may have obtained had his behavior been more appropriate to the situation; 2. Tony appeared *unaware that he influenced* the customer's behavior. In Tony's mind he would have received an inferior tip regardless of the quality of his service. By being a good judge of character, he reasons, he saved himself needless effort in having to perform well; 3. Tony is apparently *unaware of the satisfaction he derives in being "correct"* about the customer. From our vantage point we can contend that Tony gave himself the short end of the stick. Yet in Tony's mind he derives satisfaction from being a smart fellow.

The example described above is not from a group training situation; nevertheless, the basic ingredients hold constant for all situations that contain self-fufilling behavior. It is an important part of the consultant's task to help the participants appreciate the adverse effects of their self-fulfilling behavior. How does the group consultant undercut group behavior that the participants enact in confirming their preconceived notions about groups? He may do this by interpreting to the group *what it is they are doing* and *the function these behaviors serve* for the group. We can be more specific about how this is done. In an early session of a sensitivity group Edna, the heavy-set woman, and Harry, the middle-aged executive, expressed their resentment and disappointment at the consultant for not doing what was clearly his job to do. They contended that if the group experience was not to be a waste of their time each of the participants must learn ways of becoming more interpersonally competent outside the group. The group agreed with Edna and Harry that the consultant's job was to lecture the group on social behavior. He was expected to point out to each participant what he was doing to "turn off" people.

The consultant at this point intervened and indicated that there was nothing he said or did to convey the idea that he was supposed to lecture them or make them more socially competent. He wondered out loud where these ideas came from. Since he did not introduce or suggest them to the group, these ideas must have been brought in by the group members. He suggested that the members of the group would perhaps prefer to be told how to behave rather than struggle with their own intentions and silent fears about being intimately involved in an interpersonal encounter. The participants reflected on the consultant's words. They soon fell into desultory discussion. After a while tension was felt to be building up in the group. The participants were again mobilized together for another assault upon the consultant's apparent lack of responsibility in performing his job. The participants claimed that they could not work on the task at hand because they did not have the resources to do so. They disclaimed possessing training or knowledge about groups; certainly they denied having the technical knowledge the consultant must possess but was selfishly withholding. They blamed the consultant for the group's failure to accomplish something.

The consultant pointed out that the group was insisting that he feed them by telling them what they were supposed to be doing. He shared with them his impression, that it seemed incredible but accurate no less, that when he did feed them they ignored what he had said and persistently insisted that he was depriving them of his skills and knowledge. He pointed out that he had observed people in the group smiling and nodding their heads in approval of what he is saying before he had completed enough of his statement to put his point across. It was apparent, the consultant told them, that they did not want to hear what he had to say. The consultant raised the question of whether the participants actually wanted advice and guidance or an approving pat on the head.

As the foregoing incident suggests, in terms of his statements to the group, the consultant cannot simply describe what he observes to be transpiring in the group. He must offer conjunctively an explanation of the behavior. As in group therapy, as Spotnitz suggests (1961), the consultant addresses himself directly to the emotional tendencies the members of the group appear unaware of but which are significantly influencing their behavior as members of a social unit. He also deals with the mobilized feelings they are aware of but cannot tangibly fashion into words. If they could it would enable them to match their attitudes and sentiments with the observations of others and thereby test their validity. Experience remains largely unconscious unless it is symbolized in accessible concepts for the person to employ in his dealings with others. Experience must be labeled so that the conceptual ideation can be matched and properly matched and properly connected with emotional counterpart, e.g., kinesthetic and propioceptive sensation. In putting the participant's experience into words the consultant attempts to alert the members of the group to the emotional realities of

Explaining Present Behavior

the situation in such a way that will enable them to understand their behavior. As in psychotherapy, the consultant's *interpretations*, that is, his explanation of what is "actually happening" (as he views it) in the group (and which the group will not consider because of its threatening nature), will probably not sink in and be accepted the first time the participants are faced with it. It will become vivid and inescapable only after it is experienced and is pointed to repeatedly.

The Summary Period

Normally, a process group has six to twelve participants. Ideally, a session runs for two hours. The first hour and one-half is given to free discussion and group interaction. At the end of this period the consultant says something to the effect, "Now let's stop and recapitulate what went on here as a group! . . . What kind of group process did we see evolving?" During this period the participants are stimulated to conceptualize how *they as a group* interacted. What kinds of general themes and interpersonal patterns developed in this interaction? It is essential that the consultant permit the participants to struggle with the difficult task of making sense of their activity as a group. For people accustomed to thinking in terms of manifest generalizations and irrelevancies, thinking in terms of process and group dynamics is an onerous task.

The consultant who imposes his own explanation of what went on in the session, before the participants have the opportunity to express their own impressions, contradicts the message he has been trying to effect throughout the group training experience—that the group members have the resources to work effectively at the task at hand. When a consultant too quickly and too frequently "assists," the participants cannot help but confirm their preconceived notions that they cannot function by themselves. Why else would the consultant so quickly rush to their aid? The consultant intervenes in the summary session only after the participants have largely exhausted their efforts to describe the group process. To the participants' observations the consultant adds his own impressions, clarifying and explaining as well as pointing to phenomena which the participants seem to have ignored.

Frequently, what the participants fail to observe are the most cogent processes evolving in the group. The consultant's delineation of these processes often helps clarify interpretations he made to the group during the session. These interpretations may not be understood until they are set within the context of the overall group process.

At all times the consultant needs to be aware of the current mood of the participants. Timing is as vital during the summary period as it was during the group process period. The consultant must sense where the participants are in their development as a group. He must assess the nature and the degree of complexity of didactic and experiential material the group members can absorb at that point in time. If the consultant is insensitive to the group's maturity and defensive system, by imposing additional cognitive and emotional experience he will be simply lecturing to them. Here, again, he is contradicting the per-missive, nonprodding role he enacted during the group process. It is easy to be beguiled by the apparent sophistication of the participants during the summary stage; particularly when the sophistication is com-pared to their "dull-wittedness" in the emotional heat of battle during the group process. The participants, if they are reasonably literate, may be cognitively familiar with the terms and concepts the consultant employs. Nevertheless, many of the same emotions that were operating during the group process period will operate during the summary period. These covert group tensions continue to prevent the participants from successfully integrating the consultant's explanations with what they experienced during the session.

One way the consultant can avoid mobilizing the participant's defenses is by not becoming defensive, himself, during his exposition of group process. He must set aside the assumption that if he somehow could convince or persuade the participants to accept his point of view the group would greatly benefit. It is better for the consultant to present his observations *as his own impressions*, which he feels convey something about what went on in the group. He should be careful to emphasize that what he says is his own point of view. Regardless of the truth it may contain, it is only one view of what happened in the group. Whether or not he discusses the most important events which occurred, they are the events which he found interesting and considers important to study. He should convey to the group that there are no absolute truths about groups. Each participant and each observer tends to see one or another perspective of the situation's totality. Each perspective may have validity. The consultant offers the group his observations of what he sees happening in the group as well as what he observes being ignored by the group.

With groups whose members insist on "absolute principles" about interpersonal behavior, it is useful to follow Foulkes and Anthony's suggestion (1957) of leaving explanations "hanging in the air." I offer my exposition about interpersonal behavior in a way that retains the possibility of alternative notions. It is the task of the participants to pull together these explanations into a meaningful integration on the basis of what the consultant helps them realize they are experiencing as they try to manipulate the consultant into fulfilling their need for certainty. This is more valuable than pitting consultant's theories about what happened in the group against participants' theories.

Throughout the summary session the consultant tries to serve as a *role-model* for the participants. He tries to exemplify as best he can a "useful" group member, applying himself to the task at hand and following through in an objective and considered manner. Moreover, if he experiences strong feelings about the behavior of participants he lets the participants know about them as directly as he can. For example, if someone is not letting him be heard or is repeatedly distorting his words he lets him know about it; or if he feels favorably about a participant who in the summary period is trying earnestly to apply the material to his own behavior he lets the participants know about these feelings.

In short, during the summary period the consultant assumes a teaching and discussion-leader role. He asks the participants to explore the evolution of events that occurred in the session. The consultant lends himself to the impressions of the participants by offering concepts to bring together the group members' impressions and heretofore unrelated events and interactions in the current and previous group sessions. He concerns himself with both the emotional and cognitive elements of the experience. Balance given to both feeling and thought is necessary so that a holistic view of group process is presented for the participants to examine. This is necessary, as Arieti points out, because "only the most primitive emotions do not need a cognitive counterpart. It is only with full understanding that we can get to the emotional core of things. . . . What is the point of self-discovery if there is nothing or very little to discover?" (Arieti, 1968).

The Self-Actualizing Aim

The focus of the process group is on the group as an entity rather than on its individual members. This is in keeping with group training as an educational process in self-growth. In other forms of group experience, Encounter groups, T-groups, and certainly in therapy groups, the attention of the professional person in the group is on the individual, pointing to each individual exclusively, indicating specific dysfunctional behaviors and frequently suggesting more appropriate substitute responses. The therapist or group leader who points out dysfunctional behavior in individuals bases his assessments upon some specific set of therapeutic concepts. Whether they are based on theories of Freud, Rogers, Moreno, Perls, or whomever, there is the implicit assumption of an absolute and given program of growth and development for the individual. This is not inappropriate within certain contexts, such as the treatment of seriously disturbed patients with thinking disorders or in acting-out characters. In character disorder instinctual urges are rampant, and there are no adequate ego resources to critically evaluate the implications of these inner demands. A critical ego must be internalized and nurtured through identification with a strong, realistic, and consistent therapist, vis-à-vis patient-therapist, patient-group interactions.

With the neurotic, which most sensitivity training participants are, the superego is overly severe to begin with. The ego and the more spontaneous, coping, and exploratory urgings of the personality must be freed from the superego's strict restraint. A group leader who takes charge and directs the group, no matter how democratically he tries to behave, reinforces the stringent promptings of the individual's superego to view the leader as a means of enacting behavior where guilt is blocked from awareness. When an individual's actions are attributed to the leader, that individual can remain an "innocent" follower into whatever folly he is cast. The more absolute the authority figure is perceived to be, the less accountable for his actions the neurotic holds himself. "The leader's way" tends to become tempered into "*the* way." Relinquishing the direction of the group to the participants in a process group conveys to them the "authority's" contention (although the group will fight accepting it) that they, the participants, can solve their own difficulties, for the "authority" has demonstrated his confidence in them.

In a process group, there is much possibility for emotional and cognitive development because the participants are thrown, within a climate of study and observation, to their own underdeveloped but potentially capable devices. Here more can happen because less is controlled. Each individual participant can more "legitimately" go at his own pace. There are of course pressures within the group to prevent others from trying out new and psychologically risky behaviors. However, because the consultant is less emotionally involved in the group, he is less unwittingly collusive with the group and can more appropriately discern those pressures resistant to psychological growth.

155

Process Compared with Therapy Group Training

Much of the confusion and controversy concerning sensitivity training centers on the objectives of the group leader. Is it group therapy he wishes to conduct or another form of group experience? Until this question is answered it may be difficult to understand why process group training concentrates on group process and the study of the group as an entity rather than on individuals in a social situation.

A clear distinction must be made between group training, as enacted in process groups, and group therapy. Both techniques are concerned with the didactic process of self-awareness in a group situation. "Group therapy," however, "is for the person who is already hurting;" who has serious emotional problems that prevent him from adequately functioning. Sensitivity groups, on the other hand, are for those who feel that they are functioning adequately but who wish to increase their capacity for more self-actualized and gratifying living within the bounds of their present relationships (Rogers, 1967). It may be a whimsical overstatement to claim that persons entering group psychotherapy are impelled by pain and those drawn to sensitivity training are propelled by joy; it would seem accurate, however, that persons who gravitate toward group training are those seeking to expand their present personality and explore new kinds of interpersonal function, rather than those experiencing serious difficulty with present modes of functioning.

Group psychotherapy is a direct attempt by the therapist to influence the client's dysfunctional attitudes and behaviors through the skilled manipulation of his own interpretations and the proclivity of the situation. His aim is to induce transference onto himself and other group members of significant others from each client's past history. In sensitivity training the emphasis is on more conscious readjustment of role in interpersonal situations. Feedback and insight gained within the here-and-now confrontation are used. Consequently, as traditional group therapy is restorative rather than proactive, group therapy necessarily requires a longer duration to achieve its aims than does group sensitivity training. Group sensitivity training is proactive in that it is not actually concerned with the participant's past but with what he purports to be seeking. What *are* the sentiments and motives that have brought him into heated encounter with his fellow participants in the group? What is he *currently* experiencing as he attempts to make his sentiments known to the group? Sensitivity training's success is derived from its ability to implement these objectives for self-awareness. The goal therefore of group training is "exploration rather than cure" (Stoller, 1967). Its aim is self-amelioration of interpersonal "hangups." Sensitivity groups have a spontaneous explosiveness (which traditional group therapy often lacks), because they focus on the immediate here-and-now situation within the sensitivity group, not on explanations of past behavior and traumas, which are often now still and cold. Preoccupation with the past often serves as a handy justification for not doing anything to fashion a more gratifying, self-actualized existence today. Without the shackles of habitual, everyday role expectations, each participant has the opportunity to explore more freely just what he really thinks and feels about himself and others, and to experiment with ways to make his own personal strategies less self-defeating and more gratifying.

The aim is not a particular psychological state for the participant, such as being able to better trust people, or becoming less prejudiced or better able to understand other generations. Nor is the objective to remove deep-seated emotional conflicts or to modify the basic character of the group participants. If the group experience enables the individual to make personality modifications so much the better. Process group has not failed if psychodynamics aren't modified, as this is not the goal. Rather, process group alerts the participants to a greater appreciation of the uncertainty, frustration, anger, alienation, anxiety, and other intrapsychic discomfort they experience in group interaction, of their interrelationship to the resultant roles, defenses, attitudes, and sentiments they evince in reaction to these feelings.

There is also a purely technical reason for not working with the individual in groups that are short-term. To interpret a participant's behavior sufficient information and observation is needed to avoid the confusion and legitimate anger caused by a poorly conceived interpretation. Process groups are usually short-term group experiences. As a result the consultant has much less opportunity than the group therapist to get to know participants as individuals in depth. Nor can he work through with them as in intensive psychotherapy. Group training is devised as a technique that tries to best maximize short-term experience.

Confronting Frustration

A powerful and overwhelming emotion characteristic of process groups is the sense of utter helplessness and frustration the group generates from time to time. This mood is sensed in the participants' inability to achieve group objectives suitable to their own satisfaction. In therapy groups the therapist may undercut the anxieties generated by unfulfilled strivings by guiding the patients in exploration of these feelings. Analytic exploration of feelings becomes normative for therapy groups. Participants in process groups do not receive direct guidance in the exploration of feelings. The sense of utter helplessness and frustration in a sensitivity group may become intolerable at times as the participants' fantasies become nurtured by fears of being overwhelmed and destroyed. From where have these fears sprung, now so impressive? They have been present, although covert, from the onset of the group. To those attuned to their throb they were repeatedly manifested in the forceful exclamations of group members that "this group enterprise is doomed to fail." Various rationalizations were offered by group members for the group having to perish, none sounding very convincing. Beneath the pessimism of the group denigrators was a half-conscious set of statements they were uttering to themselves:

"I need to know what is going on in this group; what you, the consultant and you, the other participants are trying to do to me; you are trying to violate me (expose my vulnerability); I cannot let you do this; I must fight you; if I defeat your endeavors I'll remain safe and unchanged; *but* if I defeat you and remain unchanged, then why have I come here? I am wasting my time; I am wasting the opportunity to improve myself and feel better about myself."

These ambivalent feelings, shared to some degree by each of the participants, lie at the core of the participants' resistance to applying themselves to their task. These feelings impel much of the pathological dynamic generated in groups. To rid themselves of these uncomfortable feelings each participant *projects*, that is, attributes resistance and lack of sincerity to the behavior of the other group members and the consultant, absolving himself of the same motives. Here the consultant should intervene, interpreting the meaning of the projective behavior of the participants and indicating how it fails to achieve its purpose of resolving inner turmoil.

159

It has been charged by many critics of group training that group experience that focuses entirely upon an analytic understanding of an individual's participation in interpersonal situations is a deficient training experience. The "rugged individualist" school criticizes the sensitivity training movement for singularly excessive concern with feelings to the exclusion of attention to responsibility and task performance. Participants who emerge from group training without attention directed toward application of their group training experience to their responsibilities outside the group are likened to the proverbial psychoanalytic patient who leaves therapy with an incomplete analysis. He is highly sensitive to sorting out how he gets into situations and how he experiences these difficulties, but is at a loss in trying to put these insights together in such a way that he is able to remedy these situations. His life is devoted to a quest for why he does the things he does. Each day adds more situations to his agenda for investigation in a cycle with which he can never hope to catch up.

It was with this consideration in mind that I sought an atmosphere for trying out behaviors that participants considered adopting that was more supportive than the participant's home situation. Psychodrama was therefore applied to group training in my community center workshop. Psychodrama has proved an effective method for *demonstrating* interpersonal phenomena. Employing dramatic techniques usually captures the interest of the participants in such a way that lends conviction to training experience. Use of psychodrama was also guided by notions about role behavior. In a process group, participants are strangers and therefore are better able to shed some of the roles enacted in everyday life. The more familiar we are to others the more difficult it is to resist the pressure of being cast into familiar, stereotyped roles. Even in social situations in which we know no one else, we immediately create a certain image or role in regard to how others react to us. We are, in effect, telling others how we are usually seen. It is not strange that once a role pattern has been established, any variation may be viewed with surprise and distrust by others. Participants in our groups have complained: "I feel in a rut. I want to try something new and different, but I cannot with the people I know. I wish I could change myself."

Changing Roles

In the relatively safe group situation, under trained guidance, trying out new responses and behavior patterns is encouraged. Participants are frequently asked to take roles which differ from their everyday presentation of themselves. A rather shy and retiring young lady, Priscilla, was given the role of "mod swinger" in a singles bar. After a number of attempts and considerable encouragement from the group she played the role convincingly to her surprise and to the delight of the group. For several weeks the group had been trying to draw her out of her protective shell. In subsequent sessions Priscilla seemed more relaxed and her interactions with other participants took on a bolder quality. She left for vacation and returned for the last session with a stylish new hairdo and makeup, presenting herself as a more attractive and self-confident person than she had been when she entered the group.

For other participants the changes are not as dramatic. Perhaps there will be a gradual increase in one's awareness of his own actions and an increased sensitivity to the actions and reactions of others. A business executive in one of my groups found for the first time in years that he was not in charge. This experience was useful to him because it enabled him to see himself as others saw him. He was able to get feedback from the group members who were not restrained from telling him "like it was," for they did not have business or work relationships with him.

From time to time in the psychodrama period I have focused on specific work problems that a participant brought up in the process group. These were generally problems that had not been resolved to his satisfaction, so that he and the group were still caught up with the difficulty at the time of the psychodrama period. In such conflict situations focus is on the participant's actions, which were important contributing factors in both the external situation and in preventing the group from helping him with the problem in the current situation. And it is these dysfunctional interpersonal behaviors that the group can best help a participant work out. It is important to alert the participants to how they influence and contribute to the situations in which they find themselves. For example, Mr. Jones had spent the first two sessions quietly observing the group interaction. He sat in a stiff and Napoleonic posture, appearing to be a judgmental, disinterested observer. At the third session, unable to restrain himself any longer, Mr. Thomas, a loquacious but usually mild government employee, took Mr. Jones' body position, imitating his posture, even to the very curl of his lips. The group immediately became aware of what was going on and tension mounted. As Mr. Jones became cognizant of the situation he looked on in silent surprise. He broke the silence with a laugh, saying, "I must look ridiculous. No wonder my employees seem to find it so hard to approach me." At this point others in the group felt free to give Mr. Jones their impressions of how he acted in the group. We moved into a small psychodrama with Mr. Thomas playing Mr. Jones, as he perceived him behaving in his business role, and Mr. Jones playing one of his employees, with whom he was having difficulty. After a while Mr. Jones reversed back to his own role and another member of the group played the role of his employee. The others in the group commented on their reactions to his role playing, providing him with some appreciation of the effect he had on others.

Not infrequently participants find themselves unable to take another role. A rather conservative businessman had spent several sessions bemoaning the actions of today's youth and sharply criticizing the younger members of the group. The others suggested that he be placed in the role of a hippie. Though he tried several times he was unable to "feel the role" and act convincingly as a hippie. It is not realistic, however impressive illustrations may appear, to expect a participant to make major characterological changes from a few sessions devoted to trying new roles. Nor is this the intention. Nevertheless, the inability the participant experiences trying out new roles alerts him to his own problem areas. With this experiential evidence he can at his own choosing follow through and resolve these problems outside the group. If he feels they are serious he can pursue psychotherapy.

The question is frequently raised whether behaviors demonstrated in the group are characteristic of the participants' behavior in other situations. Participants claim that there is something unnatural about a sensitivity training group not found in other social situations. Therefore their behavior in sensitivity groups is not really indicative of what they are as people. This type of statement may be employed by a group member in an attempt to deny that he is ex-

Group Behavior and the Outside World

periencing difficulty outside of the group. This question was answered by one participant: "I was surprised to see Anna, a member of the last group, at the beauty parlor. She seemed to take over the whole beauty parlor like a queen bee with a hive. She was just like she had been in the group. And most surprisingly, my feelings about her were just as they had been in the group." Also, a participant who is treated in a sensitivity group in a way that coincides with reactions he receives from others outside the group is more likely to become convinced of his persistent role pattern.

The Consultant's Technique

A caution should be mentioned here about action methods in general. It is extremely important that the technique employed be *relevant* to the group or the individual at that moment in time. The consultant conveys a lack of confidence in his own skills and the goals of ameliorative endeavors if he utilizes a technique because the group or the consultant is bored or threatened by existing conditions. This shows a need to entertain and appease the participants rather than a concern for the difficulties they are experiencing. It suggests that whenever you are bored or threatened, try to ignore what it is that is bothering you and find something pleasing instead. On the other hand, a technique that is relevant to the difficulty being encountered conveys to the participants that the consultant is aware and concerned about their plight. He is not trying to ram a technique or theory down their throat, regardless of how it is received; instead he is open to exploring alternative ways of getting at their concerns and helping them work them out. For example, consultants who are uncomfortable with the participants' hostility find ways of averting direct confrontation of these feelings by keeping the group member dependent on them or by devising various subtle ways of draining off this hostility without having to talk about it. This points to the need for discussion after each and every nonverbal exercise (up until the point at which participants try to "talk away" what they have experienced).

The consultant often needs considerable courage to face up to the hostility generated by the participants in an unstructured group situation. These tensions are most explicitly expressed in groups that meet over a longer period of time and where a climate exists for free expression of feeling. Hollister (1957) has pointed out quite correctly that despite Bion's claim that the hostile feelings are directed toward the role of the consultant, not toward the person of the consultant himself, the leader nevertheless experiences the feelings as "real, personal and threatening. . . . During this stage only the leader's firm belief in people and in the group, and his knowledge that this is a normal stage of group growth" help him risk loss of prestige and tolerate the psychological abuse directed at him by the group.

The psychodrama period is concerned also with group tensions. *Warmup* exercises employed by psychodramatists are helpful in working out various group tensions. Before a group of participants can be moved to concerted action a certain degree of trust, support, and mutual liking must be developed. Warmup activities permit each participant to make himself better known to the other group members and reciprocally helps free others to make themselves known to him. Here, unlike in other parts of process group training, specific activity is suggested to the group by the consultant, and each participant who

Warmup Exercises

165

wishes or requires his active guidance and support receives it. The participant who is not warmed up to the group has been cogently described by Jourard (1964) in another context as confronted by a choice whether to permit others to know his as he currently experiences himself, to remain a nebulous quantity, or to be seen as something he is not. "When we are not truly known by the other people in our lives, we are misunderstood. . . . No man can come to know himself except as an outcome of disclosing himself to another person." Each participant in the group has a responsibility to each other participant. Whenever a group member discloses himself to another he makes it easier for others to make themselves known to him. This applies to other areas of group concern as well: attendance, trust, and commitment. Each participant is responsible to be on time and attend all sessions. The group may be able to carry on without him, but his lack of commitment to them tends to make their commitment to each other (and of course to themselves) more tenuous. Each participant acts as a maximum for the others; not because it should be that way but because this is what happens in groups.

To return to warmup techniques. An illustration of one such technique I have frequently employed may be helpful here.* A group of about ten participants sit around in a circle, close enough so that their arms and legs may be in contact. They are asked to bend forward and cast their glance at a spot on the floor, in the center of the circle. This physical arrangement serves to reduce perceptual stimulation and other kinds of sensation people depend upon for getting their bearings in the everyday world. Each of the participants in turn is asked to think about how he feels *right now* and to name a color out loud which best

---

166 | * This exercise was originally suggested to me by Jim Sacks, a member of the Moreno Institute.

describes his feelings. Each participant having given his color; each is next asked to tell the group which animal best represents his feelings; next each participant is asked to choose someone in the group and give him an animal shape which best represents his current feelings about this person. This is followed by each participant choosing someone else in the group and saying one negative thing about him and one positive thing. When the consultant feels the group is sufficiently warmed up he may ask the participants to look at the persons they are describing. This may continue until each participant has been described or the descriptions are allowed to make several circuits of the circle. Several rounds may be required as the first round is often superficial or contrived.

To enhance the emotional aspects of the experience the participants are discouraged from discussing, elaborating, or explaining their statements until the exercise is completed. Verbal explanations tend to dilute, mask, and devalue feelings during warmup exercises. Nevertheless, in order to take hold of insights generated by the participants during the exercise, discussion of feelings and perceptions of other participants is encouraged after the exercise. Note the gradual progression from less to more threatening expression of feelings employed in the exercise. (No participant is coerced into making a statement. After some initial encouragement by the consultant he is allowed to pass.)

Variations of this technique may be employed with the same group. The consultant may use nonverbal techniques to specifically address the problem which the group is "hung-up" on at that moment in its development. Once the group is sufficiently warmed up the consultant "finds that potential members who have been excluded before, now become acceptable. Whatever threat was involved has been resolved through catharsis, relearning and great objectification which has been taking place on the part of the group" (Enneis, 1951).

Short-Comings of Process Group Training

In recent years a well known law firm in Washington, D.C., developed considerable friction among its law partners. The venerable older gentlemen in the firm, after considerable urging from some of the young junior partners, agreed to recruit a consultant to conduct Encounter groups. These groups, they were told, were marvelous for "getting to the bottom of things." To everyone's surprise rapport vastly improved in the firm, and the biweekly and occasional weekend marathon groups were enthusiastically endorsed by all, including the skeptical senior partners. During the course of the second year, however, without anyone actually being able to indicate why or how, attendance in the groups dropped. Some of the partners complained that biweekly groups were now impractical, for their caseload had greatly increased since the inception of the group training. Other partners simply found convenient excuses not to attend. The group consultant and clinician recognized this resistance against bringing the problems that prevent individuals from working cooperatively with others as a form of "acting-out". Acting-out by members of a group suggests that some important need is not being met by the group. The need cannot be met because the conscious acknowledgement of the need is a threat to the members of the group. This group of law partners, because they were so astute and sophisticated as individuals, could not function effectively as a group. Their sophistication blinded them from the problems that beset them. The partners had become highly skillful in locating hidden agendas

168

and isolating problems but they could not seem to transcend this phase and put their insights to some useful function.

Their group probably approximated the proverbial group of elderly medical pathologists sitting by the shore of a large lake. One of them pointed to the water. A man was struggling to stay aloft. Soon he gave up and began to drown. The pathologists with scientific precision described to one another the man's symptoms as he passed from them. They were unable to aid the drowning man because none of these learned gentlemen claimed to be able to swim. The two examples I have cited illustrate that what may appear to be sophisticated work in a group may become a compulsive ploy fashioned to avoid facing the risk and uncertainty of applying our insights to situations that most vitally concern us. Groups, like the play, in the sense Hamlet uses it, are no longer the thing, when they are used as devices to avoid facing that which most concerns us. Process groups reach impasses in their development when they become expert in enumerating the skills and resources needed to tackle vital concerns of the members, and at the same time tacitly agree never to actually put these "tools" to work with the real issues. The group of law partners did splendidly with issues of no real emotional concern to them. Symptomatically, they never brought up in the group the feelings that led to the group's dissolution. Their group then served them as an exercise in futility.

Process groups have their limitations, as do all techniques. Process groups as I conduct them, where the consultant acts as a detached observer, create, or perhaps uncover, such tremendous feelings of dependency that the group seldom develops effective leadership to formulate group goals and persistently work at implementing them. There is something | 169 about the stark vacuum of a leaderless group that continuously activates powerful and contagious emotions in the group. So much time is devoted to studying and reducing tensions that little opportunity is available for concerted group activity. Balanced group experience requires attention devoted to the cognitive aspects of the participants' human character as well as the emotional. After a period of intensive involvement with interpersonal and intrapsychic tension in process groups, participants are encouraged to act on the basis of their own decisions and procurements of feedback from other group members in becoming the person they wish to be. However, it has been found that this cannot be effectively done until the participants have had considerable experience in studying the influence covert tensions have on their "rational" attempts to effect their needs. Therefore, I conclude each sensitivity training conference with the provision of one or more application groups.

Application Groups

In an application group the consultant takes an active leadership role. He steps out of his detached observer role and establishes a *focal problem model* for the group. This means that the consultant seeks to locate one or more central problems which concern the majority of the group members. Generally, due to the homogeneous selection of participants in a sensitivity training conference (e.g., a group of teachers, social workers from the same clinic, a group of supervisory managers), these shared concerns are not difficult to locate. Initially, the consultant helps the group to clarify the problem that most concerns them, e.g., "How are we going to explain to our supervisors that there is a better way of making decisions than the off-hand way they make them?" Then the consultant refers the participants back to their recent group training experience for "tools" acquired from the experience, which may now be useful in dealing with the problem at hand. "It seemed to me earlier this week that this group felt that its way of working on problems could not be improved by sensitivity training," the consultant told the management interns. "You people seem to feel differently now. What went on in you to cause this change? Is there anything you learned from this week-long conference that might be helpful in effecting a change in your agency's system similar to the change you have experienced?"

The consultant then showed the management interns how to apply the concepts and experiences acquired in the conference to the group's central concern. "What have we learned about how people change their attitudes and begin to engage in honest dialogue with others during this conference? It seems to me some of you were suggesting a developmental process beginning with expression of hostility, then looking at what the anger was all about, seeing which aspects were justified, removing these threats, dropping the irrational anger . . . I wonder if this kind of perspective could not be applicable in your work situation!" The consultant indicates the rationale behind his observations and the reasons he makes the suggestions he does. Unlike the process group situation he may also specify his theoretical sources for his suggestions. Intellectual tools are valuable here as it is in an intellectual task participants perform in an application group. The consultant, in short, does as much as he can to enable the participants to put to immediate use whatever tools they have acquired for solving problems.

By successfully applying their new learning to problems at the termination of the conference the participants leave the conference with some degree of 171 satisfaction with their endeavors. Success experienced in applying new learning to "real" problems probably increases the participants' willingness to apply their "information" to their everyday situations.

In summary, the function of the consultant in the application group is to facilitate group communication through understanding and skill in group dynamics and learning processes. The consultant guides and encourages the group members to impart information and work strategies among themselves. The application group tries to impart information to the participants in the most clear and expedient manner, suggesting how the concepts and skills acquired in the conference may be utilized. To do so the consultant takes a more active and directive role than he did in the process group. The most salient learning feature in the application group is the role of the consultant. In the process group the focus is on the study of group tensions. In the application group the emphasis is on the role-model which the consultant presents. By working on problems in a rational and considered manner, asking clear and meaningful questions which elicit relevant data necessary for formulating plans and making decisions, the consultant demonstrates to the group members the steps necessary for developing and implementing their own goals in situations where consultants are not present to guide them.

The 10
Consultant

The starting point in conceptualizing the role of consultant to a training group is to view the consultation process in much the same way as it has been traditionally used by community institutions. My purpose at this point is not to promote favorably the consultant role, but rather to lay bare some of the manifest and implicit expectations about the role.

Foremost there is the spatial consideration. The consultant does not belong to the institutional system with which he consults. He is an outside expert—at least those who confer with him generally regard him as such. He is called in to assess internal system problems to offer assistance in the form of recommendations. As an outsider he has neither the formal authority nor the responsibility to make decisions or to see that they are carried out. He is an outsider without preferential attitudes arising out of relation- 173 ships with system members, and without vested interest in the consequences of the institution's actions, and he is regarded as more impartial in making observations and rendering judgments than are members of the system. Because he is generally known to the members of the system by reputation rather than as a person, his opinions are generally more respected; however, they are not necessarily better liked or more likely to be acted upon than are those of others in the system. When his recommendations are felt to be inadequate the system members may dismiss them; but due to his status there is the assumption that his opinions will at least be heard and considered regardless of how the institution decides to employ them. The consultant's relationship to the system is regarded as temporary. He generally works with the system in such a way that the autonomous resources of the system may eventually take over his function.

The Consultant's Task

The consultant should look at the participants' behavior as a *process* which has a beginning, a middle, and an end. Each behavioral event must be explained within the context of what has gone on before and what follows. It cannot be explained as a discrete event. The consultant's theoretical orientation need not be of foremost concern, provided he feels comfortable with it and it does not force undue theoretical prejudice on his perceptual faculties. The consultant must initially attempt to view the behavioral field with a naive or common sense attitude (Heider, 1967); that is, the consultant attempts to look at the people he views before him as simply as possible. He tries to make clear to himself what he perceives with no attempt to explain what the participants are doing to one another. When he feels he has painted for himself a fairly accurate description of what is taking place before his eyes, he asks the logical question, "Why?" This question is an attempt to explain the *function*, or *payoff*, given behavior has for the person who evokes it and for those who contribute and participate in maintaining it.

A quarter-century of psychoanalytic thinking has impressed social scientists and clinicians that behavior is *overdetermined*. That is, a given behavioral pattern becomes associated with a number of unconscious and preconscious drives, each of which under certain sufficient conditions triggers off the behavior. Profuse reinforcing responses for such a behavioral pattern renders it resistant to modification or elimination. Therefore, many causal factors are necessary for the explanation of a behavioral act. The social scientist, although generally less convinced than the clinician of the potency of unconscious factors, agrees with this view. But he will state behavioral determination in such a manner as to make clear that a single behavioral event may be described from a number of different perspectives or levels of analysis. For instance, the observer may describe the same event at the sociological level in terms of social systems requirements; at the social psychological level in regard to role occupancy; at the psychological level by enactment of the individual's unique personal strategy (e.g., risk taking); and at the unconscious level in terms of intrapsychic urges and stresses. In

Over-Determined Behavior

175

my view the competent group training consultant needs to be conversant with the concepts and methods of inquiry necessary for intelligibly assessing behavior at each of these levels of analysis. By so doing he can then verify and cross-check his observations and thereby free himself, to some degree, from the theoretical bias of his preconceptions about human behavior.

Parsimony

Also important for explaining behavior is the principle of parsimony: "Of two equally meaningful interpretations the one that is less complex, the one that requires fewer assumptions, fewer data in general, seems in general to be preferred" (Heider, 1967).

The consultant makes a statement to the group only when he believes that his intervention will illuminate what he sees happening in the group. He seldom speaks, therefore, until he has some evidence on which to premise what he has to say to the group (Rice, 1965). In this respect the consultant generally has an advantage over the participants. The participants are involved in an intense emotional encounter, impinged by a welter of confusing and unclear ideas, feelings, and sensations. The consultant, by employing a conceptual model built upon a series of comparative situations and a series of generalizations derived from experience, is able "to strip away some of the redundancy of stimulation to describe or encode incoming information in a form more economic than that in which it impinges on the receptors" of the participants (Attneave, 1954). The economy of this process often permits the observer to glean the essence of the matter.

In-depth investigation of groups may be approached in three ways. The consultant may focus on the group as an entity, attempting to ascertain what general mood, emotion, need, or apprehension is being experienced in common by the group participants. This approach has been called "Group Dynamics," "Group Process," "Systems Analysis," and so forth. Perhaps Parloff's term, "integralist," is best for a general term. It is not partial to any one approach and yet encompasses all the approaches where major concern is studying the group in depth. Some of the best known proponents of integralism are Bion, Ezriel, Foulkes and Anthony, Whitaker, and Lieberman.

They believe that the study of the group as an entity reveals the functioning of the individual member in his full complexity, since all group activity reflects overt or covert aspects of the behavior of the individuals composing it. The group as a unit engages in activities which provide the individual with experiences and responses which are different in degree and perhaps in kind from those found in the dyad. The integralist believes that a major aspect of the patient's problem is his inability to be an effective member of a task-oriented group (Parloff, 1967).

The consultant may concern himself with a subgroup within the larger group entity, and investigate, for instance, the interaction of the three group members who appear to have the highest regard for one another. This second approach is advocated by those who attempt to focus on some small unit or subgroup within the larger group proper. They concern themselves more with the psychodynamics of individuals than with the dynamics of the total group. Since their unit of study is personal relations and transactional units, they have been referred to as "transactionalists" and "interpersonalists."

It is difficult to designate the theorists who best represent the transactional position since there is no single individual or group that is acknowledged as a spokesman for this wide ranging "school." The transactionalists include such divergent views as those held by Frank (1957), Bach (1954), Berne (1966), and Mullan and Rosenbaum (1962). All these perceive the group as providing stimuli which permit the individual member to demonstrate his idiosyncratic modes of relating and responding to a broad range of individuals . . . (Parloff, 1967).

If the consultant wishes he may simply disregard the group as a configural reality and concern himself with each participant as an individual within a situation in which other social objects are present. This third position is held by therapists and group practitioners such as Locke, Wolf and Schwartz, and Slavson, whose work and major theoretical interest were initially the individual. For various reasons they have become interested in groups and group phenomena. In turning their attention to the group they have been unwilling or unable to view the group as anything other than a collection of separate individuals.

Proponents of this approach to treatment insist that since intrapsychic change may be best affected by analytic methods, then analytic theory and practice would be adopted insofar as possible in the group treatment setting. Such theorists appear to acknowledge that the group setting represents a challenge to the application of such formal techniques of the analytic method as free association, genetic review, dream interpretation, and the establishment of a transference neurosis. They respond to this challenge in two contrasting ways: by conceding that the aims and patients appropriate for analytic group therapy are restricted (Slavson, 1964); or by admitting no important differences yet reinterpreting the meaning of various psychoanalytic concepts to fit group treatment practices (Wolf and Schwartz, 1962; Locke, 1961) (Parloff, 1967).

Naturally, the consultant does not have to maintain one of these focuses of attention exclusively. His emphasis may shift during the course of the group's development or even several times within a single session. He may test his observation by attempting to conceptualize the phenomenal data before him at different levels of analysis for each event. It is nevertheless characteristic of group leaders that they generally focus on one level rather than balance the three described.

Attention to the group as an entity, that is, the integralist point of view, permits access to the participants' shared hopes and fears. Each participant enters the group with his own idiosyncratic rumination of problems, issues, and concerns. Certain common motives are activated in each of the participants as a result of his endeavor to relate to other group members in order to achieve personal goals. The integralist position permits investigation of the social and personal forces that prevent the articulation of personal incentives as well as of the forces that foster them. The integralist studies how to recognize, appreciate, and employ these forces in a constructive manner. In short, the integralist position states that groups are not perpetuated by manifest objectives alone but also by latent purposes, which often stand in direct opposition to the articulated stated group and personal

The Group as an Integral Entity

179

goals (Parloff, 1967). Without attending to the underlying common group tensions we are unable to grasp those socio-emotional dynamics that bring men together into groups to satisfy their wants.

Trans-Actional Analysis

The transactional or interpersonal focus permits the consultant to observe mirrors of interpersonal groupings that are most common to and characteristic of daily life. Although we live in a family generally consisting of several persons, we rarely come together as an entire family; though we may be employed by agencies comprised of a large number of other employees, large staff meetings are infrequent; we ride in buses and trains with scores of people but in all these instances we seldom interact with more than a few others. Most of our interactions at any one point in time are with one or two other individuals. Transactional analysis consequently imparts information about a salient natural interpersonal subgrouping.

Intra-Personal Emphasis

The intrapersonal emphasis is predicated on the observation that skin and other physical attributes separate one organism from another. Accordingly, we refer to each of these bounded organisms as an individual. The intrapersonal approach assumes that the best way to understand the individual is to observe what transpires within his skin and body shell. His goals and ambitions will then become clear, and we will see why he behaves as he does with others. Intrapersonalists often make the further assumption that social objects have little meaning beyond their transference value or value as persons for other group members. Individuals, instead, serve as transference

180

screens of the individual's experience with previous significant persons in his life.*

One participant obviously does not comprise a group. Nor are two persons a group. Two participants constitute an interpersonal situation and a field in which social influence can be effected. Sociological tradition as far back as Durkheim does not recognize an interpersonal situation as a group situation unless there is an existing superstructure in which the interpersonal interactions are rooted. This means that an interpersonal situation is not recognized as a group situation unless the effects of existing social norms and traditions transcend the immediate interactional relationships, influencing the participants' behavior in ways that cannot be properly explained on the basis of their present interactions alone. In short, a group situation prevails only at such time as the interactional situation is influenced by a previously established set of rules and role relationships. (Members of a group who interact with disregard for the group's established way of conducting business are no longer functioning as group members, and their status as group members may be called into question by the other members of the group.)

In the same way three or more persons collectively do not constitute a group unless they have some previous knowledge and regulated expectations about what is expected of one another.

What importance does this rationale have for group training? If two participants are not a group the presence of the consultant may make it a group. And

The Influence of Group Size in Group Dynamics

* As it is not my intention here to present theoretical views about groups in detail, the reader who is interested in a detailed overview of the approaches to groups in depth should refer to Parloff's excellent chapter.

181

by extension there are greater pressures to draw the consultant into the group when there are fewer than three participants present, other things being equal, than there are in group situations in which larger configurations are present. Two participants unable to establish a regulated interactional pattern by themselves will apply more or less subtle pressure on the consultant to become a group participant, whom they hope can provide help in regulating their relationship to one another. The consultant may be perceived by the participants as a parental figure who is judging their sibling-like interchanges. It is suggested, because this model lends itself so cogently, that if a consultant were to work under these conditions that he intentionally use the family model as his prototype. Depending upon the ages, social maturity, sex, and so forth he could conceptualize group process to capture the mother-daughter, mother-son, father-son, father-daughter, husband-wife interactions that the dyadic group configuration activates in each of the participant's behavior. The consultant, in interpreting the interactional pattern of the dyad, impresses upon them how each is behaving with the other as if the other were "mother," "father," "brother," "sister," or "spouse."

What if three participants show up for a session? By this definition three participants constitute a group, providing that they have some prior interpersonal dealings sufficient for developing regulated expectations in regard to their interactions. A three-person group is, however, rather unstable. Only two persons can directly relate to each other at any one moment. One participant is therefore excluded. Each participant harbors a fear of being excluded from the interaction, which activates primitive fears of abandonment. These primitive feelings precipitate dominating and alliance-seeking reactions. In such a provocative setting, process generally moves at a rapid pace. The consultant will not be called upon to use his interventions to stimulate group process. In a sense his primary role with a triad is to disarm the volatile climate in the group. He should try to convey to the group, by pointing out what is going on between and among them (interpersonally and intrapsychically), how fears of loss of protection and feelings of insignificance lead to strong anger and aggressive behaviors. With four or five participants present there is a viable group that generally gets to know itself rather quickly.

At all times the consultant should be intently observing and analyzing what is going on in the group. Even when he is silent he continues to make interpretations of the group process. This is usually not a difficult task for someone with theoretical knowledge of groups and human behavior. The crucial factor is, of course, that of *timing*. Bion provides an explanation of timing:

Making Inter-Ventions

> Interpretation itself is an attempt to translate into precise speech what I suppose to be the attitude of the group to me or to some other individual, and of the individual to the group. Only some of these occasions are used by me; I judge the occasion to be ripe for an interpretation when the interpretation would seem to be both obvious and unobserved (Bion, 1961).

Bion's statement, however, does not make it clear enough when an intervention is required. We must know what group unit we are interested in and therefore which theoretical model best captures that unit. Also, how do we wish to employ the anxiety being experienced by the participants? Interpretations should facilitate participants' awareness of their implicit assumptions that are interfering with the group task. These assumptions have not been tested out and are being acted upon as if they were already valid and proved. Group interpretations based on the awareness of the latent meaning of attitudes and behaviors permit and enable us to consciously influence and redirect irrational behavior.

Interventions should be withheld when they will impede group process (and at the same time impede the participants' readiness to process new informational input). The group is not "ready" to handle certain hidden agenda and must be allowed to discover the material at its own pace. Interpretations should be held back when they facilitate only a temporary solution to communication problems. Interventions are disruptive when the group seems on the verge of creating a more pervasive interpersonal quality among its members, e.g., trust, frustration-tolerance, mutual respect. A group operates on many levels. A group can be concerned on a manifest level with making clear some vague statements a participant has made, while on a deeper level it is developing "tolerance" and "respect" for those group members who have difficulty expressing their thoughts. Consequently, an interpretation by the consultant directed at the communication confusion may clear up the misunderstanding and enable the participants to get on to other business, while at the same time nip in the bud the respect and tolerance being expressed for group members who are not attuned to the rest of the group. In many instances draining off the tensions of surface problems in a group tends to suppress work at a deeper level of process.

In a sense this method of making interventions is parallel to permitting a young child to learn by his own mistakes, provided the required task doesn't greatly exceed the child's development. I prefer letting a group struggle with a difficult task rather than suppressing its opportunity to develop responsibility. My model for this role is that of the ego-oriented psychoanalyst:

> Interpretation, however, if it is performed by the analyst as an exclusive function of *his* ego, may be too active and, therefore, in Greenacre's sense, damaging to the patient's autonomy. The growth-promoting function of the analyst requires that he relinquish *some* of his function of interpretations and help the patient arrive at his own interpretations *whenever possible*. Kris (1951) thinks that this will promote ego-growth, diminish the analyst's omniscience, and pave the way for ultimate independence. He advocates that, rather than interpret for the patient, the analyst should substitute a question designed to stimulate the development of the patient's own interpretative skills. The synthetic and integrative functions of the ego are thus exercised with the encouragement of the analyst. If the patient is slowly educated to such procedures at the outset of analysis, it can become a powerful ally in the terminal phase when the independence of the patient is put to test. The analyst must be constantly alert to the patient's increasing skills, their emergence, and must be ready to relinquish the exercise of his skills even though the patient may perform less elegantly (Blanck, 1966).

In general, as the ego-oriented analytic position above would seem to suggest, I tend to make more interventions in an active, verbal process group. These group members are using their verbosity to interface their inner tensions and the ineffectiveness of their functioning as a social unit. Interventions are also needed when the group is intellectualizing about the here-and-now and avoiding its own anxiety about being a group. Participants often pose as "therapists" who render one-sided, perhaps psychologically brilliant, but irrelevant analysis of some participant's behavior. This kind of collusive group behavior keeps the other participants from having to look at themselves. Active intervention is clearly required when the participants are caught up in an obsessive flight into trivia, or when the group appears comfortable with present restrictive solutions to its focal problems. Here interventions are posed as a catalytic agent to disturb the group from its uneasy equilibrium.

I tend to make the fewest interventions, in keeping with my ego-analytic orientation, in a group that is struggling with anxiety which members acknowledge and seek to both explain and regulate. Interventions on the part of the consultant are disruptive when the participants are consciously attempting to confront their tensions. Unless the tension level is clearly unmanageable the consultant should not hinder the work of the group by oversolicitous guidance. The consultant should be mindful that the value of group experience is to a considerable extent "a function of the emotional tension that can be engendered without harming the weakest member" (Taylor, 1961).

According to A. K. Rice, director of the Tavistock Institute, where the Bion method was developed, there are three basic responses to the consultant's interpretations:

> When, as a consultant to a group, I make a comment on group behavior that is immediately accepted as correct by all members of the group, I usually feel that my interpretation must have been so close to consciousness as to be of only small value in advancing the member's understanding of what is happening. Such acceptance is, of course, at first both gratifying and reassuring, but within a short time I cannot avoid feeling that the group has "presented" me with material for an agreeable interpretation as a means of

hiding more obscure behavior which, if examined, would give rise to more painful feelings. If I make a comment which members immediately deny—often aggressively—only to behave subsequently as if they had accepted it, I feel the interpretation may have been of greater value . . . an interpretation that is overtly ignored . . . in the long run turns out to have made a greater contribution . . . than . . . either (Rice, 1965).

In the exposition of my role as a group training consultant I have been imposing my own value system. I need to place these values on the table. My message is simple: I am asserting that the group has the necessary resources to work out its own difficulties. The means to this end is to face up to feelings instead of fleeing from them. Anxiety and discomfort in participants are therefore positive and healthy indicators. They are communications from the deep recesses of the self that some important parts of the personality are protesting against the neurotic defenses and self-defeating life style the person has evolved.

Change can only come about when there is a disequilibrium (anxiety and discomfort) in the personality, an unbalance which demands change and can bring about that change. The therapist works with the forces engendered by this disequilibrium, his task is to direct a new balance in the personality which will be more stable because it does fuller justice to inner needs and the demands of outer reality. For this reason, if a patient has achieved a state of equilibrium, if only by means of his symptoms . . . there is little the therapist can do (Foulkes and Anthony, 1957).

Group training consultants must create an atmosphere in the group in which the healthier aspects of the ego can emerge and assert themselves. Through interventions and didactic discussion the consultant attempts to convey that anxiety in itself is not something to fear (and avoid) but is an indication—as is a toothache—that something is amiss and needs attention. In other words, the participants should come to live with anxiety. Better yet, they need to *work with anxiety*, to use it as a constructive tool in their amelioration. Once the individual can live with anxiety his security operations become considerably less vital and he can devote more of his attention and energy to achieving gratification.

The Consultant as an Emotional Being

A consultant cannot effectively observe and comment upon group behavior if he is prepared only to acknowledge his cognitive experiences in the group. The consultant should act as neutrally and consistently as he can—"stay in role"—the rationale for which was discussed earlier in this chapter. I am here concerned with the consultant's activity in a group and the effect it has on the level and quality of the participants' functioning.

A foremost concern is the question of responsibility. In formulating his role in a group, the consultant (regardless of his theoretical persuasion) must decide who he thinks should take responsibility for group functions, e.g., who should admonish or sanction behavior; who should foster relationships among the group members; who should administer to the group members' personal chafe and hurt and to all the other important group functions. The directive consultant or trainer assumes that most, if not all, of these tasks are his own responsibility (at least initially). He either carries out these tasks himself or, if he regards them as the group members' responsibility, works on the participants' resistance to carrying them out. He does not stop until the functions are taken up in a definitive manner by the group members. The directive consultant therefore limits the latitude of freedom accorded to the group members in defining their own roles. The directive consultant generally has a clear idea of what he expects and wants to happen in a group experience (and he is not hesitant about communicating it to the participants). Consequently, the more active the consultant is the less freedom the participants have to develop their own ideas about their roles. The nondirective consultant, in contrast, sets limits on himself instead of on the participants. He is generally less clear (perhaps it is more accurate to say he has a less developed notion) about what the participants should be doing and is more explicit about what *he should not be doing*. Restricting his own freedom of activity, in terms of the guidelines here proposed, affords the participants the opportunity to develop their own inventions into effective psychosocial functions.

The group training role of my choosing is that of the nondirective consultant. However, he should not emotionally remain neutral or indifferent to the feelings being generated by the participants. It is neither realistic nor useful for the consultant to be emotionally removed from the tensions, anxieties, frustrations, threats, and ambitions that participants in a group, in the same room, are experiencing. Vicarious experience must guide and shape his work with groups. His activity should be a creative blend of his knowledge, training, and intuitive sensitivity. His consulting style cannot be effective if it is not consistent with his personality and temperament. His viscera can serve as a barometer of the emotional climate in the group. His own internal sensitivities may help him heed

Bion's warning to be suspicious if he feels that he is dealing with the problems the participants think he should be.

The consultant must continually evaluate his own role in the group. By doing this he can at any point question the role the group has placed him in and which he has apparently gone along with. The consultant must then question his own motives for collusion with the group, thereby permitting them to avoid looking at some important process taking place in the group. This difficult introspective task may be performed, by dividing his own ego, which is both a perceptual and emotive organ, into observing and experiencing selves. As an emotive self he "participates" and affectively responds to the tensions existing in himself and by extension in the group; as a "trained" cognitive self, he interprets and makes sense of what he is experiencing. The consultant or group trainer who perceives himself as another member of the group "free to be himself" in the group is not capable of making this valuable ego division, and as a result negates his effectiveness as a trained observer. (The therapist is always running into this dilemma.) The need to assist patients by becoming involved with them may, however, justifiably override his value as an observer. On the other hand, being aware of and able to conceptualize his own feelings the consultant can use these experiences as a tool to assess and explain the phenomena which he himself has been drawn into.

In summary, the consultant's own emotions are barometers of what is going on inside of him as he is being affected by the interpersonal field of which he is part. He cannot lie to these "gut" feelings as easily as he can to his head.

The *zeitgeist* of our times—in the professional arts and sciences as well as among the pseudo-informed populace—has encouraged lip service to a diluted understanding of existential thought. There is a general feeling—and Esalen is an obvious example of this—that if people would just lower their defenses and reveal their inner selves all intrapsychic conflicts and interpersonal misunderstandings would vanish instantaneously. This is a pipedream. People employ defenses because they feel incapable of adequately handling the situations they find themselves in.

Close attention to the issue of acting-out is important here. *Acting-out* is a type of transference phenomenon described by Anna Freud as an intensification of transference in which the ego "behaves wholly as an infantile ego" (A. Freud, 1966). The male who experiences intensely ambivalent feelings toward women who betray his trust or prove unreliable can handle these feelings by acting them out when he experiences inner tension. He may enter into brief, violent, and assaultive relationships with females. By aggressive sexual powers he periodically vents his anger and concomitantly satisfies his lust. However, only certain kinds of women will accept this type of relationship—women who he undoubtedly experiences as degrading. Instead of relieving his intense feelings he may be further chafing his deep-seated hurt. Unable to consciously explore his feelings he is unable to remedy his situation.

Participants in groups who act out feelings they experience when tense, frustrated, and confused need not experience these feelings consciously and work on them in a constructive manner. A group may be exploited by the very feelings they fear expressing, for by expressing these feelings they fear they will

Non-Clinicians as Consultants

191

lose control over them. In process groups I frequently observe group members denying an interpretation that they are angry at the consultant; they follow this up by lashing out at a group member who dares to suggest that the group should reconsider the consultant's remarks. In pointing out that people who are not already angry are not likely to become so agitated at a mild suggestion, the consultant is told by the participants that they refuse to accept that their anger preceded the "deviant" group member's suggestion. The participants refuse to accept that they welcomed the opportunity to vent their built-up resentment of previous "wrongs;" they insist their rage was justified.

We cannot rationally modify our behavior unless we are aware of what it is that is bothering us. By acting-out rather than talking about their feelings, participants in sensual-sensational groups lose the opportunity of exploring their inner turmoil. The acting-out techniques as employed by some of the group training approaches rest on a false and rather destructive implicit assumption: by acting in ways that are more comfortable and pleasant all our problems will disappear. If the participants' temporary discomfort is dissipated but its source is not revealed, a valuable opportunity for remedial attention is forfeited.

In process groups members are encouraged to explore and reconsider interpersonal strategies, the rules and attitudes which guide the participants' interactions with one another. But there is a mindful caution about telling participants that they *must change* their behavior *now* or at any other specified time. The clinician recognizes that an individual must work out his own behavior at his own pace. If defenses are knocked down and not replaced with a better way of handling those situations in which the individual feels distressed and inadequate, the individual has no place to go but into a psychotic reaction—the psychological escape from an impossible situation. It is also important to keep in mind that not all the participants in a group are at the same level of psychological maturity. Too frequently, group leaders are unaware or unconcerned with this consideration. They expect people to drop their defenses and disclose themselves frankly and openly because somehow their notions, derived from a superficial understanding of existential and humanistic thought, suggest that ideally people should be so inclined. The consultant's job in a sensitivity group "is to confront the group without affronting its members; to draw attention to interesting group behavior and not to individual behavior; to point out how the group uses individuals to express its own emotions; how it exploits some members so that others can absolve themselves from the responsibility for such expression" (Rice, 1968).

The Consultant's Counter-Transference

Consultants for training groups may experience difficulty in their groups that is intricately related to their own psychodynamics. At such times they appear perplexed and perturbed about their adequacy as consultants. One clear symptom of this difficulty is that they face their groups at times as an odious task, yet this attitude doesn't seem to be substantiated by their verbal statements of the difficulty the group is presenting, nor is it consistent with their training and experience in groups. Extensive investigation of hospitalized psychiatric patients demonstrates that exacerbated pathology in the patients' behavior, especially in their interactions with other patients, is closely related to perceived disagreement and conflict with the professional staff (Stanton and Schwartz,

1954). Group participants may experience similar confusion in trying to work out difficulties in areas in which the group leader himself experiences difficulty.

A consultant relatively free of conflict, or at least aware of his difficulties (e.g., his own participation and reaction to problem areas), can constructively guide the group in working out difficulties in these areas. The consultant who has unresolved difficulties in areas the group needs to deal with is understandably defensive or insensitive in regard to these issues. The consultant's nonverbal cues and his expressed directives heavily influence the issues to be considered and the manner in which they are dealt with. The group will quietly realize, consciously or otherwise, that certain areas are taboo for discussion. Partly in fear of judgmental retribution from the consultant, the participants will give up attempting to resolve these conflict areas. The group's development as a mature, well functioning organism is thus retarded in areas in which underlying group tensions cannot be permissibly confronted and rationally dealt with.

The development of the group skills of the sensitivity training consultant, no less than those of the clinician, is closely related to the development of his own intrapsychic and interpersonal life. Group work, like psychotherapy, is a relationship after all—a relationship with the depths of being and the craving to absorb and participate with a greater sense of being in relation to others. Consequently, disturbances in the growth and realization of the leader's interpersonal and inner life severely impede his effectiveness as a consultant. Consultants should participate regularly as members of other consultants' sensitivity groups, a group experience which will provide the experiential bond between leader and member roles in groups.

Frequently, however, because process groups and other forms of group training are more concerned with the participants' proactive strivings for new kinds of interpersonal functioning than they are with intrapsychic conflicts, some of the consultant's personal difficulties may be ignored or insufficiently worked out in a sensitivity group. Individual psychotherapy is, in this case, a valuable adjunct to group experience. Regardless, however, of his intrapsychic health and his training in groups, the consultant must at all times be aware of his limitations. By so doing he can more effectively assess difficulties the group is having when these difficulties seem unexplainable by other more objective kinds of assessment.

The 11
Conceptual
System

W hatever system the consultant employs to explain behavior in the process group, it is essential that his theoretical position conceptualize this behavior in a consistent and logical manner. He can then relate his observations to other events which replicate or contain elements of the present event. Replication is useful for confirming or rejecting the ways he has come to understand group events. It also provides the consultant with additional information which enables him to modify his initial impression. These data ideally should provide the consultant with a multidimensional explanation of group phenomena. It is the essence of science that knowledge is one definitive body of information, which is applicable for understanding each and every aspect of existence. The complexities of a single event are so enormous, how- 197 ever, that it is impossible for any individual to grasp the event in its entirety. The disciplines of science and the various schools of the arts seek explanations at different levels of analysis or, if you will, from different perspectives of the same phenomenon. These areas of knowledge and explanation, therefore, are not distinct, except in man's arbitrary attempts at subdivision. No one level is the "real" or correct explanation of an event. Each is but a different perspective of the same event, described by the observer in conceptual terms which he is familiar with by virtue of his training, skill, and experience. Edwin Boring, the historian of the experimental method, has pointed out that the true interdisciplinary approach would be to integrate the various spheres of knowledge in one head. Since this is probably not possible, the methodological suggestion of the social psychologist Muzafer Sherif is worth noting. (Sherif has repeatedly indicated that if the social scientist (or the clinician, for that matter) is seriously concerned about the validity of his findings, he needs to ascertain if the observations he accrues at his customary level of investigation are consistent with the findings collected by other scientists at the levels of analysis at which they are operating. If there is any disparity, he needs to recheck and find out why.

Unlike the physical and behavioral scientists, consultants in a process group are not able to validate observations or group interventions based on these observations. The consultant cannot replicate the process group situation, controlling all but those conditions he is interested in influencing. He has neither the time nor the control over the situation to do this. In order to guard against distortion resulting from the inadequacies of the conceptual framework on which process groups operate, data must be viewed from several different levels of analysis. How would this work? At the societal level, for example, Talcott Parsons' social system analysis might be employed. The functional imperatives that Parsons (1959) finds operating in all social systems may be seen as fitting closely with Bion's basic assumptions, which are conceptualized at the psychosocial level. The extrapolation of social system theory and Bion's psychosocial theory is as follows:

Functional Imperatives (Parsons)	Basic Assumptions (Bion)
Goal Attainment	— Work Group
Latency Management	— Pairing
Integration	— Dependency
Adaptation	— Fight-Flight

Furthermore, when a group is in fight-flight there should be manifested on a psychodynamic level those activities recognized as passive-aggressive behavior. *Passive-aggressiveness* is a character trait disturbance of nuclear conflicts centering around perceived powerful, significant social objects which are transferred from childhood to social objects in the present interpersonal situation. In this conflict authority figures cannot be confronted directly but are subtly demeaned. The feelings activated by earlier conflicts are acted upon as if the genetic situation were still prevalent. If the consultant perceives the participants as a group to be in fight-flight, he gains confirmation of his observation by noting individual behavior that indicates passive-aggressive strategies are being employed. At the social system level Parsonian theory would suggest that during fight-flight, in Bion's terms, the group is concerned with adaptational needs, such that structural, normative, and regulatory processes are manifested in the group's concerns. As a result participants are ignored as individuals. Verification of such group 199 processes adds further confirmation to the consultant's initial observation of fight-flight. Refinement of the level of analysis approach for making audits on our group observations has still to be worked out. Before this can be done useful concepts for investigating process in training groups need be formulated. As an initial step in this direction key concepts from in-depth study of process groups will be discussed in the following pages.

If behavior is multidetermined then no one interpretative concept entirely explains a given event. Instead, to some degree, each concept offered may be useful in pulling together and delineating several of the dynamic properties that comprise a given event, in such a way that an understanding of the event can be communicated to other persons. Concepts as employed here are not intended as "domains of truth" to be pitted against other social scientists' "truths." They are instead expressions of my own understanding of interpersonal behavior. If they communicate this understanding then they have served the purpose for which they were designed.

Inter-Personal Dynamics

The sensitivity group consultant's task is to facilitate the participants' understanding of their own and others' behavior in an ongoing interpersonal situation. The clinician's task is to bring to light self-defeating attitudes and behaviors in terms of the individual's conceptualization of and emotional reaction to himself and social objects. To perform these difficult charges the first task is to select a unit of analysis which is not only logical, consistent, and economical but also one that best serves the pragmatic mandate of enabling the participants to understand their behavior in such a way that they may influence it in a desirable direction. Consequently, whereas behavior in a social event may be described accurately on the one hand on a physiological, chemical, or physical plane, and on another on a historical, cultural, or metaphysical level, none of these perspectives is especially viable for discerning human behavior in such a way that alerts people how to use it for *immediate interpersonal modification*. To do so demands indicating the goal-directed or functional aim of behavior as a realistic integration of various wants, emotions, and cognitions; sometimes concordantly, sometimes disharmoniously operating to influence action (Krech and Crutchfield, 1962). In this chapter I describe events in a group setting in interpersonal and transactional terms. The focus is on *personal strategies* enacted by each of the participants vis-à-vis each other. These transactions are to be understood within a group context, influenced and shaped by the emotions permeated by the shared implicit assumptions and common group dynamics of people who, as members of a social unit, have a history, a culture, a normative range of acceptable and rejectionable behavior, goals, and so forth. The transactions of any participant are seen in reference to each of the other participants in a group. Each participant takes account of the other for some purpose so that "the actions of each are at once a *result* of and a *cause* of the actions of the other" (Krech and Crutchfield, 1962).

The transactional and interpersonal position is the meeting ground between the intrapersonalist position, concerned with individual psychodynamics, and the integralist position, concerned with the shared unconscious and preconscious emotions and motives of group membership. Considerable attention in the following pages is given to concepts taken from individual psychology and interpersonal theory (not necessarily from a group context) because these positions need the most attention. Transactional theory, for example, has only recently come into vogue as a viable modality for investigating groups. Of the three major approaches to groups, the integralist, the transactional or interpersonal, and the intrapersonal, I feel that the integralist position from the work of Bion, Eszriel, Whitaker and Lieberman, et al., contains the best developed models for studying groups in depth. Having decided that the interpersonal and transactional position needs the most attention I have in this chapter brought together an interrelated series of concepts and theoretical descriptions of behavior from individual psychology and interpersonal theory which have been helpful to me in explaining the behaviors of participants in a process group.

Role A group is a social system circumscribed by more or less permeable boundaries. Each social system has "needs" and required functions which are carried out by its constituent parts, the group members. The term "role" is the social system appellation for the ways in which group members relate to one another and articulate group functions. The term does not necessarily embrace the composite of participants' behavior in groups. Initially, group members' activities in a group are rather idiosyncratic. They reflect the norms, values, and culture of the participants' previous and existing membership and reference groups. When these participants' characteristic ways of responding to other participants in the group become regulated (stabilized through a process of modification and readjustment to the membership of the present group), and are therefore predictable to the other participants, these behaviors can be referred to as role. These regulated actions cannot be explained on the basis of the participants' personal dispositions alone. It is meaningless to speak of a role in isolation. A role can be meaningfully understood only in relation to other regulated modes of behaving of the other role occupants within the social system. Behavior is a function of the psychosocial field which exists at the time of the enactment (Lewin, 1951). A role in psychosocial terms is a compromise between how the role aspirant wishes to present himself in the group and what the other group members impress upon him as being available and indigenous activity for group goal achievement and group maintenance. As a minimum requirement, if a participant's behavior is to meet the needs of the group, it must be predictable to other group members.

In studying sensitivity training groups, instead of using the term "role," I prefer to view the structural quality of interaction within the groups as interpersonal encounters. The term "role" by virtue of its frequent loose usage to explain a variety of diverse and often contradictory theoretical conventions about social behavior does not suggest the spontaneous, dynamic quality of interaction so frequently observed in process groups. An interpersonal encounter is a clash or interchange of different perspectives of group members. Within these encounters each participant enacts diverse personal and interpersonal strategies, sentiments, and attitudes with other group members. The behaviors enacted in an interpersonal encounter become seen as role only when they become highly characteristic of that individual in his transactions with other participants.

Encounter

Personal Flexibility

The effective calibration of one's behavior to that of others demands flexibility. It means that the individual cannot behave in the same way in different situations, or with different people, or at different times. Individuals who cannot make these adjustments are often considered to be neurotic because of their behavioral rigidity (Abrahamson, 1966).

The participant must relate to what is realistically going on in the group rather than to some highly personalistic (autistic) stimulus. Where egocentric needs and unresolved internal conflicts interfere with the participants' objective assessment of the interpersonal situation in the group, his behavior will not be very useful to the group. The impulse-driven individual who cannot internally inhibit his craving for immediate gratification until a more suitable occasion cannot accommodate himself appropriately in an interpersonal encounter. "Readjustment requires not only acquisition of new behavior, but the inhibition of old" (Abrahamson, 1966). In an encounter where the "thou" is treated as an "it" or an impersonal object, he feels used, manipulated, and exploited, creating tension and strain within the encounter. Only where both agents within the encounter can cast aside reactive fears and the need for safety can they personally accommodate themselves to the other; and in so doing explore their interpersonal domain, each coming to know himself and the other with increased meaningfulness.

Inter-Personal Transference

204

Participants relate to one another in an interpersonal encounter heavily influenced by preconceived notions about the other carried over from relationships with others in the past. The thoughts and feelings generated in conflictual relationships with significant others, which have been unsuccessfully handled in the past, tend to be taken as accurate descriptions of what the present objects think and feel. Transference-imbued relationships, because they are inaccurate descriptions of present relationships, impede interpersonal accommodation. Interpersonal transference leads to a vicious cycle of misinterpreted perceptions, intentions, and communication. This is vividly described by Laing. The following is the implicit dialogue of two participants caught up in this vicious cycle:

PETER: I am upset.
PAUL: *Peter is upset.*
PETER: Paul is acting very calm and dispassionate.
PAUL: *I'll try to help him by remaining calm and just listening.*
PETER: If Paul cared about me and wanted to help he would get involved and show some emotion also.
PAUL: *He is getting even more upset. I must be even more calm.*
PETER: Paul knows that this upsets me.
PAUL: *He is accusing me of hurting him.*
PETER: If Paul knows that his behavior upsets me, he must be intending to hurt me.
PAUL: *I'm really trying to help.*
PETER: He must be cruel, sadistic. Maybe he gets pleasure out of it, etc.
PAUL: *He must be projecting.*

(Laing, 1966)

Functional Autonomy

Transference-imbued relationships would not be reenacted by participants unless they served some "useful" function. These unconscious attitudes were once appropriate to the needs of that person but are no longer conducive to personal growth and interpersonal maturity; this leads both to their persistence and the self-defeating nature of transference-imbued relationships in present encounters. Functional autonomy implies that the repetition of attitudes toward significant persons from the past no longer serves the same purpose in the present. Some other "payoff" has been substituted for the original aim of the behavior. The employment, for example, of stereotyped responsiveness to others, although often dysfunctional in adapting to new circumstances, offers the person a consistent frame of reference for making meaning of an otherwise chaotic array of sensations impinging upon him. Modern theories of perception are based upon the view that the person makes an effort after the meaning of his experiences. Correspondingly, each participant in a group is "always consciously or unconsciously forming an estimate of the attitude of his group towards himself" (Bion, 1961). In this way he tries to assess his own meaningfulness in terms of others.

Psychologists have tended for the last half century, largely from the impact of psychoanalytic libido theory, to describe motivational explanations of human behavior in terms of hedonistic (pleasure-pain) promptings. I on the other hand hold, along with theorists of humanistic orientation, that the individual's need to make meanings of the events in which he is caught up in is a rather basic and generally more adequate motivational imputation than are purely hedonistic accounts. Lecky (1961) pointed out that rather than pleasure man craves a sense of unification and meaning to his existence. Each participant's continual struggle to make meaning of his experience in the group is a basic process permeating the life of a group. Accordingly, therefore, as long as communication among the participants is open and clarity about what is happening is sensed by all, a low state of tension in the group is evidenced. There are, in other words, minimal indicants of anxiety and discomfort when pressures for clarifying confusing experience are absent. Junctures in the life of the group where communication becomes blocked radically affect the group mood. At such times participants are observed to regress and employ modes of functioning typical of earlier periods in their lives. They employ behaviors which have proved effective in reducing tensions in the past (functional autonomy).

Cognitive Balance

Why do people persist in acting in stereotyped ways with others when time after time these people find these behaviors do not lead to the results toward which they are directed? The concept of cognitive balance is important here. The world in which we live, devoid of the myriad of theory, explanation, and preconceived notions, is a big, booming, buzzing confusion. There is no direct correlation between the objective dimensions of the world "out there" and what registers on our sense organs.* In order to meet and master our world, that is, survive within the precarious confusion that engulfs us and pervades our thoughts and feelings, we need to make some semblance of meaning of these sensory and kinesthetic experiences. Without any assurance of a correct interpretation of our experiences we are constantly forced to make inferences about what is going on around us. Some of these inferences are of rather incidental importance and we need not be concerned with them here.

Other inferences, particularly those concerned with

* I am indebted to Professor Alfred F. Glixman of the Menninger Foundation for much of my thinking about personal strategies.

our physical and psychological safety, are of more vital concern to us. These may be called *core attitudes*. It is these inferences which comprise our attitudes about ourselves and others, and which in turn serve to steer our interpersonal transactions. Not only do core attitudes influence how we treat others, but as Kelly (1963) suggests, they shape the very manner in which we perceive the universe. We generally respond to the universe in a twofold manner. We behave in a manner which is intended to achieve a preferred state of affairs, while at the same time acting in such a way as to confirm our core attitudes about what we have predicted would happen as a result of our interaction with the environment.

Often we achieve the confirmation of our inferences at the expense of what we "consider" to be a desirable state of affairs for ourselves. A person acts as he believes. If he believes that he has some choice over his own behavior he generally acts in ways to maximize choice. A participant in a process group who denies that the group's behavior is influenced by its emotionality but instead by some natural law of group dynamics is attempting to minimize his behavioral choice. He is saying that if my emotionality is affecting how I behave in the group then I would have to seek to understand my feelings and try to deal with them. I am unprepared to do so. I have always found it more convenient to think that people are the way they are because they have to be that way. This kind of thinking can be explained by two quests that each individual becomes caught up in: a quest for certainty and that for freedom. These quests may not be mutually exclusive—as most people seek both— except in extreme (pathological) states. A quest for certainty seems to be an extremely exerted effort to maintain a fixed, stable level of organization over one's cognitive belief system. The person who seeks personal freedom is also seeking organization over his cognitive system. However, he seems better able to withstand disorganization or imbalance (anxiety and uncertainty) for a longer duration in attempting to gain a new and more complex (comprehensive) cognitive organization. People are from this perspective not equally capable or desirous of risking chafe and insult in the pursuit of more effective personal functioning. This is understandable in that confirming our expectations about the world accrues a great deal of certainty because it affords us the security of believing, however mistaken we may be, that we are able to take care of ourselves in the precarious world in which we live. Where perceptual feedback and existing beliefs about ourselves are consistent they coexist without tension and are perceived as belonging together. In such instances there is no pressure toward modifying either the reception of the new experience nor the existing belief system. On the other hand, experiences which do not agree with our existing beliefs are perceived as threats to our ability to survive, and the self builds up defenses which tend to deny the awareness of this unwelcome prospect. In short, there appears to be a natural proclivity toward maintaining a consistency between our beliefs and our experiences. Information from the environment which is inconsistent with our core attitudes are referred to as being *cognitively dissonant*. The self has three basic techniques for handling dissonant information. One is to deny or suppress the existence of the information; second, the self may distort or convert the information in such a way as to render it consistent with the person's core attitudes; third, at such times, as where incoming information leads to the realization that two or more vital core attitudes are in sharp disagreement, there is an impetus in the self toward modifying one or more of these core attitudes. In an interpersonal encounter the selected perceptions, the distorted or denied meanings of communication, the manipulation of other participants' words and actions we observe can be understood as attempts to maintain a consistent cognitive balance among the participants' core attitudes.

Self-Fulfilling Prophecy

The self-fulfilling prophecy is a vivid instance of circumstances set up in such a way that a "predicted" occurrence inevitably results. How this comes about was discussed in some detail in Chapter 8.

Manipulation of the Inter-Personal Encounter

Within each interpersonal encounter it is possible to discern the twofold nature of human behavior described in the cognitive balance concept. In communicating with others we attempt to treat the other in a manner that brings about a preferred state of affairs, while concomitantly confirming our expectations about this interaction. This process is discernible by regarding the two levels of interpersonal communication. There is the content of the discourse and there is the manipulation of the relationship, existing or potential, between the social agents involved in the encounter. The agents are not merely exchanging information, they are simultaneously attempting to establish a relationship with the other by creating a particular image of themselves in the eyes of the other. The participant in the group who is always answering the questions of the other group members may be trying to establish his relationship with the others as the person who should be turned to for direction and leadership. The group member who frequently relates accounts of participants in other groups who became distressed from sensitivity training experience is alerting the others not to ignore him as he needs their protection. The relational component of communication described here is referred to as *metacommunication*. The twofold nature of communication may be apparent in the following account of a married couple group. A couple were engaged in a heated argument about what they had observed taking place earlier in the session between the leader and two other participants. The others in the group were rather puzzled about the argument. They were certain that there was no disagreement in the couple's respective observations of the event in question. Yet, if this were the case, why were the couple's words drenched in such strong anger? Later it was revealed that in this couple's home situation it was the wife who habitually initiated discussion about their neighbors' conflicts and the husband customarily followed the wife's lead. During the group session the husband had usurped his wife's role. The seed of their covert and rather pungent discord was not a factual disagreement, e.g., about what was observed, but rather *who was supposed to* express it. They were arguing therefore over the terms of their relationship.

Similarly, in relating to another it makes some impact whether we regard our discourse as talking *with* another or talking *to* another. We change the nature of the relationship, regardless of the constancy of the content, by modifications in vocal inflection and by various kinds of cues nonverbally enacted. Moreover, what is not being spoken about in a discourse may be more crucial to the relationship of the discussants than what is being said.

Double Bind Messages

There are countless instances in interpersonal situations in which social agents convey messages to one another by word and deed of such contradictory nature that the agent who receives the message is "damned if he does" what the other seems to be asking of him and "damned if he doesn't." A participant may declare that he wishes he could get closer to others in the group. His determined countenance and arms tautly folded across his chest conveys simultaneously that a barrier on his part awaits any invitation from the others for including him into the group. On the other hand, a group may convey to a reticent participant: "Be at ease . . . We like you . . . We want you to be one of us . . . You have nothing to fear." But by the manner in which they indict the participant for his nonparticipation—frequently rationalized as, "We're only jumping on you because we really care about you"—by their previous demonstrations of insensitive conduct when other participants disclosed their feelings, a very different message is conveyed.

Personal Strategies

The concepts employed in this chapter have been attempts to describe how and explain why participants treat each other as they do in interpersonal encounters. The pivot concept in our exposition is that of personal strategies. The attitude a person takes toward himself and others can be understood in terms of the choices he makes. People regulate their behavior in terms of the assumptions they make about the contingencies in which they find themselves. These assumptions have varying probabilities of confirmation or rejection. According to assertion-structured theory, "Life is a constant actuarial process; the individual is betting on his assertions (assumptions) and winning (confirmation) or losing (disconfirmation). The neurotic is essentially a person who is constantly betting on a set of assertions that have a high probability of disconfirmation" (Harper, 1959).

The neurotic's behavior becomes highly redundant in a self-defeating manner. The stronger the assumption (the more vital the core attitude in the hierarchy of a person's belief system) the greater is his need to confirm the assumption based on whatever evidence he has at hand, be it faulty or even contradictory. In other words, the more vital an assumption is for an individual in maintaining a comfortable attitude about himself, the greater is that individual's need to set himself up for conditions that "prove" his position. To insure that these conditions occur, people generally posit certain rules (assumptions) that govern their transactions with others. Our lives abound with such rules, e.g., "Honesty is the best policy except if it hurts someone's feelings," "It is better to give than to receive," and so forth.

I refer to this whole packet of behavior as *personal strategy*, to emphasize the rather obvious but frequently ignored fact that an individual has a choice about the rules he makes for himself. They are of his choosing because he believes that they have a "payoff" for him. That many personal strategies operate from unconscious motives does not mitigate the fact that these choices are preferable to others and that they would not be maintained if they were not. Personal strategies taken together are then the manner in which a person organizes his world and commits himself to that organization. Once he has fashioned a way of gaining satisfaction (be it that of simply making meaning of his experience) he is reluctant to give it up and face the threat of not being able to continue to secure satisfaction (e.g., understand his experience) as he did in the past.

I once encountered a male patient in my psychiatric ward who tried to commit suicide the night before because his wife had left him for another man. His self-regard had been severely assaulted because he felt that he was not masculine enough to hold his wife. This view of himself was inconsistent with his core attitudes about the kind of person he should be. He could no longer deny, distort, or defend himself against the realization that his wife didn't regard him as sufficiently masculine. He experienced himself as emotionally unable to revamp his need to be regarded as masculine (his core attitude) and accordingly preferred instead to do away with himself. My patient had made the implicit assumption to himself that to be masculine is to be sexually virile and, given the slightest provocation, physically assaultive. These "virtues" are supported by his cultural institutions. They were nevertheless dysfunctional to my patient who had tried to enact them uncritically. In the past when his son acted up he felt compelled to discipline him by "belting the hell out of him"—doing what he believed his parental duty to be, consistent with his conception of the masculine role. Not surprisingly he was bewildered by his son's lack of respect for him. He attempted to resolve his conflicts with his wife by impressing his sexual powers upon her. He was unaware that she was frequently asking for other kinds of contact and consideration. When she left him he could not therefore but believe, consistent with his implicit assumptions about male-female relationships, that his wife's lover was preferred because the latter was more virile than he was.

We should be mindful in considering the above clinical description that the implicit assumptions a person makes about himself and others, which are acted upon as if they were valid and proved without being critically tested, lock the person into a limited repertoire of alternatives which are frequently inappropriate to the demands of the situations in which he finds himself. Freedom and choice in behavior have a psychogenic origin. An appropriate mode of behavior is possible only if it is conceptualized as a possibility. Otherwise it does not exist. The nature of beliefs not only influences the personal strategies a person enacts but reinforces the continuity of the strategy long after the behaviors cease to be efficacious. Beliefs being integral in the maintenance of present behaviors require critical evaluation before behavioral change occurs.

People habitually operate by way of least effort. There is a characteristic proclivity in all of us to avoid expending excessive energy in dealing with others. This may be a remnant of an archaic survival mechanism for maintaining a reservoir of energy to meet threat and exigency to the organism's survival. Self-growth and actualization are those ego-promoting strivings in the person which clash with this archaic defense. The conflict between these two ego processes, I suspect, lies at the heart of the individual's ambivalence and supports personal strategies which no longer serve their purpose. Certain personal strategies, although no longer effective, nurture the fiction that the individual's present mode of functioning is adequate and no further expenditure of energy is required to improve his life style. The *psychic economy principle* in part also explains why people try to deny their responsibility for their own actions. If people claim to have choice over their behavior energy must be expended in dealing with the way they act. If on

Psychic Economy Principle

the other hand one claims no control over his behavior his actions are beyond his purvey and they can be disregarded for all the good concern over them will accomplish.

The Responsible Person

The most crucial personal strategy a person enacts in interpersonal encounters, or in any other area of his existence, concerns the accountability he takes for his own thoughts, feelings, and actions. The things a person does and that which takes place in his encounters with others do not happen fortuitously. They occur because they serve some "desired" result for the individual, although in the long run the behavior may be self-defeating. The responsible person recognizes that if his behavior is self-defeating it behooves him to find out how it serves him.

A basic principle of human behavior is that no one enacts any kind of behavior unless he "wants" to. Whatever choice we make we do so because we find that particular choice preferable to the other choices we conceptualize as possible. People enact self-defeating behaviors because other alternatives are more distasteful. Many of us are locked in with insoluble problems because we are reluctant to believe that we have a choice in improvising our fate. We assume society, or any other convenient external agent, dictates what the payoffs of interpersonal encounters will be: status, security, emotional gratification, whatever. These payoffs we infer can only be achieved by playing by certain rules which exist prior to any specific encounter. Eric Berne has described the rules by which people play as a *life plan,* "formulated in his [the person's] earliest years, which he takes every opportunity to further as much as he dares in a given situation. This plan calls for other people to respond in a desired way and is generally divided, on a long-term basis, into distinct sections and subsections, very much like the script of a play" (Berne, 1963).

The rules are frequently based on fantasy and preconceived notions which are seldom put to critical assessment. They are in turn acted upon as if they were valid and proved, as they tend to confirm core attitudes and generate feelings of security. The cost of this pseudo-security is an inability to modify one's behavior in regard to internal and external environmental demands. Frequently we observe participants in sensitivity groups who are so intent in presenting themselves in a certain manner that they are constantly preparing their "presentation" ("script" in Berne's terms) in their own head. As a consequence, they do not attend to what is going on in the group. They miss important interactions and events and as a result react inappropriately with what is going on in the group.

Masochism

An understanding of masochism helps explain the function of pseudo-securing attitudes which have self-defeating consequences. The maintenance of security mechanisms as we have already said results from a need to defend against anxiety and uncertainty. The person who experiences a lack of control over his existence is flooded with the perturbing anticipation that an adverse event may occur at any moment which will threaten his well-being. Anxiety is experienced. Anxiety, being perhaps the most unbearable of human experiences, is the emotion most likely to lead the person to drastic maneuvers to prevent its occurrence. The person who has not developed reliable personal strategies for ascertaining with some fair degree of fidelity the onset of adverse events may find that by setting himself up for certain dreaded events he has greater control over its severity. A person who feels lonely and unattached, who typically encounters rejection in forming social relationships but doesn't know why, may be expected to be rather apprehensive of his reception by others in a new social situation, say, a sensitivity training group he plans to participate in. He may tell himself that if only he knew how others were going to treat him he wouldn't be so anxious about the group experience. If he is going to be rejected, he tells himself, he can accept that. He is used to that. It is the uncertainty whether it will or will not happen that he cannot tolerate. He tries various roles to test out his reception by the group. One session he is passive, the next critical. Regardless of his carefully thought through preparation his behavior in a group sooner or later stimulates an adverse reaction from someone, resulting in the rejection he anticipated.

A self-fulfilling process may be involved here. By unconsciously bringing on the dread event the participant need not have to bear the anxiety of waiting for it to occur. The viciousness (the strength) of the event's unpleasantness may well be inversely proportional to the duration of anticipation. The participant may be saying in effect, covertly, to his feared event, "Hit me quickly while I have my teeth clenched and am gripping on with both hands!"

Narcissism

Self-defeating and masochistic behavior are reinforced by narcissistic attitudes. Narcissistic attitudes are refusals to give up one's image (core attitude) about the kind of person he is and his expectations of how others should and in fact do treat him despite contradictory information. Narcissistic attitudes are characterological strategies used to compensate for injury to a person's ego, particularly to those parts of the ego that are associated with autonomy and self-exploration. Narcissism is a characterological scab that binds around an emotional wound suffered during the tender developmental years. It develops most tenaciously as a result of emotional and social deprivation. The child who learns at a tender age that he cannot depend upon significant others in the family grasps early in life that there is a lack of regularity between his needs and nourishment from those who care for him. He must then find for himself a way to survive without depending on others. At the same time significant others treat him as a means to their own satisfactions rather than as a person who possesses intrinsic self-worth. Taking this as his cue he learns that manipulation has a payoff. Fear of others induces him to pay off to others and he in turn employs the same threat-imposing strategy on others.

This does not do much to foster deep feelings of self-respect and self-worth. To compensate for his inability to develop those aspects of himself involved with self-worth he employs denial in the form of a reaction formation. He says, in effect, no further work or effort toward improving himself is necessary because he is already a very special person. For Freud, narcissism was an introverted investment of libidinous energy and fear of external manipulation; for Adler, a compensation for inferior development of some capacity; for Jung, a complex, the manifest behavior conveying a very different attitude toward the self than contained in the dynamically potent but consciously repressed attitude. We are indebted to Jung for the understanding that narcissism is not necessarily self-love. The grandiose person who emulates self-importance has at the core of his own feelings considerable self-depreciation which he seeks to conceal. On the other hand, the depressed, self-depreciative introvert silently treasures with considerable pride his importance, having been so singly inflicted with an onerous burden.

Social Revenge

According to Alfred Adler the two major interpersonal needs of an individual are attention and power. *Attention* is a striving to be accepted and taken notice of, a desire for intimacy and respect. *Power* is the ambition to be successful and in control of one's fate. When these motives are frustrated and the individual feels unable to satisfy them he may give up hope of attaining attention and power and turn to revenge.

"If I can't get what I want no one else will either," is an implicit statement of this motive. Social revenge becomes manifest in an individual's "tyrannical nature; nagging; a tendency to depreciate . . . to domineer over [others] . . . the misuse of valuable ideas and movements in order to depreciate others. . . . Also heightened affects like anger, . . . grief, habitually loud laughter, inattentive listening, and looking away when meeting people, directing the conversation to oneself, habitual enthusiasm over trivial matters. . . ." (Ansbacher and Ansbacher, 1956). Such participants seem inveterately bent on "screwing up the works." They insist that the group is worthless, totally incapable of helping anyone or learning anything, and has no business even operating (and these adverse group agents do their best to fulfill their prophecy). I agree with Adler that there is a struggle in these persons for power and obtaining the expression of concern from others. It is not as Adler suggests, however, that they find the group impotent because they unconsciously identify with their own impotence. Precisely because they sense that the group has sufficient power to engulf them and deprive them of their freedom, their only hope for control over their fate is to resist the group and disrupt it rather than participating in it as forces influencing constructive objectives. The course of their existence is a constant struggle to deny their uncertainty about what they want from others, others from them, and the feelings of helplessness their perplexities arouse. They prefer the security of old pains rather than uncertain thorns of new joys. It is my impression from psychotherapeutic work with persons with serious acting-out tendencies that persons who have grave doubts about their ability to control their own behavior get involved in antisocial acts so that they may feel guilty and humiliated and as a result retreat from situations which they regard as more highly threatening to them than the events in which they were "humiliated." By so doing they are able to seek comfortable and protective states of depression. The events in which they act out are public enough to insure the disapproval and disgust of others; this provides external constraints to keep the person away from the threatening situation.

The Nature of Group Process

12

Group process "has to do with what constitutes a group, how it operates to develop and maintain its groupness, and what effects it has upon the individuals who comprise it" (Hopkins, 1964). Group process includes all those acts, behaviors, thoughts, and feelings, both overt and covert, that are activated when a group of people come together and are aware of one another's presence. The word "process" is employed to suggest that behaviors in a group usually called "action," "movement," "development," and "change," and generally regarded at first glance as discreet units, are not separate and unrelated to prior events in the group. All the group behaviors that comprise group process are interrelated and influence subsequent trends in the group's activity. Group process is therefore continuous and directive. Further- 223 more, if the underlying disturbances in a group could be specified, then the interrelationship of observed events and unconsciously registered data could be readily understood. Group process includes the ways in which group members interchange feelings, thoughts, and values, and the precise types of relationships and activities that result from these interchanges. Seen from this perspective, it seems reasonable to contend that the behavior of any participant in a group cannot be properly understood unless consideration is first given to what is happening to the group *as* a group, in which the participant is a member.

Theorists interested in group process further contend that every group has its own dynamics and processes, which are not observed in a study of the sum of the individuals who comprise the group (Hopkins, 1964). This does not, however, give a metaphysical quality to groups, such as a group mind that exists apart from the mentalities of the participants. Nor does it imply a functioning that is inferior or superior to the individuals in it (Hopkins, 1964). Psychodynamics of individuals in ordinary life and the processes generated in groups are not antagonistic (Foulkes and Anthony, 1957).

Furthermore, like an individual, "a group cannot choose to have or not have group dynamics. It has some kind of dynamics going on in its activities. What it can choose is whether or not it will improve its way of functioning by trying to understand its own dynamics" (Laubach, 1968). A group exists so long as it is conceptualized by its members and so long as the relationships, rules of conduct, strategies for solving problems, and achieving goals are taken into account— intentionally or unwittingly—in the group members' transactions within each other.

224

In the Bion method (of which the process group is a derivative) the consultant observes manifest action and makes statements indicative of the unconscious passions being experienced by the group members. This approach has been criticized for making interpretations of a group of people which may only characterize a few participants. We are told that to analyze group functions is to deny individual differences and personal distinctions (Wolf and Schwartz, 1962). Furthermore, some critics claim that a group is not an individual, and therefore individual psychodynamics cannot be appropriately applied to a group as an entity (Wolf and Schwartz, 1962). Some critics claim that even when group interpretations are representative of the membership, they are so broad and general in nature that they indicate little or nothing that we do not already know. And, finally, and most important in the mind of the psychoanalytically trained critic: Attention to group dynamics even where it is relevant tends to divert the group leader and the participants from the essential task of exposing and solving transference distortions (Wolf and Schwartz, 1962).

The last criticism, which questions the consultant's purpose in conducting groups, has been addressed in earlier chapters. The former criticisms point out that the Bion-type group interpretation does not cover all that goes on in a group or catch the most important dynamics. I feel these criticisms are pale. Behavior is multifaceted: no stimulus ("cause") leads to any one response. The nature of experience is not so constituted. The consultant cannot, and should not be expected to, be able to comprehend all the determinants of participants' behavior in a process group. The consultant describes what he observes and attempts to explain these events in terms of the conceptual system he finds most acceptable to himself. At best, due to the relative immaturity of the social sciences as exact sciences, these are incomplete explanations of behavioral events. This does not prevent the group experience from being worthwhile. To be meaningful for the people who participate in it, group training must rely on a two-way interactive process. Participants will not understand their behavior in groups merely from the consultant's explanations of their experiences. The participant needs to be reminded that if the consultant or any other group member is not meeting his needs, it is the participant's responsibility to make himself known to the other, so that his needs can be related to appropriately.

An
Action
System

Group process has the properties of an *action system*. It is a system of tensions and energies created by the participants' need to make meaning of their participation in group events, and, by the reactive hopes and fears aroused by their understanding or lack of understanding of these events. A group is not simply a hypothetical construct used to explain psychosocial events. Indeed, processes generated by groups are registered in the muscular-glandular activity of the group members. Just as physiological manifestations of stress and attraction indicate what is going on in the individual's intrapsychic life, the physiological activity of group members denotes the inner life of the group. Group emotion, for instance, consists of that which each individual participant contributes through his verbal and nonverbal communications of what the group experience means to him. Like any other action system, the group as a system has subparts, functions, and boundaries. In the process

226

group there is a major concern with the here-and-now. Desultory discussion of events beyond the immediate group interest generates tensions as the boundaries of the group become taut and strained. All action systems, moreover, have the problem of allocating energies among different subparts and functions in an economical and efficient way for the system as a whole. Action systems therefore, employ *adjustive* functions in attempting to maintain a "steady state," a comfortable level of functioning which maintains the pre-conflict organization of the system. In performing adjustive measures, action systems are generally thought to be hierarchically organized. Progressively more central and total system adjustive functions are made, in order to handle disturbances in the system and to establish a residual energy, a level of tension, which is tolerable and supportive of the system's safe and productive functioning. In one group, two participants were engaging in a heated encounter to the exclusion of other group members. Their exchanges seemed sufficiently absorbing (gratifying), such that the other group members felt excluded. Such a pairing-off cast the pale of death for a group that already harbored concerns about its ability to exist as an entity. Feelings of abandonment and neglect, as well as exclusion from powerful, exciting, and tender relations, were expressed by the other group members. Suddenly, without the consultant quite aware of how it started, the other members of the group pushed the dyad to make far more exaggerated statements about their intimate intentions than the pair claimed to want at that point. Since the pair were unwilling to fulfill the ideas that abounded in the images of the other group members the group spun a fantasy about the pair. The story took on such an intimate, sexual nature that the group members were forced to break off the tale. By this time, however, the pair had been sufficiently "warned" about the dangers of their pairing, and they desisted from further interaction with each other for the remainder of that session. This is an example of a group employing adjustive measures to extricate an internal system threat.

Group Pathology

Oftentimes have I heard you speak of one who commits a wrong as though he were not one of you, but a stranger unto you and an intruder in your world. But I say that even as the holy and righteous cannot rise beyond the highest which is in each one of you, so the wicked and weak cannot fall lower than the lowest which is in you also. And as a single leaf turns not yellow but with the silent knowledge of the whole tree, so the wrong-doer cannot do wrong without the hidden will of you all (Kahlil Gibran, *The Prophet*).

There has been considerable concern about some sensitivity training leaders' lack of discretion in accepting highly distressed participants into their groups. It is feared that these participants may become more disturbed as a result of their group training experience. There are occasional reports of a participant experiencing a psychotic break during a sensitivity group conference or soon thereafter. On more than one occasion I have seen participants trying to relate to the group in primary process terms, indicating thinking disturbance and a breakdown of the ego's capacity to censor publicly inappropriate thoughts and feelings. I have observed, however, that the underlying pathology present within the group activates, encourages, and supports this disturbed behavior. Indeed, "behavior of a deviant individual is per se no problem; the problem is that the group

228

does not know how to respond to particular types of communication. Anger or bullying of individuals is seen not as a response to the individual; but as a response to the members' own anxieties set off by the more or less accidental behavior of the deviant. Deviant behavior that is disturbing must nevertheless be seen as speaking for the group. Otherwise, why is the group upset by it?" (Thelen, 1954.) Disturbed behavior is due to conflicts within a person, but its specific manifestation reflects the anxieties and aspirations of the society in which one resides (Bettelheim, 1967). Sociologists and social psychologists have delineated the instrumental or task roles and functions that exist in groups. As groups grow in size and complexity participants tend to jockey for position, and gradually certain group members are seen by the others as addressing more of their energies to certain group problems and functions than do other participants. The relationship between how a group member expects to behave in a group and how others "require" him to specialize in the interaction process of the group is conceptualized as "role." Patterns of behavior, attitudes, and capacities revealed by each group member are accepted or rejected by the others according to whether they hinder or stimulate the other group members' own personal goals. Participants tend to perform their roles in groups in ways that will facilitate group goals, for unless a group is unfettered of its internal conflicts it cannot achieve the personal goals of its membership. All this seems clear, but I become puzzled when I observe groups acting in ways that seem quite contradictory to the manifest personal and group goals the participants claim they are bent on achieving. Certain events in training groups seem unexplainable by means of the current body of social scientific thinking. I have observed participants in process groups state that they have entered group training to become more self-reliant, for their lack of autonomy as individuals has prevented them from achieving what they want in life. They then spend session after session demanding that the consultant lead them like little children; they ask him to reconsider his misplaced confidence in their ability to solve their own difficulties. How does one account for the outrageous indignation of group members directed toward a fellow participant when in fact these indignant participants are subtly but nonetheless clearly encouraging the "deviant" to sidetrack the group? Investigation of the personality traits of individual group members leads nowhere, because the behaviors enacted in groups are related to the personality dynamics of other group members. A study of personality dynamics alone will not reveal under what conditions one rather than another group member may display certain group behavior. In short, social scientists and others concerned with group process have found that knowledge about each of the group members' individual psychodynamics is insufficient to explain the subtle, elusive, and complex inner life of group activity.

Underlying Themes

The integralist perspective may provide some enlightenment. In the life of any group numerous topics, issues, and events come to the fore to be discussed and dealt with by the group members. Each group has certain topics which it discusses more frequently than it does others. They may be politics, education, heterosexual relationships, whatever. To call these areas of discussion "topics" is however to address only their obvious and manifest content. To locate

230

the themes that pervade these topics is to explore below the surface of the discussion and attempt to sort out the pressing concerns of the group members. A single theme may underline a number of different topics. Thus, while a group may be discussing last night's television address of a politician to his constituents, a recent and embittered teachers' strike, or the lack of teamwork of a basketball superstar, the theme in each instance may be whether a man has the right to interpret and perform his job as he feels he should or perform it in the manner in which the members of the social grouping he represents expect him to.

Regardless of the topic, each underlying theme has its own unique, accompanying emotional mood, which remains committed to that theme unless the group tensions tied up in that mood are resolved. Thus, not knowing what is expected of themselves in a group, group members will accompany a topic of the dependency theme with feelings of helplessness, despair, demands for attention, and irrational expectations of themselves and the consultant.

I have found in process groups that the prevailing mood of the group is most represented or embodied by one group member. This participant appears to be more attuned than is anyone else to what is going on in the other group members. When for instance, a group is skirting an issue, developing subtly restrictive means to avoid threatening feelings, this one participant is more sensitive than the others to the uneasy solution being formulated. He is willing to express his own discomfort in some discernible, although often nonverbal, manner.

231

Some of these moods are positive and acceptable to the other members, and there is a positive identification with the group member who represents this mood. Generally these participants are referred to as "leaders." When the mood is positive the group member who best represents the mood is looked to for direction and sustaining the good feelings in the group. However, leadership is given to all group members who *move* the group in some direction—for "good" or for "evil." A group *uses* its members to serve its purposes and functions. There are also unpleasant, threatening, and disturbed feelings aroused in a group. Often without realizing how they are encouraging him, a group member can act as a "leader" for a group when the others look to him to "act out" and express adverse feelings which they also are experiencing and are unable or unwilling to consciously acknowledge. The group member who best embodies adverse feelings of the group comes to be rejected, pitied, ignored, "scapegoated," or whatever. Every group at some point in its existence crucifies some of its leaders and extols others. The aim in both instances may be similar: to vicariously and silently express through others what the group members have difficulty articulating and dealing with for themselves.

The group member who best represents the group mood might be called a *polarity*. The dictionary defines "polarity" as "any tendency to turn, grow, think, feel, etc. in a certain way, as if because of magnetic attraction or repulsion." In a group where the feelings expressed are pleasant and acceptable to the membership, the group representative seems to push the others to greater articulation and awareness of their experiences. In the dark and deep intrigue of adverse moods, the group representative appears to be used by the other group members to bear away dark and guilty burdens.

232

The perpetuation of mood by group polarity, with the more or less insidious impetus and support of the group is so highly interrelated that I refer to this group phenomenon as "group collusion." Bion has pointed out that it is indeed very "difficult for an individual member to convey meanings to the group which are other than those which the group wishes to entertain" (Bion, 1961). First of all there is an unconscious endeavor by the other group members to integrate the various behaviors and interactions of the polarity in order to make his behavior seem consistent and predictable. Secondly, the interactive pattern of the polarity in fact becomes increasingly more consistent and circumscribed, as a function of his polarity role and the support of reinforcing reactions by the other group members to hold him in that role.

Group collusion results from the resonance in each of the group members of the discord struck by shared and unacceptable emotions evoked by others. As Thelen implied in the passage cited a few pages back, if we did not fear that expression of forbidden urges by others is contagious and hence could arouse our own latent disturbed proclivities, we would not feel threatened by their expression. Denial and distancing are not very efficacious strategies for a group. The group that denies its emotions becomes exploited by them. Ironically, groups often act out the very feelings and actions they deny. The group members in one Encounter group repeatedly pointed out that one of the group members was clearly vulnerable to an emotional collapse. They felt concerned about him, they claimed, and desired to protect him. The group member in question, to the others' dismay, indicated that he neither wanted nor felt in need of their protection. He said that he did not experience himself as inordinately unprotected. If some of the other group members wished to feel concern and to protect him,

Group Collusion

233

he continued, then that was their problem not his. Several of the group exploded at his refusal to feel vulnerable and pointed out that his statement was a clear indication of the near collapse of his defenses.

I felt the need to point out to the group what in my mind seemed ubiquitous, but which the rest of the group apparently wished to ignore: the group members were trying to assuage their guilt for their sadism. The group member in question was regarded as a deviant because he would not accept their attack on him as dangerous. They were ready to decapitate him in order to prove their point. The group, by use of a self-fulfilling prophecy, would prove him vulnerable. They would not desist their attack until he became disjunctive. At the same time, the participants wished to expiate their culpability over their dastardly behavior. They tried to do this by demonstrating that weakness and vulnerability were inherent in the deviant. If the deviant collapsed it would not be their fault. They in fact had tried to protect him by alerting him to his disability. Nor were they at fault if he was so fragile and defenseless that he wouldn't heed their warning.

In my view, what they were attacking in the deviant was an uncomfortable attitude that each of the other participants himself experienced: a reluctance to give in and admit he needed someone else's assistance. At some level of awareness they sensed that this attitude had impeded their own interpersonal growth. At one level therefore they were sincerely trying to indicate to the deviant the imprudence of an "I don't need anyone's help" attitude. Because each of the group members felt uncomfortable with these feelings about himself, he could not acknowledge them as his own. Instead of relating to the deviant group member as a kindred soul, they tried to split off the rejected part of themselves and place it onto the deviant, regarding it as his problem not theirs. It was to be something which he had to work out himself, not a concern with which they were also struggling.

Instances such as these of group collusion raise the following questions, which the consultant needs to pose for the group so that their work as a group may be meaningful:

Does the group recognize and acknowledge those who give it direction? How do polarities obtain their "powers" from the group—by possessing resources to move the group in directions the participants have acknowledged as desirable, or by representing fears and threats that rise in them in ways they wish to avoid?

Group collusion is familiar to all those who have conducted intensive group experiences for any period of time. They have no doubt observed in their groups a phenomenon which may be referred to as "self-flagellation as a defense against anxiety." A member of the group will confess to any of a number of personal liabilities: being mentally "sick," homosexual, criminal, irresponsible, etc. The confession does not seem to ring true. We are struck with the uneasy feeling that the confessor "doth protest too much." I have found it helpful in this situation to put aside consideration of the manifest content and to pay close attention to the manner in which the discussion is being transacted between the "discussant" and his "audience." This kind of scrutiny shows that the confessor is actually speaking a soliloquy in a group setting. Whenever another participant tries to relate to what the confessor is pleading, the confessor cuts him off. He conveys by implicit statement or more frequently by verbal intonation and gesture that he does

Self-Flagellation

not wish to hear what the other participants have to say about him, such that he cannot bear to face them and tries to shut off his interactions with them. The participant's nonverbal cues then contradict his statements asking for the group's help and good wishes. Participants in groups may use self-humiliation to protect themselves against experiencing the precise personal liability they are confessing to possess and wish to change. "They indulge in this moral self-flagellation to avoid the hurt, the anxiety, and the deeper guilts" which squarely facing their feelings would arouse. The group, by not picking up on the participants, nonverbal signals, may travel under the fiction that he is asking for their help. Or, correspondingly, "in order to protect itself from being excessively stirred up, the group may overidentify with (the confessor) and prematurely 'absolve' him of his guilty feelings. This promotes a short-circuiting and dissociation of the guilt, which cannot get worked through to its origin" (Schecter, 1959).

And last, but not least, it should be pointed out that each group polarity serves as a barometer of underlying group emotion that the group cannot afford to avoid investigating. When the group develops solutions to its conflicts which are too abstract or too fanciful for concrete application, there is generally someone in the group who characteristically voices her (in mixed groups females generally take this function) confusion about what is going on in the group; something to the effect, "There must be something wrong with me but I don't understand what we just decided to do!" A participant who questions a solution the group has spent considerable time and sweat over formulating proves to be a thorn in the side of the other group members. Such a person may be dismissed as "a stupid, labile hysteric who never understands what is going on." However, to so dismiss her uneasiness is often to discard rather sensitive intuition and a valuable diagnostic tool for the study of ill-advised group solutions. The question the participants need to ask themselves is whether the "deviant" is alone in her "naïveté," or is she voicing the silent questions of others?

To investigate a group in depth is in large measure to be increasingly appreciative of a myriad diverse and highly complex nonverbal signals being transmitted by the participants. These signals, or cues, as they are frequently referred to, communicate powerful and urgent emotion. Shifts in the mood of the group are reflected in changes the participants make in posture, gesture, facial expression, and muscular tone, as well as in verbal expression. The emotional climate we sense in a group though not verbally articulate is the result of bodily cues, emotionally responded to, without cognitive mediation.

Nonverbal Signals

In groups during states of high tension and anxiety a process which has been referred to by analytic group therapists as *de-egotization* may occur. Each of the participants, as a condition of his belonging to the group, gives up part of his own ego by dissociating conceptually certain of his own personality attributes. In turn, he regards his relinquished ego as an attribute of the group or of the leader of the group as its representative of the group (Slavson, 1964). In so doing what has been referred to by group dynamicists as a *de-individualization* process occurs in the group. Unconscious drives and impulses are acted upon by the group. Unconscious drives and impulses are acted

De-Egotization

upon by the group members, which under other circumstances would have more successfully restrained. "Anyone who observes persons in groups and the same persons individually is forced to conclude that they often behave differently in these two general kinds of situations. Casual observation would seem to indicate that one kind of behavior difference stems from the fact that people often release in groups, that is, are sometimes more free from restraint, less inhibited, and able to indulge in forms of behavior in which, when alone, they would not indulge. There occurs sometimes in groups a state of affairs in which the individuals act as if they were 'submerged in the group.' Such a state of affairs may be described as one of de-individuation, that is, individuals are not seen or paid attention to as individuals." Under these conditions there is "likely to occur for the members a reduction of inner restraints against doing various things. . . . If individuals, then, have needs which they are generally unable to satisfy because of the existence of inner restraints against doing certain things, a state of de-individuation in a group makes it possible for them to obtain satisfaction of these needs . . ." (Festinger, Pepitone, and Newcombe, 1952).

The composite of these otherwise inhibited needs and strong feelings freed from the group members' usual characterological restraints comprises, what for a choice of a better term, may be referred to as *group mentality*. Derived from a primitive system of signaling and deciphering, the group mentality contains hopes and reactive fears contained within each of the participant's images and shared in common with his fellow group members. In this condition the participants are difficult to differentiate, for they do not stand out as individuals but are a horde. Rather striking are the group members' demands for attention, protection, and reassurance. Similar to the classical Freudian id, a

238

group mentality possesses no critical attributes and no negation of urges. The "conception of the group as guided by common unconscious forces is consistent with Freud's (1921) observation that to the degree that a group lacks formal organization, its members are stimulated to display basic similarities in their unconscious drives. Such groups encourage members to throw off, albeit temporarily, the repressions which contain the expression of their instinctual impulses" (Parloff, 1967). Groups under these conditions are highly unstable. Initially most, if not all, of the process groups I have worked with could be so characterized. They appear to be under the assumption that differences breed discontent and will inevitably lead to group dissolution. The process group becomes "our group" and frequently a preoccupation of its members in their everyday existence. In the group sessions the expressed possibility of satisfying their needs in other social situations seems negated. Apprehension is sensed that unless the group continues to survive the participants' needs will never be met. Arduous efforts are made to erect normative limits for fostering group behavior that will keep the group in existence. Tension, however, becomes overwhelming when the participants discover through obsessive-compulsive scrutiny of their rules for procedure that numerous loopholes still exist. The participants express a common fear that they have no time to waste in keeping the group alive. They propose simple and inadequate solutions to plug the loopholes that more sophisticated, critical judgments have previously failed to avert. Seldom do participants in this stage of group development question why the group must survive. They seem unwilling to grapple with their reasons for having a process group in the first place. They seemed to be operating under the assumption that they have already justified the existence of the group. There are no "ifs" or "buts" about the importance of the group, as if it were a natural and inscrutable law that the group must survive at all costs; some catastrophic event would occur if it didn't. The participants appear to be desperately seeking some object or agent, preferably an external one, to be named as the threat to the group's survival. At the same time they refuse to consider their own shared fears about what it means to be in an intimate interpersonal encounter with others.

Origins of Nonverbal Signals

It may be helpful to trace the source of the group members' fears as an evolutionary process in man's social development. In the animal kingdom, including the primitive *Homo sapiens*, sophisticated consciousness and its result, intentional language, were only rudimentarily developed. In order to survive the perils of an uncertain and precarious world the solitary beast needed protection from those who stood consanguineously within his species. Without digressing to speculation about specific evolutionary processes (although there is some evidence that we smell fear) it suffices to say that certain means of alerting others of the species that danger is imminent were adopted. We may additionally assume that these modalities developed idiosyncratically and largely unconsciously, initially within the primary group—the family—and by successful adaptation in others of the species. It does not seem unreasonable that these modalities for signaling danger have been passed down generation after generation. We no doubt witness from our own experience that we relate to intimates and relatives on a nonverbal level more than we do with strangers. Each of us retains within his own makeup the remnants of a primitive biological signaling system. Due to its archaic and partially innate nature we share this system with other humans. In a series of studies Fisher and Cleveland (Fisher, 1968) have demonstrated "that the individual's manner of distributing attention to his body is intimately related to the traits, conflicts, and personality defenses characterizing him." There is further evidence that these somatic reactions to stimulation are socio-culturally determined. Body language was originally a warning system to alert fellow creatures to hide, flee, or fight in face of danger; and our derived rudimentary signaling system has tremendous communicative impact. "The more a human expression approaches an archaic form of communication, the more contagious is the meaning it conveys" (Meerloo, 1959). Archaic forms of communication instantaneously touch off primitive emotional reactions, and "the closer a human expression approaches an archaic form of communication, the more unobtrusive is the communicative meaning it conveys." (Meerloo, 1959). In 1965 in a high school in Blackburn, England, the local medical health department received an urgent call for help. A few girls had fainted earlier in the day; now the girls were falling over like ninepins. One hundred and eighty students were affected and eighty-five required hospitalization. The school had to be closed for the remainder of the week; only then did the students begin to recover. Mass hysteria in the Blackburn incident, like other instances of mass hysteria, was triggered off by some sudden expression of emotion within a group of unsophisticated people united against a vaguely conceived but strongly feared threat.

"Mental contagion is the result of a common backward pull, a mutual pushing of people into reminiscence, regression, and infantilism" (Meerloo, 1959). Under these conditions people are unable to exchange their ideas and feelings freely with others. 241

The opportunity for critical reconsideration of thoughts and sentiments is impeded, and thinking proceeds along highly autistic channels.

Consensual Validation

Thinking that is reality-oriented requires consensual validation. *Consensual validation* is an interpersonal technique which all of us generally employ without giving it much thought. We use it to ascertain if our perceptions, thoughts, and feelings about events and other people as well as ourselves are experienced correspondingly by others. Consensual validation is an indispensable social necessity. Nonvalidated thinking breeds delusion and susceptibility to contagion.

In a process group comprised of six females (five social workers and a nurse), the participants insisted that their difficulties in the hospital were attributable to not having a male to depend upon for protection against the aggressive females and an overly powerful male administrator. Since the consultant was a male and had supervisory status the participants insisted that he desist from what they regarded as his aloof, detached, critical attitude and become part of the group, giving them the understanding and guidance they required. In the de-egotization process the rational, self-critical capacities of the ego, which serve to realistically evaluate and take heed of the complexities of the variegated world in which we exist, are given up to the group or paralyzed within the personal ego of the participant. These mature, critically evaluative attributes comprise the group ego. The de-egotization, or splitting of the ego, is performed in a rather simplistic fashion. In the female process group reported above the participants split off their human capacities in order to attribute to weakness and helplessness to themselves and strength and wisdom to the

242

consultant. The female professional workers could therefore blame the consultant for their dependency ("It is he who is an expert on groups—he must be running the group for some good purpose—but how can we know *what he wants*—it is his obligation to inform us so that we can *do what is expected of us.*") The group, by relinquishing responsibility for what *should* happen, gave leadership to the consultant and did not test its capacities for discovering, exploring, and implementing goals for themselves. It was for these very reasons they could make no headway with their supervisors. In groups where two consultants or co-therapists are present a parallel process occurs. The participants try to separate the "leaders," attributing to one the role of "good parent" and to the other that of the "bad parent" (in Sullivan's terms, the mother who makes them feel anxious). Thus they try to benefit from the one and avoid the other. The turmoil of escaping from the "bad parent" makes learning untenable. The participants act as if they are compelled to imitate what others act out for them, without understanding what is happening inside themselves to produce this behavior (Meerloo, 1959). Relinquishing ego functions leads to *depersonalization,* a feeling in which their sense of their own identity as a person is paralyzed. The more depersonalized a person experiences himself to be, the less he is able to organize his critical faculties and stand up and confront his hidden terrors alone.

The same holds true for process groups. Conflict areas that are skirted and unresolved serve as impediments to group development. This hinders the group's effectiveness as a social unit over and over again, and the participants are not aware of what the problem is and how it can be removed.

What is particularly disruptive about the de-egotization process is that intellect becomes separated from emotion. Without the appropriate cognitive

243

endeavor emotional activity is elicited in a chaotic and blind manner. Without sufficient emotional contact with the object or issue under consideration, intellectual activity is a remote, lonely, and unsatisfying experience for those engaged.

In sum, without a continual confrontation with reality by means of the reflected appraisals (consensual validation) in deep and meaningful relationships with others, repressed infantile concepts and reactions come to dominate our mental life (Meerloo, 1959), and we become dominated by our own and others' irrational thinking.

Nonverbal Signals— A Door to the Unconscious

Important for our understanding of nonverbal communication is the influence of the economy principle, which was discussed earlier. Nonverbal cues are automatic, unintentional signals which expend little energy, since they do not require the concentrated efforts of the central nervous system. Not being cognitively processed, these messages frequently consist of intentions which are logically inconsistent with our verbally professed statements. Perceptive group members pick up these inconsistent messages and understandably ask for some clarification from the communicator of what he actually wants of the group. Frequently this is based upon a false assumption that people at their innermost core are uni-dimensional. Most of us seem to believe that a single "real" motive or goal lurks somewhere beneath our polite social behavior, covered up by pretense. The human potentials people often make this assumption. People, fortunately or unfortunately, are more complex organisms than the uni-dimensional rationale assumes. People have mixed feelings about most of the things that are important to them. It is not that one imperative covers up a person's true desire, but that people often want rather contradictory commodities simultaneously. Likewise, people at one and the same time have contradictory feelings about themselves and others.

In matter of fact then, nonverbal communication is the organism's vehicle for expressing *ambivalence*, laying bare the core of the double-bind situations we place ourselves and others in and the double messages we "thrive" upon in our interpersonal encounters. Nonverbal communication, hence, is a door to the unconscious.

Paradoxically enough, activation of archaic reactions to threats evoked by social contagion is actually self-defeating and wasteful. The fears ignited are no longer appropriate to the present world. The dangers modern man faces in the twentieth century are no longer external but almost entirely psychological. The primitive could escape danger by flight, because it was external. Can we flee and hide from our inner tensions, from the burning desire to cast aside our stifling inhibition and make meaningful contact with others? In the young child, the ego was weak and immature; instinctual urges rode herd. Forbidden wishes were immediate and potent dangers to the survival of a young organism in a world of powerful adults which might destroy him for his socially forbidden acts. As a result, the reality-adapted aspects of the personality perceived each instinctual urge, whether in action or fantasy, as a peril to the survival of the organism. Unlike the primitive the child has grown to maturity. He is capable of refining his urges into socially appropriate gratification. The primitive fears remain, however. By habitually devoting his endeavors to avoiding threats to his security, he has impeded access to the gratification he claims to crave in his more conscious communications: ". . . if a person must devote any part of his activity to a defense against anxiety, there is to that degree a decrement in the attention he can give to the resolution (or satisfaction) of the situation in which he finds himself" (Cohen, 1950).

Silence in the Group

As we are presently concerned with nonverbal behavior, it may now be opportune to discuss one of the more sticky problems for group trainers: how to regard the silent members in the group. First we need to ask, what does silence in a group mean? It of course depends upon when the silence occurs. (What, for instance, has happened prior to the silence.) It would seem that silence in a group may have one or a combination of three precursors:

1. *Silence may represent anger.* Communicating is figuratively giving of one's self. When we feel angry at someone we generally don't wish to extend ourselves to them. We would prefer to vent our wrath but generally hold back because of the consequences of acting on our anger. This has its origins in the early characterological development of the person. About the end of the first year of life the mouth begins to share its pleasure-giving role with that of the organ of elimination. Cleanliness is one of the major problems of this period and one of the touchiest from the point of view of parent-child relationships. In many families it represents the first major source of conflict between the child's desire for pleasure and distaste for restraint, and the wishes of the parents to regulate the child's behavior. Substituting voluntary control for what was initially an involuntary reflex process earns approval for the child in the eyes of his parents. The child quickly learns that withholding is an effective means of manipulating their approval and for getting back at them when they displease him. Silence and

246

withholding is then a characterological response to angry feelings representing threat or expectation of disapproval for expressing anger; fear of losing control over impulses and actually doing what we *feel* like doing to someone.

2. *Silence may represent fear.* When we are afraid we often pull within ourselves and shut ourselves off from the threat we find convenient to regard as external. Fear and anger are closely interrelated. We get angry at people who expose us to danger. Our silence is often an attempt to mask our fear of appearing vulnerable.

A silent participant in sensitivity training may be perceived by the other group members as a *potential* danger to the more actively involved members of the group. Fear that someone in the group will breach confidentiality is a reaction to having disclosed intimate feelings and experiences. No one can guarantee that tales will not be told outside the group. One safeguard is having every group member make intimate disclosures about himself. This serves to counterbalance the threat. The silent participant, not having opened up to the group, has no restraint on telling what he knows about group members. Pressures are therefore borne on him to open up and provide the group with "blackmail insurance" in respecting group confidentiality.

3. *Silence may represent an integration of cognitive and emotional input.* When our experiences make an impact upon us we may endeavor to retard our attention to additional external stimulation for a sufficient period in order to relate these impressive events to our past experiences.

Each of these three factors in group experience may affect silence. There are manifest indicators which differentiate each of these factors, however. The emotion experienced in each is different. When verbal

247

language is not being employed nonverbal cues become particularly salient. Persons communicate by means of body-language when experiencing difficulty expressing their thoughts and feelings through verbal symbols (Ruesch and Bateson, 1951). In a schizophrenic-patient group Ronnie rarely spoke. He could best be seen as a group polarity representing sexual tension in the group. His body position—rigid, slouched, swinging leg—often helped mirror the mood of the group when anxiety began to build up about heterosexual relationships. Each individual has his own characteristic way of reacting to the emotional climate in the group. The alert consultant picks up these cues and relates them to what is being experienced. A participant rhythmically pounding on his chair conveys a very different impression about what is going on in him (and by extension in the group) than does a participant brushing his brow. When participants become astute at discerning nonverbal cues and relating them to others' characteristic ways of reacting to situations, they help one another understand what the other is experiencing and under what circumstances. This is frequently a valuable kind of information for a participant. Interpretations, based solely on what a participant said and what it "really meant," can be defended against by intellectual mechanisms, such as rationalization and denial. Interpretations are inferential and indirect assumptions about what someone is experiencing. Feedback of how one behaves under actual interpersonal conditions makes it difficult for a participant to disown his true self. Being a more direct kind of observation, it is made of sterner stuff.

Group 13
Themes
and
Moods

"A theme is a topic and point of focus in discussion, with a clear beginning and a clear stopping point. There may be one or a number of themes in a single session, usually there are several. For each theme, there is a major participant [a group polarity] who is the center of focus, and there are minor participants whose number and intensity of involvement are short-lived" (Hobbs, 1951). Some group therapists have referred to these themes as "G-responses." "Almost all G-responses represent attempts at some kind of homoestasis. The group constantly seeks to strike a balance among the anxieties of its different members. This balance represents a kind of homeostasis which keeps the anxiety of the members on a tolerable level" (Kadis, Krasner, Winick, and Foulkes, 1963).

Group themes or motifs are therefore in this sense the group's history of enabling solutions (which Whitaker and Lieberman referred to as a group 249 *culture*). These solutions are called into play by the participants because in their minds these solutions have proved effective in reducing group tensions in the past. In Chapter 12 I spoke of group moods that group polarities came to represent. I have not yet explained the reasons for their occurrence. A group mood contains the feelings excited originally by focal conflicts, which are subsequently revoked in dealing with a theme in which the same or like reactive motives (fears) of the original conflicts are aroused. The experience of these feelings may be thought to trigger off the mnemonic reenactment of interpersonal behaviors (solutions) that in the past have proved "successful." There may be considerable value in regarding intensive group experiences from a focal conflict model:

> The manifest content of discussions in groups may embrace practically any topic . . . but it is one of the essential assumptions for psychoanalytic work with groups [for the study of any group in depth for that matter] that, whatever the manifest content may be, a *common group tension* of which the group is not aware but which determines its behavior [is present] (Ezriel, 1950).
> We view the covert, shared aspects of the group in terms of forces and counterforces, particularly those involving the shared impulses, wishes, hopes, and fears of the [participants] (Whitaker and Lieberman, 1967).
> The wish and the fear constitute opposing forces. The fear prevents the wish from being expressed directly or perhaps even recognized. The wish cannot be pursued actively or thoroughly satisfied. At the same time the wish cannot quite be given up and keeps the fear in the foreground. This situation creates tension in the group and provides the impetus that keeps the group in almost constant dynamic flux (Whitaker and Lieberman, 1967).

A group solution represents a compromise between the opposing forces; it is primarily directed to alleviating reactive fears but also attempts to maximize gratification of the disturbing motive [the wish] (Whitaker and Lieberman, 1967).

In my work with process groups I have attempted to locate and sort out common group themes, that is, themes that seem so highly interrelated with the properties of process groups that they manifest themselves in all or most of the groups I have observed. Naturally, every observer cuts into the group using his knowledge, training, and interest to make topical distinctions so that he can discern what is going on. Consequently, the themes which I have observed and regard as rather distinctive (but nevertheless highly related to the stream of ongoing process in the group) may be less distinct or undifferentiable to other observers. Mindful of this I nevertheless offer my observations as a frame of reference for investigating the topical dynamics of group process and for providing an explanatory rationale for these dynamics.

Each motif is best understood from its focal conflict aspects: as a wish that strives to be achieved; as a fear that impedes the expression of the wish; as the resultant compromise which alleviates the tension generated by the conflict between expression and prohibition. One caution should be made: group motifs are regarded as the "as if" stances the participants take toward real or fantasized objects with which they are concerned. These conceptualizations are not meant literally in the sense, for example, that

Common Group Themes and Moods

the group consciously regards the consultant as a messiah and expects him to come into a session with sandals and a camel. Rather on a covert level they act toward him as if he were a person from whom all wisdom flows. Referring to their attitude toward him "as if he were a messiah" is a graphic way of expressing what we infer their attitude toward him to be, not necessarily how the participants might consciously describe him.

Dependency

One of the most impressive phenomena observed in process groups is the never-resolved dependency striving of the participants. There appears to be something harrowing and depersonalizing about the amorphous structure of a process group which accentuates the need of the group members for a dependable, strong, parental figure. The participants as a group express the need for nurture and protection. They treat the consultant as a messiah who has all the answers and necessary resources for conducting a worthwhile group. Where there are two consultants or a consultant and an observer, the participants try to separate them, regarding one as the "bad parent," who is to be avoided, and the other as the "good parent," from whom to suckle. If the consultant does not satisfy their dependency needs, as he inevitably fails to do, they look to their membership for a leader or to the external environment for absent members or strangers to serve as prophets to lead them out of the wilderness of confusion about what is happening in the group, and reduce for them the tension they are experiencing. When these endeavors fail, as they inevitably do, a pairing phenomenon usually occurs. A group member will offer cigarettes, chewing gum,

252

or whatever other oral gratifications are presently available. The curious thing about the dependency theme is that the group is not able to masticate whatever nourishment it claims to crave from the consultant. The participants ask the consultant to feed the group information and instructions for properly working at their task. They inevitably disregard whatever assistance he offers them. Events observed in some of my groups have led me to believe that dependency needs may be temporarily suspended or partially resolved if in an interpersonal encounter the reciprocity of expectation and communication of explicit rules is sufficiently established such that each of the participants stands in a more or less definite status and role relationship in matters of consequence to the other.

Narcissism

The participants in this mood attempt to assert their individuality. They express in both subtle and direct manner resistance to changing their habitual ways of relating to others and a stubborn unwillingness to question their preconceived notions about themselves and the group situation. All the process groups that I have worked with had had considerable difficulty accepting the premise that they are a group, bounded by certain limitations and specific considerations by the very fact of their interacting over time and subtly setting up regulations for their interactions, rather than simply being an assembly of individuals together in a room unaffected by the presence of and their social relationship with the other participants. They act as if they each lived in a vacuum. They frequently distort, ridicule, and deny the consultant's statements. They claim that they cannot understand how a group can have emotions—emotions that affect everyone in the group. The participants in this mood express fear of being influenced by the other participants. Wary of influence the participants reject being relegated to a single emotion shared by all. They are unwilling to work as a group because they claim that a group by its very nature is alien. Beneath their apprehensions are remnants of magical thinking. They fear that if they are regarded as a group their individual personalities will be submerged. If their behavior is predictable to the consultant their freedom and individuality will be diminished. They insist that science and psychology are imperfect, as if a more perfect science implies control over their behavior. The group gets angry when the consultant suggests that the members need to know more about themselves because they feel that he is suggesting that they are less than perfect. It often appears to me that the group is desperately trying to work on the consultant to avoid looking at themselves. They regard the group situation as a combat where the consultant is trying to do something to them which is ill-advised. As a result they project their feelings of inadequacy and confusion about their own intentions onto the consultant. By so doing there is the hope that if they stay active and put the consultant on the defensive he will not be able to pass judgment on them—a fear which their interpersonal strategies are designed to avert. In this mood participants react angrily when other group members make statements about what they appear to be like as people. They claim that they have not disclosed and cannot disclose themselves because there is so much to them as people that whatever they might reveal would only be superficial and hence a misleading glimpse of what they are really like. They claim they wish they could become more intimate with one another. They appear unable to do so because they are preoccupied with their own needs, particularly that of remaining a mystery to others. During the narcissistic mood the group members find it very difficult to work constructively because they are concerned, not so much with what they have gained from the sensitivity training experience, but, in fact, with what they have lost of themselves. They resist confronting their own and others' feelings by various more or less sophisticated adages about people not being able to depend on feelings if they are to look at the world realistically. Explaining their behavior on the basis of feelings they are experiencing in the group is regarded as an arbitrary and unsound practice.

Guilt

This is the mood in which fear of calamity and need for punishment are expressed. The participants regard the consultant's comments as evaluations (or proscriptions) rather than observations (or descriptions) of what he sees going on in the group. In this mood I frequently sense that the participants have come to the group to be approved of, especially by the consultant, and do not care a hang about learning about themselves or about group functioning. This mood often occurs after there has been a heated leadership struggle. Being too competitive in process groups is regarded adversely by most participants. They consequently attempt to reject in others what they find unacceptable in themselves—asserting leadership. After attacking the consultant for not giving the participants what they expected to derive from him, members of the group will suggest ignoring him or retaliating against him. Other participants react strongly against this suggestion for fear of receiving punitive action from the consultant.

Hostility This is the anger and frustration that seems such an integral part of the development of a process group that I would scarcely recognize a process group without it. The anger is generally subdued but lurks ever presently below the surface to intermittently break out in episodes or staccato abruptness; then to recede under the embarrassed and upset demeanor of the participants. These feelings remained generally curbed because there seems to be the notion that if strong feelings (not exclusively angry emotion, however) were expressed in words the participants would have no choice but to act upon them. The participants find it safer to discuss intellectually the nature of emotions rather than express concern and involvement with the other participants. In spite of the manifest fear of expressing anger in a group, I frequently get the feeling that the reluctance to express anger is a cover. Most people in our day and age do not find the expression of anger a particularly difficult chore. The expression of anger is after all not an altogether unpleasant experience; it often carries a feeling of potency and mastery with it that many people find difficult to obtain in other ways. At a deeper level many of us feel barren, lacking in the necessary tender and loving resources to meet others' needs. If we placed ourselves in a place of being intimate we fear that we would prove ourselves to be inadequate and would be rejected for our worthlessness. For those of us with such a concern the expression of anger is easier to induce than is tenderness. Conveniently, in terms of their defenses, preoccupation with anger prevents the group from attaining the intimacy it claims to desire.

According to Bion, whenever two participants pair off in disregard of the presence of others in the group a sexual coupling is being represented, the aim of which is to conceive a genius (a messiah or leader) to mobilize the group and lead it away from dissolution. Symptomatic of pairing is the apt attention and concentration of the other participants witnessing the dyadic interaction of the pair. Bion's explanation is too restricted by his psychoanalytic bias. It is my impression that the pairing phenomenon reveals dynamic properties in the group's attempt to cope with and reduce tensions by permitting the pair to explore means for obtaining interpersonal gratification. Having found successful strategies and modeled them for other members permits the others to emulate a gratifying interpersonal relationship. The purpose of pairing consequently is not to produce a solitary group leader, although certainly this sometimes occurs. Participants tend to reject encounter with the other participants *as a group* when their needs are frustrated by the group, e.g., their striving needs for inclusion as an esteemed member of the group, their need to obtain affection from the group for being a person whom the other participants are comfortable and pleased with, and their reactive needs for centrality and solidarity of their psychological integrity. When the group as an entity fails to satisfy a group member as an individual, he seeks a particular individual in the group with whom he can develop a more satisfying relationship. In short, what the participant feels he

Pairing

257

cannot get from the consultant or the group as an entity, he hopes to secure from a relationship with another who is exclusively his.

**Fear
of
Injury
and
Exploitation**

Fear of exploitation perhaps dominates a process group to a greater extent than any other mood. Whereas it is generally more characteristic of the initial sessions of a group it is nevertheless a mood and caution that the participants never appear willing to cast aside. We recognize the participants' reluctance to reconsider their preconceived notions about themselves and others as an unwillingness to look at the perturbing and vulnerable aspects of themselves. In this sense this mood is closely identified with that of narcissism. Change is regarded as dangerous. Becoming "sensitive" is regarded by the participants as permitting their defenses to drop and risking getting hurt. The participant feels threatened by sensitivity training experience because he interprets it as dropping everyday roles and the protection these roles have bestowed. The participants develop checks and balances to protect themselves from being exploited. In terms of the focal conflict model they give up attempts to achieve wishes and concentrate on trying to reduce the tension generated by reactive fears. The participants may discuss jungles or other perilous places as a reaction to being exposed to unknown dangers. They discuss the limitations of psychology, psychiatry, and education, reflecting their fear that sensitivity training is an unpredictable and potentially dangerous experience. Participants become angry at the member (or the consultant) who does not realize the tremendous destructive forces that lurk beneath the surface. The group is wary of every conceivable indication of disturbance in its participants. If a participant does not appear for a session, the group discusses with considerable apprehension whether his absence is due to pathology in the group or to the absent member's extragroup involvements. The participants scrutinize late or previously absent members in an attempt to isolate the "dangerous germ" in the group and to develop an effective immunity against the germ. The group members in this mood return to their fundamental doctrines: they treat what was said or done in previous sessions as a form of Bible (no matter how controversial the original statements may have been to the very group members who now hold these statements in sanctimonious regard) and defend it against exploitation by dangerous and heathen ideas. In this mood participants who emphasize individual differences in others are regarded as dangerous because the group members feel unable as individuals to protect themselves from attack. There is a tendency in this state for the participants to point out their commonality—not in terms of personal characteristics but as members of a group who have shared experiences together. Implicitly this is taken as their bond not to tear each other apart. Moreover, to temper assertiveness by participants with strong leadership proclivities the participants try to convince one another that nothing gets done with people of similar status or equal competitive strivings.

While this theme is most characteristic of the terminal states of the group, it may be reflected in the earliest moments of the initial session of a group. There is a certain sadness in the group about participants getting close to one another, for if there is no birth then there can be no death. Consistently throughout the course of the group experience the participants feel that unless someone can point out some achievement the group will realize or has already obtained—either individually or as a group—the group will perish and be forgotten. The participants have difficulty confronting the group's termination. They seem to wish to perpetuate each session, to say nothing of the course of training forever (yet paradoxically, many participants in my community groups did not re-register for an additional series of sessions once the series was *formally* over).

The participants in the mood of termination discuss various kinds of locomotion: vacations, trips they have taken, pending plans, and past experiences of travel. They seem to be trying to anticipate where they are headed. The process groups I have observed generally have been unable to stay for any protracted period with their separation anxiety. Moreover, seldom has any participant explicitly referred to his feelings of separation in the last session. The issue was usually alluded to by intervention. Even then the participants seemed to prefer to stir up ghosts of former groups, discussing their terminating experiences in these groups instead of dealing with the demise of their current membership in such a way as to lay bare to the other participants what the group has meant to them.

Work

This is the mood in which the group appears to appropriately apply itself to the task at hand. From Bion's writing may be derived some intellectual appreciation of a work-group prototype. I have endeavored accordingly to specify for myself the precise expression the word mood takes. I find this a most elusive task. Sometimes participants in particular groups seem to be realistically working at the task at hand: they appear appreciative of the irrational and preconceived notions they have been or are currently operating under; they are able to relate to one another with what appears to be more sincerity and candor than they have had at other times. Nevertheless I am still at a loss to delineate precisely what expression the work theme takes *at the moment it occurs*. Perhaps the very manner in which I couch the question for myself is an inaccurate and misleading one. Like pleasure or satisfaction, effective psychosocial functioning may not be one discrete moment, period, or specific act encapsulating appropriate emotional expression or constituting the sophisticated cognitive activities referred to by Bion. Effective psychosocial functioning may be a general feeling and affirmation of aspects of one's self that fears and challenges have been met head on, hopes and aspirations articulated and pursued. There may be an accentuated awareness of feelings about one's self and others in the participant fully engaged in mature work activity. This permits an immediate and open contact with the otherwise fragmented processes of ego that typically shield and decompartmentalize human experiences into neat and depersonalized objects. As a prototype, it seems that a group is doing its work when each of the participants has a clear and explicit conception of how each of the other participants in the group feels about each other; most specifically, how he regards each participant and how he actually reacts to him. To achieve this goal a clear understanding of how a group uses the members to serve its purposes is prerequisite. I am speaking here among other things of the shared participation and collusion of participants in replacing lost objects from their past experiences by unwittingly relating to the recovered object (strangers) with the same intention, affection, and perception given the earlier object. A study of this process should lead to insight into the dysfunctional requirements the participants are demanding of themselves and their recovered objects in order to maintain inappropriate object relationships. With insight the participants will be better able to lessen their need for distorting perception, denying communication and feedback from others, and repressing intrapsychic signals that are contradictory with conscious perceptions and purposes. With improved communication and clearer understanding of one's own intentions, the provisions for more meaningful encounter and mutually gratifying negotiation can be established.

A process group is a created situation in which each participant is "encouraged to bring his own beliefs and attitudes into open debate, and in which those beliefs and attitudes might be objectified, integrated, and tested by the standards and methods that a *group* can develop with more authenticity than a single mind can be trusted to" (Powell, 1949).

Allen (1942), according to Lippitt et al. (1958), has described interpersonal health as a process of "uninterrupted personal change in accordance with changing biological and cultural imperatives, with a progressive relinquishment of old interpersonal satisfactions in favor of new ones. When [participants however cannot relinquish] old satisfactions growth is interrupted and neurosis results."

Having come to a greater understanding of himself and others with the help of the group, e.g., through feedback, confrontation, support, and insight, the participant is then able to explore how he may affect the group to meet those needs he seeks for himself. In short, a sensitivity group is a reexperience and confrontation with one's own habitual stultifying modes of functioning. It also simultaneously constitutes an experiment in new and improved ways of functioning.

Alienation and Estrangement

Participants in process groups have considerable difficulty expressing their loneliness and dejection. A good deal of trust in the other participants needs to precede the explicit and candid disclosure of feelings of alienation. In the initial session feelings of loneliness and dejection are sensed in the participants' painful pleading for satisfaction of their wish to be led and told how to behave in a group. The participants seem lost and bewildered by being in a situation in which they are not told what to discuss, how to behave, or what the results of the experience will be for them. The agenda-less format of the process group is experienced as intolerable because the value of the group, in the imago* of its members, resides in the group's ability to structure time and divert attention from themselves and their inner turmoil. By ridiculing the consultant they hope to shame him into responding to their needs. They are confused as to why the consultant has such a strong effect on him. They try to discuss whether or not he is human. In the highly charged struggle for leadership, group members express difficulty getting close to one another as everyone is competing and cutting each other down. As the heat of the battle cools participants who are willing to express feelings of loneliness and dejection and relate them to their reasons for coming to the

* The imago is a set of notions or implicit assumptions about what a situation is or should be like. In terms of groups the imago is a mental picture at some level of consciousness about what groups are all about and how participants should behave in groups.

263

group emerge as group polarities. Commonly, we find such a person to be a depressed, forlorn individual who heretofore has been unable to achieve much recognition as a valued member of the group. In essence, the question the alienation mood poses for the group is: Can a group of strangers come together under unfamiliar conditions without resorting to discussion of outside activities, pursuits and achievements, or making cocktail party identifications and approaches to have their needs met?

Need for Certainty

This is the mood in which the need for confirmation and security, discussed in the last chapter, is activated. Sullivan posits that there are two basic kinds of human needs (a) the need for satisfaction, the attainment of bodily gratifications, whose aim is a state of quiescence; and (b) security, the attainment of reliable techniques for thwarting threat to the organism's physical and psychological integrity. The need for certainty falls in the latter category.

Man is an organism in a precarious world. As such he bends his efforts to protect himself from injury. It is perhaps this need then that thwarts the most arduous attempts of the participants to reconsider their beliefs and habitual modes of functioning. Participants prefer discussing past events. There is considerable certainty about past events. No matter how unpleasant or unfortunate the original experience was the most terrifying aspect of the original situation is no longer present—apprehension (anxiety) about the outcome of the event. Anxiety is perhaps the most intolerable of human experiences. We will undergo any chafe or ordeal to forestall it—even pain. Thus the need of certainty filters all our experience and we prefer to discuss the already disarmed pains of the past, the there-and-then, then try to deal with the uncertain and discomforting feelings generated by our immediate experiences, the here-and-now. Participants in a process group struggling to maximize certainty act as if they believed that the success of "treatment" (sensitivity training) is due to its guarantee. They spend considerable time and effort trying to cajole or coerce the consultant into proving his skills. They concomitantly disregard his statements that he cannot demonstrate such proof as the success of the group experience is the responsibility of the participants. If interpersonal strategies do not get the participants what they want they employ personal strategies to maximize certainty about what is going to happen to them. Through selection, denial, and distortion their perceptions are modified so to conform with existing attitudes. To avoid the uncertainty and discomfort of testing new behaviors the participants fall back on familiar ways of functioning and familiar points of view. They fall into the rut of saying: To be in the present is not to know. Once the group finds a Bible it follows it through the wilderness. In their singleminded pursuit of an absolute standard of conduct they neglect to realize that the group situation has changed since the normative rules were laid down.

Flight

This is the theme in which confrontation of immediate experience is avoided. In this mood underlying group tensions are circumvented as if they were active third rails. To the foreground come peripheral and trivial issues which are seized upon with ardor and urgency as if these were the real issues that the group convened to adjoin. Flight, it appears to us, is not one of the more basic motifs in process groups. Flight may be, rather than a basic theme, a mechanism or medium for avoiding the potentially dangerous and unpleasant experiences aroused by the need for certainty, dependency feelings, narcissism, and so forth.

There are many ways in which participants express flight motifs. They may vent anger about unacceptable behavior in persons outside the group so that they need not confront unacceptable behavior within the group. They may "short-circuit" threatening here-and-now confrontations by referring back to what a participant previously had said; by the time it takes the group to get back to each previous discussion the issue is no longer pertinent to what is currently going on in the group and is a "dead circuit." The participants may catalog all the appropriate skills necessary for meaningful confrontation of their experience in the group, but with the tacit agreement that it is better to use the group's time to invoice interpersonal skills rather than actually employing them. The group may encourage certain participants to "entertain the group" so that the other participants do not have to face the task at hand. Participants may talk about trips and vacations, anything to avoid what is being currently experienced.

Autonomy and Achievement

Individuals enter the group generally with some nefariously conceptualized wish to escape their problems by fashioning themselves as autonomous people. This aspiration is so ill-defined and fettered by unconscious fears, reinforced by an achievement-oriented culture, that the participants feel sorely frustrated unless they can point to tangible results of their group experience. When the group is in this mood dialogue along the following lines may be heard in the group.

> MR. A.: "Jo-Jo is talking much more than he did in the earlier group sessions."
>
> MRS. B.: "Yes, but was he merely playing a silent observer role or was he actually reticent?"
>
> MISS C.: "Maybe Jo-Jo just feels like talking more today."
>
> MRS. B.: "How about it, Jo-Jo, do you feel that *the group has changed you?*"

Competition

The process group is seen as representing the participants' original primary group, reflecting with vivid impact unresolved feelings and implicit and untested assumptions about the similarity of the membership of the process group and those of the original primary group. The consultant is the object in the competitive mood most likely to be perceived as a father figure, with the other group members representing other familiar figures. Intense sibling and generation rivalry is observed in the group. The group may view its task as a contest between it and the consultant and feel that if they can put the consultant down they emerge victoriously. Themes of parricide are espoused at such time. Participants are trying to prove something instead of fashioning a remedy. The more hopeless the prospect of cooperative endeavor the more relief they seem to experience. Because each of the participants has leadership aspirations each prefers to attack the leadership of the consultant rather than attack other group members and expose themselves in return to attack. In this mood participants who wish to assert leadership but are afraid of being castrated by the group for doing so push others out to test the group climate to see if it is safe enough to expose their own ambitions.

Transference

Transference is a phenomenon which occurs in all interpersonal situations. It stems from man's cognitive capacity to generalize about the dangers, to say nothing of the sources of pleasure, from an earlier situation to subsequent situations in which similar components are present. As we have suggested earlier it is the common emotional impact from one situation to the next which brings about transference. Inappropriate transference, that is, generalizing on the basis of irrelevant or misleading resemblances, leads to dysfunctional interpersonal accommodation in that motives are unlikely to be satisfied. The *projection principle,* claims that people tend to attribute more of their own thoughts, feelings, and actions to other objects in unstructured situations than they do in more structured situations. I would therefore expect considerably more transference in process groups than in more defined groups. The members of a process group frequently wonder why they, as relative strangers, have axes to grind with one another, not realizing that strangers represent embodiments of fears and sentiments from another time and place.

Selection of Participants | 14

Individuals who gravitate toward sensitivity training may be those who perceive their problems differently, as suggested earlier, than people who become patients in individual and group therapy. The severity of a person's protuberance cannot be judiciously discerned by his choice of ameliorative experience. Patients in psychotherapy are not necessarily more disturbed or less self-reliant than participants in training groups. Training groups have their share of acting-out characters, hostile, and paranoids, and more than their share of depressives. I have seldom seen participants in training groups with clear-cut thinking disorders. But few groups I have worked with were conspicuous by the absence of one of two rather perturbed persons.

Disturbed Participants The healthier part of a person's ego drives him toward seeking help. He may seize upon group training as a compromise for an ego not sufficiently able to grapple with the full gravity of his disabilities, which attendance in psychotherapy signifies for him. At the same time he may view training as an opportunity to demonstrate his frustrations to others, whom he hopes will be sympathetic to him. Consultants in training groups should realize that many people coming to groups are asking help for rather serious problems, which may be better handled by endeavors which emphasize individual psychodynamics rather than group process. The efficacy of group training has not been ascertained. It has not yet been clearly defined who will profit from sensitivity experience and who will not. It has been argued that if there is no empirical support for group training in handling serious emotional perturbances, the consultant's responsibility to his professional obligations may be called into question if he permits disturbed participants in his groups rather than referring them to traditional treatment that has demonstrated beneficial effects. (Of course many argue that traditional psychotherapy itself has yet to empirically demonstrate its efficacy.)

Screening Participants Many critics of group sensitivity training maintain that there is a need to screen out participants who may be seriously and adversely affected by sensitivity experience. But many advocates of group training reply that interviewing and screening out candidates for group training are often impractical. The problem critics respond in turn, is that many group training

270

leaders seem to believe that prior information about participants in their groups is not necessary, even if it were available. These trainers with undaunted confidence seem to feel that they can work with anyone who finds his way into the group. The critics of group training are alarmed at this attitude, which they consider a naïve, grandiose disregard of the problem. "What," they ask, "is going to happen between sessions or after the often brief but explosive period of sensitivity training to participants who come to the group originally disturbed?" Furthermore, they point out, since group training is generally terminated at the end of some specified period of time rather than when a participant is "ready" to leave the group (as in psychotherapy), participants may leave the group more anxious and upset about their functioning than before the experience began. Therefore, the critics insist, it is important to know if a participant is capable of handling the tremendous anxiety that sensitivity training groups can arouse.

It is my view that while these criticisms are often valid and a necessary precaution, they may frequently be overstatements. I have come to realize after experience in hundreds of sensitivity training sessions that training groups have a number of built-in protections against exacerbation of a distressed person's pathology, and group training may be no more jolting to him than to the healthier egos in the group. Participants in training groups are usually concerned about others in the group becoming upset and will support a group member from excessively becoming so. I am certainly not going to contradict the evidence of group pathology described earlier; nevertheless I am equally impressed by the understanding and support group members show one another. Even were this not

271

true, a consultant qualified to take a group should, by being "qualified," be able to handle stressful process and support agitated participants if the group members fail to do so.

The Influence of the Disturbed Participant

A sensitivity group is not made more disturbed by the presence of a seriously distressed person in the group. On the contrary, the other participants may become so supportive and docile ("so that no one will get hurt") that they cannot effectively work at their task. Mindful of this, a serious objection I have to permitting a distressed person in a training group is that because he has such a ravenous need for attention, protection, and consideration, he prevents the other participants from devoting their energies to important phenomena going on in the group (or could potentially be transpiring in his absence). There is, however, nothing absolute in what I have said in view of the paucity of sound research. Distressed participants, particularly vociferous, overly defended persons, may benefit from the group in sufficient degree to justify their presence. This is because these overly defended participants who "come on" too strongly can be "attacked" or confronted constructively. In such situations the group and the consultant have less apprehension that confrontation feedback will demolish their defenses, as with the easily upset participant. Participants who are forcefully confronted and who are able to withstand the attack generally develop more effective defenses because they have had the opportunity to discover which defenses work and which need to be additionally fortified. The easily upset participant who flees or feels demolished is unable to discern which of his defenses worked and which did not.

272

One danger is always imminent, however, with a distressed participant in the group. He may not be able to continue the group experience. Such tremendous feelings of guilt may be generated by the other participants that the group can no longer deal with any issue but the departure of a participant or superficial attempts to disguise their concerns. It is better for the group, if there are no serious counterindications for the distressed participant, that he stick it out to the end.

If participants for sensitivity training experience (process group) were evaluated, there are several individual characteristics which my own experience (and the reports of other group trainers) suggest may be useful indicators as to how the participant may function in a training group. Whereas the composite of these factors should not be construed as absolute assessment indicators, they are relevant to the participant's ability to make use of the group training experience.

Persons who take responsibility for their own thoughts, feelings, and actions. The things that happen to us do not occur capriciously. They take place because they serve some desired function for us, although in the long run they may be self-defeating. Participants who seem to profit most from group training are those who accept the responsibility for their own actions and seek to find out why they often act in self-defeating ways. They do not come to the group to persuade others to accept their attitudes and beliefs about themselves but for a candid exchange with others. This requirement discourages, perhaps eliminates,

Criteria for Participants

273

the character disorder personality, both of culturally deviant and psychopathic types.

Persons who experience anxiety. People who are comfortable with their present modes of functioning have no compunction to modify their behavior. Actually, in their own minds they have reason to maintain their present behaviors. Only people who are uncomfortable with their present functioning seek other modes of functioning. This requirement would eliminate the dominant character, the chronic monopolist, who tries to dominate the group in attempting to avert anxiety and resist inducement for change. However, like Mullan and Rosenbaum (1963) I have found that a *provocateur* can stimulate interaction in a group of stolid participants, provided he is not so overbearing that he becomes more of a nuisance than a group catalyst.

Persons who are verbal. Process groups are enacted through the use of verbal communication. This restriction eliminates not only seriously withdrawn and recalcitrant persons but also those individuals undersocialized in verbal skills. Unless a person verbalizes there is generally little opportunity to assess what is going on in him. It is possible and indeed likely that nonverbal participants can profit from group training (particularly where nonverbal techniques such as psychodrama are employed). These persons generally, however, require more individual attention than sensitivity training provides.

Concern about other participant's approbation. Unless a participant is concerned about his *persona*, the way he presents himself to others in the group, there is no need to place himself under their influence and open himself up to others. To those individuals who have given up hope of gaining others' approval and wish merely to avoid their disapprobation, the group situation is a place in which they have nothing to gain and everything to lose. This restriction would eliminate seriously guilt-ridden individuals who should be in psychotherapeutic treatment.

The person must be able to tolerate tensions engendered by the hostile expression on the part of the self and others toward him. The participant must be able to evoke anger without fear of loss of control when he experiences the situation warranting it. This would eliminate the seriously self-denigrated and impulse-ridden personalities (Bach, 1954).

The person must be in sufficient contact with the environment. If the participant is unable to relate with a fair degree of fidelity to what is taking place in his external environment, possession of the other attributes we have described above are not very useful. Flight mechanisms are defensive strategies to avert threats with which the individual fears he cannot contend. A person's need for flight is predictable. If, for example, he has given up hope for securing approval from others and is only concerned about avoiding disapproval he is more likely to employ flight techniques than if he were actively seeking approval.

Selecting Sensitivity Training Groups

It is no less important for the prospective participant to know what to avoid in selecting an experiential group than it is for the consultant to know what kind of persons to turn away from his group. Dr. Everett Shostrom, a group therapy pioneer with considerable experience as a sensitivity training consultant, has postulated a number of sensible precautions for prospective sensitivity training participants (1969). The following are factors which he regards as "fairly strict no's":

275

Do not respond to the announcement of available sensitivity training without giving the venture careful consideration. Be particularly wary of experiential groups widely advertised on the mass media. Not infrequently, enterprising peddlers of group experience lure naïve persons with false and mythical promises of cure, intimacy, and joy. Groups run by responsible professionals abide by the ethical regulations of their profession and refrain from making public announcements. They rely on referrals from other professionals and the good reports of previous participants.

Be wary of groups that make promises (be they intimacy, cure, or simply friendship). No trainer is able or should attempt to intimate that he can guarantee "interpersonal goodies." Consider, the following advertisement from a west coast center which claims to be dedicated to research in the unlimited multiple approach to life enhancement (UMALE). This includes physical, the emotional, spiritual, philosophical, religious, nutritional, and other approaches. They promise precision psychodrama demonstrations in which one can "see and feel how emotional problems are solved in this new fascinating, exciting harmony using the 'Harmony Role' of psychodrama. How to create joy for yourself at all times through a special combination of psychodramatic and sensory awareness techniques, participate or observe as you choose. You will enjoy and benefit either way. Watch the role players unfold a problem scene by scene to a solution. No problem is too deep for precision psychodrama. It might be anything from how to meet and hold the opposite sex, to a life-long phobia . . ." (UMALE, 1968).

Trainers may suggest that they can create such an atmosphere by keeping the participants to a limited number. Shostrom recommends that a prospective participant never participate in a group which has less than six members. "The necessary and valuable candor generated by an effective group cannot be dissipated, shared, and examined to too small a group, and scape-goating or purely vicious ganging-up can develop. Conversely, a group with more than sixteen members generally cannot effectively be monitored by anyone, however well trained or well assisted" (Shostrom, 1969).

Before joining a group give considerable thought to why you want to participate in a group. Having clarified for yourself what you want you can more properly decide which kind of group experience is best for your deeper rather than your more transitory needs. "Any important crisis in your life has been a long time in preparation and deserves reflection. If you are sanely suspicious of your grasp on reality, be doubly cautious. The intense, sometimes apocalyptic experience of the experiential group can be most upsetting, particularly for persons who feel that they are close to what one layman calls 'controlled schizophrenia.' A trained person responsible for a meaningful session would not throw precariously balanced persons into a good encounter group. Nor would he allow persons who are diabolically experienced in the ways of group dynamics to form a group. If you find yourself in a group in which everyone talks jargon, simply walk out" (Shostrom, 1969).

Never join a group with intimates, people you have close working or social relationships with, to say nothing of relatives, unless the group is specifically for participants with such relationships. A colleague of ours, a man with eminence both as a scientist and a clinician, reported with disgust and puzzlement the consequences of a training group experience of a friend of his. The friend attended a week-long conference at one of the famous summer sensitivity training centers. The friend apparently had a psychotic episode during the conference. A report of this was received by his employer and he was without any inquiry fired. It is not sufficient that you be told everything that is discussed or happens in the group will be considered confidential. Precautions on your part may be necessary. If you feel you cannot comfortably discuss your feelings in a group because of certain *external factors*, then you need to find a group where these external factors are absent. Resistance to disclosure due to characterological defenses is quite another matter and reason to seek therapeutic consultation.

Do not be sold by the trappings of the sensitivity training venture. Neither the surroundings in which the training groups convene nor the backgrounds of the participants guarantee a good group experience. Shostrom points out that group sessions can and have been held in ghetto classrooms and storefront buildings. A good session may include persons and exposure to ways of life which you do not closely associate with in your existence outside of the group. On the other hand if you are interested in a comfortable, luxurious country club setting with interesting clientele, a sensitivity group may not be the place for you.

Be wary of groups with ideological axes to grind. Steer clear of groups with a doctrine to sell. Avoid groups which coerce reluctant group members to acquiesce instead of being concerned with creating an honest dialogue, with the resultant give-and-take among the participants.

Check on the training and credentials of your trainer or consultant. If he is a member in good standing in his professional organization, his organization may be consulted for his affiliations and formal training. In checking the credentials of a group leader one should be mindful of what are the specific requirements for membership in his organization. For example, to be a full member of the American Psychological Association, one need have at the minimum a Ph.D. or its equivalent in psychology from a recognized college or university; to be a member of Division 12, the clinical psychology division, a psychologist must have additionally one year of internship in a clinical setting with an A.P.A.-approved curriculum and adequate supervision. On the other hand to obtain membership in the Esalen Association, Shostrom indicates, all you need to do is pay annual dues, which indicates neither control nor approval of any sort from the Esalen Institute.

Potentials | 15

Is the whole movement just a fad, designed to
fade from memory like the Hadacol, the Twist,
wheat germ, the Holy Rollers and the Maharishi?
(Howard, 1968).

Sensitivity training in groups is a complex and
elusive interpersonal endeavor that has evoked excitement and anger, to say nothing of appreciation
and compassion, from its participants, critics, and
defenders. As a result it is difficult to evaluate with
any degree of objectivity, let alone the empirical
evidence it deserves (Greening, 1964). Even if group
training were a less emotionally involving issue,
experimental evidence of its efficacy would prove
rather difficult to produce. "Scales for measuring
change in psychological states are difficult, at best, to
come by. Part of the problem in such scales lies in their
lack of sensitivity to change [which is of course
precisely what we wish to assess in sensitivity training 281

research]. This inadequacy can be due to confounding properties such as response sets, halo effects, and social desirability, notwithstanding issues of reliability and applicability" (Hartley, 1968). Hartley correctly indicates that in developing a measure to reflect change in psychological states due to group training experience, the following criteria must be met: 1. The measure should reflect significant differences in a hypothesized direction over a period of time; 2. The "change" should be some measure of distance between the participants' psychological states on two or more occasions; and 3. The measure should be relatively short and easily scored (Hartley, 1968).

Assumed Goals

The problem for the researcher of group training as Sata and Derbyshire (1967) have indicated is that group training has a number of assumed goals, and these goals are seldom made explicit at the beginning of the training experience. Frequently the consultant or trainer may modify the group's goals during the course of the life of the group. There would be no point trying to list these goals as the list would run into the hundreds. Thus with little regard to what specifically happened in his group and what he initially intended to effect in his training group a consultant can claim that the training experience was successful if any of the hundredfold list of training goals were achieved.

Four major reviews of group training literature have appeared to date (Stock, 1964; Buchanan, 1965; House, 1967; and Campbell and Dunnett, 1968). Each of these reviews has been devoted almost entirely to the investigation of T-group training. The reviewers can hardly be faulted for this shortcoming. Except for a few recent studies of marathon groups, none of the other group training approaches have felt it necessary to empirically investigate their work. Consequently, what I know of group training, other than my own experiences, word of mouth, or literary exposition in popular journals, is chiefly of the T-group approach.

It is not my purpose to review the entire group training literature. I am primarily interested in the personal and social conditions that stimulated the demand for group training and the effect group training has had upon correcting these conditions. How effective has sensitivity training been in getting the individual to feel less alienated from himself and others? How successful has group training been in enabling the individual to affect social conditions, so that they are more in tune with his better interests? Sensitivity training literature, although not directly dealing with these questions, has replied to an inquiry of group training's efficacy by citing changes produced in the participants' psychological state. Both critics and defenders of group sensitivity training frequently contrast the effects of the training experience with its influence on psychodynamic factors. These factors may be grouped generally under modifications in the individual's inner- or other-directedness. Some investigators see sensitivity training as providing greater appreciation of the psychosocial cues for appropriate interpersonal behavior. This view regards group training therefore as conditioning in other-directedness. These investigators claim that one of the most important goals of training groups is the acquisition of new cognitive skills and information. This provision will enable the participant to modify his overt

Group Training Literature

behavioral responses in the training group and ultimately in other social interactional situations. Sensitivity training, according to this point of view, develops perceptual clarity both in terms of how the participant perceives himself, in his self-concept, and in terms of the congruence of perception of him by various members of the group (Bass, 1962; Bennis, et al., 1957; Burke and Bennis, 1961; Clark and Culbert, 1965; Gassner, et al., 1964; Grater, 1959; Stock, 1964). In summarizing the studies in this area Campbell and Dunnette (1968) report, "It seems relatively well established that the way an individual sees himself may indeed change during the course of a T-group. However, there is no firm evidence indicating that such changes are produced by T-group training as compared with other types of training, merely by the passage of time, or even by the expedient of retaking a self-descriptive inventory." Correspondingly, a number of studies have tried to assess how effectively a group training participant can predict the beliefs and sentiments of other participants after a group training experience (Bennis et al., 1957; Gage and Exline, 1953; Lohman, et al., 1959; Harrison, 1962; Oshry and Harrison, 1966; Bass, 1962). Campbell and Dunnette (1968) report that those studies which incorporate "a measure of how well an individual can predict the attitude and values of others before and after T-group training have yielded largely negative results." Even in those studies that seem to verify that group training participants are more apt, but not necessarily more accurately able to describe others in interpersonal rather than impersonal terms, "there is the more important question of whether this finding actually represents increased sensitization to interpersonal events or merely the acquisition of a new vocabulary" (Campbell and Dunnette, 1968).

284

Various other investigators have claimed that the essence of experience in groups is tied in with changes in the individual's intrapsychic structure. Group training "opens up communication channels within the person so that he may become more aware of the basic values and standards he has incorporated and allows him to behave in a congruent fashion with his unique need-value structure" (Kassajian, 1969). Hence group training is in their view a reeducation in inner-directedness. (Masserik and Carlson, 1962; Kassejian, 1965; Smith, 1964; Schutz and Allen, 1966; Baumgartel and Goldstein, 1967; Kernan, 1964). Results have been encouraging in those studies in which the test items appear "to be geared to the stated goals and the content of the training program [so that] the 'correct' answer was apparent to the respondent; changes in basic personality variables seem unconfirmed by group training experiences" (Campbell and Dunnette, 1968).

Finally, still another direction for investigating changes in the participants psychological state is found in the literature. Some investigators have disregarded elements of inner- and other-directedness and have concerned themselves with the participants' ability as a result of group training to disclose aspects of the self which were initially held private. There is some evidence that participants are able to make greater disclosures of themselves following group experiences, but that this proclivity soon diminishes after the participants return to their native environment. A number of investigators who have found that changes in the participant's tendency toward self-disclosure don't hold up over time have employed Lewin's notion of a power field to explain their findings. The *power field* concept implies that personality change is initially an unstable process. New behavior will not be maintained unless it is sufficiently regulated with the individual's existing psychodynamic structure. An important influence in inculcating new behavior is the support the social environment gives the enactment of the behavior. Consequently, in a social field in which openness and honesty about feelings are threatening to the other social agents there will be pressures directed toward the person with the recent group training experience to desist from being overly honest about his feelings. He may be treated as if his T-group experience were a vacation in a foreign country where the customs and ways of life are different (and unacceptable) to the way things are done at home.

Inter-Personal Knowledge

This suggests to us that the real value of group sensitivity training may not lie in its ability to foster new interpersonal styles of behavior (e.g., make therapeutic changes). Certainly not if these styles are neutralized by powerful, adverse environmental conditions. Unless people with sensitivity training experience find environmental conditions supportive of their new "personality," their new style will not carry over into everyday life. The value of group training instead may reside in interpersonal knowledge, both on affective and cognitive levels, which the participants acquire to effect mature working conditions in the groups of which they are members. The objective of these groups can be to create a situation in which each group member is encouraged to bring his own beliefs, attitudes, and sentiments into open debate. In this process ideas and feelings can be objectified, tested, and modified by the standards and methods of inquiry that a group can develop with more authenticity and effectiveness than a single mind can be expected to do (Powell, 1949). It is not reasonable to expect a number of "sensitized" persons to make their way in an alienating society if, at the same time, society is not "sensitized" to appreciate and nurture their contributions to a better life for all.

Lewis M. Killian (1964), in his recent summary on the status of social movements (we have already identified sensitivity training as an important social movement), contends that social movements have received relatively little emphasis by social scientists. This is because men in groups have been too frequently regarded by social scientists "as the creatures rather than the creators of social change" (Killian, 1964). Where this attitude prevails science scrutinizes cultural forces in a search for the impetus for change rather than the actions and reactions of men. The traditional approach to the study of social movements has taken the form of histories of social thought, ideas, and theories. These theories are treated very much as other systems of philosophy: by critical analysis; the application of logic; "armchair" conceived theories of social dynamics; and, eventually, rules of ethics. The implications of a one-sided cultural force pressing down on a mass of stolid men should be painfully obvious as a self-fulfilling prophecy and needs no further discussion here. The belief that the individual has impact on and is accountable for his presence as a social being lies at the core of the sensitivity training movement. The foregoing exposition of group training experience has attempted to locate and delineate what it is about participants' functioning in interpersonal encounters that furthers their personal

The Promise of Sensitivity Training

287

and social ends. Correspondingly, we have explored what it is that happens in groups which is dysfunctional both for the individual and the social system in which he resides. Heretofore, in our society it has been the disjointed, alienated, private citizen who has had to seek remedial treatment for his distress.

> Society has not yet been driven to seek treatment for its psychological disorders by psychological means because it has not achieved sufficient insight to appreciate the nature of its distress (Bion, 1961).

Groups as has already been shown prefer to express ills through the behavior of their polarities. They then attempt to rid themselves of these ills by disowning these group representatives. Investigating sensitivity training groups affords us the opportunity to study the strains and tensions engendered through group process when a collection of strangers are thrown together on their own resources in an attempt to have their needs met; it is a situation where the explicit goals of their coming together are so ill-defined that serious consideration of deep-seated motives for being involved with others is aroused. Group sensitivity provides an unrivaled opportunity for the study not only of the foundation of social groups but also the most basic psychosocial processes influencing personality development and interpersonal competence. Small groups are "the meeting ground of individual personality and society. It is in the group that personality is modified and socialized; and it is through the working of groups that society is changed and adapted to the times" (Thelen, 1954). Studying how the individual comes to terms with his own unconscious drives and sentiments in group training I hope to eventually develop a model of psychosocial behavior that clearly delineates the group process of all groups, e.g., whether they be training groups, therapy groups, task groups, social groups, whatever. Hopefully this model can suggest to the social practitioner and individual citizen alike how citizen and interest groups can more successfully implement their aims. On the societal level this model can serve existing institutions in more effectively modifying their services to meet current societal demands. Greater understanding of the dynamics of groups will have proactive value in indicating how citizen and interest groups can implement their aims and resist the alienating forces that are reflected in the attitude many of us hold today—that the individual has little or no impact on the societal or intrapsychic pressures shaping his existence. Group training is seen as an ingenious way for "educating" citizens to the effect norms, values, and processes of the groups in which they find themselves influence their behavior, and how in turn they can harness these forces in their own behalf. To resist the imposition of negative definitions of himself the man in the street has generally espoused grand plans of what he would do if he "were running the show rather than those 'big shots' in Washington." Greater interpersonal competence in affecting action groups may enable him to create a more constructive and gratifying definition of himself.

The study of sensitivity training groups affords the social scientist the opportunity of being able to study events he is interested in comparing with one another within a convenient range of time and space. Participants in small groups carry out relationships vis-à-vis each other by rather direct and intimate interaction to an extent not found in the events the social scientist is usually witness to in society-at-large. In the larger community the types of events the scientist investigates are frequently defused by lengthy series of time and place. It is therefore possible in training groups for the social scientist to make actual observations required by his theories without encountering many of the difficulties present in examining interpersonal and social phenomena on a larger scale (Hare et al., 1955). Furthermore, the study of sensitivity training groups provides the social scientist with a unique opportunity to study groups without the profusion of contaminating factors that contribute to his theoretical prejudice. As such, it may prove to be a jolting experience for the social scientist, as many of the accepted statements about groups may not hold up in the light of new group experiences and will require reconsideration.

Appendix

The following is a protocol of an actual process group session, with explanatory footnotes. The group was formed about one and one-half years prior to this session. The present group consists of three female social workers and a male vocational rehabilitation worker. All are employed by the same agency. Two of the social workers, Marion and Greta, were members of the original group (which consisted of six members: five social workers and a nurse). Paula joined the group about a year and Tom about six or seven months prior to this session. Ann, another member of the original group, dropped out of the group about one week before this session.

TOM: The chairs are arranged like they were last time.

GRETA: (*laughs*)

TOM: That little microphone . . . it is still here. (*pause*) I just got out of *some* meeting.

291

GRETA: Is this the first time that you were in that meeting? I was just thinking that you sat through a lot of meetings. You had very little to say about the meeting.

TOM: Yeah, that is about the size of it. (*pause*) I am going to tell them to cancel all appointments with the social workers. It is very uncomfortable sitting there for an hour.

(*Paula enters the room.*)

TOM: Here's Paula! (*pause*) That chair is arranged so that you can always back away from the microphone. It is an electric chair or something (referring to the chair in which the consultant usually sits; the consultant had taken another chair for that session).[1]

(*Tom and Greta laugh together for a moment or two.*)[2]

GRETA: Is he (*referring to the consultant*) with us? What Paula (*picking up a non-verbal question from Paula*)?

PAULA (*Explains that yesterday she had completely forgotten about the last session. She said that she had called Marion, another group member, about some other matter, and Marion asked why she hadn't been in the group session. She then realized that she had forgotten about the session and so she called the consultant, who explained that the other members of the group had also forgotten about the session. "What's that all about?" she wondered.*)[3]

GRETA: I feel like guessing you why you and Marion were talking.

TOM: I was also.

PAULA: I had called about admissions procedure and for some information, and Marion asked, "How come you're not in time for the group?"

(*Marion enters the room.*)

GRETA: (*to Paula*) Do you know what happened?

PAULA: No, I don't. All I know are a lot of excuses but (*pause*) it was a little strange, my thinking I was saying that I needed some regular hours for seeing people (referring to patients and patients' family members).

GRETA: I meant, what happened yesterday?

PAULA: Oh! I assumed that you and Tom came and then decided to leave at four P.M. (*pause*)

MARION: (*cautiously*) What are we doing with the taperecorder on?[4]

TOM: We now again have a silent member in the group (*referring to the consultant*).

MARION: Come again?

TOM: I said, we have regained our silent member.[5]

MARION: Our consultant is not going to answer me, is that what you're saying?

TOM: As best I can tell.

MARION: He's got a new taperecorder or something. (*pause*) I just don't like things sprung on me, that's all!

TOM: We got a warning in that it was sprung on us yesterday.

MARION: Oh! You had the taperecorder sprung on you yesterday?'

GRETA: It was sprung on us yesterday. (*pause*) Maybe that is why we felt sort of really let down because we had to start dealing with the taperecorder. (*laughs*)

PAULA: I am thinking at this point about all kinds of things. My first feeling is that not coming (*yesterday*) has something to do with you (*to Tom*) having to decide on a specific time for the group. (*Tom had recently asked the group to change the time of the sessions because of a conflict with his own schedule.*) Now I'm feeling that the taperecorder is on the floor so now you (*to Marion*) are going to set the rules, you are going to set what's going on for the group. Why are we just sort of pussyfooting around? Whether the taperecorder is there or not. (*laughs*) What is going on?[6]

MARION: (*with some zest*) Yeah, we can turn it off! We have that option.[7]

PAULA: I don't object to the taperecorder; I just object to it just sort of being on the floor, just being there.

GRETA: I am wondering how you feel about the consultant not saying anything about the taperecorder.

MARION: You don't!

293

GRETA: I said I *am* wondering.

TOM: Oh! Yeah, that was what my major concern was—with with taperecorder being on.

GRETA: Because I didn't think that was the understanding. (*pause*) If he doesn't tell us what the understanding is, we won't know except by behavior. (*She is probably referring to the consultant's behavior.*) (*pause*) I don't know even if I dare ask him. (*giggle*)[8]

MARION: (*quietly*) I didn't get an answer, but you might.[9]

CONSULTANT: The group is so concerned with my behavior that it need not look at what is happening in the group. Because the people in the group have not really decided what they want to do as a group, they prefer to question what my roles are.

GRETA: I guess that puts us back where we were!

MARION: I have heard that sort of thing once too often, I think!

TOM: (*agrees*) (*pause*) You can't expect the group to react in a way that is normal to react when things are set up in a way so that the group could not have had a chance to talk about it before . . . I mean, like the group could have talked about the taperecorder and all those other things. I mean, you can't expect the group to react differently when we ask questions and we don't get answers. To me that is just passing the buck—to throw it back on us.[10]

CONSULTANT: There seems to have been a lot of resistance in the group, even prior to what happened yesterday, but the group doesn't seem very interested in exploring this. One member of the group brought it up but the group then just let it drop.

TOM: What do we want to do with this group?

CONSULTANT: It seems the issue the group wants to avoid, because we sense a hornet's nest lurks underneath, is what is happening in this group. (*long pause*)

MARION: I think we are frustrated. I think that is what happened to us yesterday. You know like I didn't come and you

294

(*to Tom*) weren't here Friday. I don't know if it is frustration. I know I am frustrated. I got still . . . (*pause*) not still frustrated but again got demands on me—which we talked about considerably. (*She apparently discussed this in an earlier process group session which met formally as a leaderless session.*) I'll give up, I guess, I'll give up the package (*the supervision of her own psychotherapy group and the sensitivity group*).[11]

GRETA: What are you talking about?

MARION: I'm talking about the Admissions Center. No, I'm not leaving the Service . . . not at the moment. (*pause*) I have been through this before and I'll be through it again. It doesn't justify my job, but at the moment I've justified it. At the moment I'm at the point where Doctor Klutchmire has said to me, "You have to be here more than you are!" (*pause*) That means three hours a week. I wouldn't be in Admissions. These groups (*supervision and sensitivity training*) take three hours a week.

GRETA: That doesn't make any sense!

MARION: It doesn't make any sense? (*pause*) I'll be in Admissions during the time I'm at duty at the Hospital. And that is another problem. (*pause*) But I'll be at Admissions all the time. I wouldn't do anything else. (*pause*) You know I have been doing other things, but at this point the job will call for Admissions. Starting in April, I won't be here until ten o'clock. So I'm going to work on an adjusted kind of hours—which has been approved and so this is something also I have to work with.

GRETA: (*asks about the adjusted hours*)

MARION: Yes, I have to work comparable hours, like to six, six-thirty P.M. (*pause*) which is another concession. (*She seems to mean that the Administration is doing her a favor.*)

PAULA: You are doing the same thing again that you do over and over again: "That I am powerless, that there is some power and it is outside there somewhere."[12]

MARION: (*firmly*) No!

295

PAULA: That someone is saying that you *have* to be in Admissions full time.

MARION: No, I *want* to be in Admissions full time. (*Paula tries to break in.*) No, it is too much time (*supervision and sensitivity training, apparently.*)

PAULA: Maybe that what Greta is saying doesn't make sense— to say that you have to be in Admissions full time. It doesn't make sense to say that you don't want to be in this group.

MARION: (*with an acclimated attitude*) O.K. It is too much time!

GRETA: Who said so? Doctor Klutchmire?

MARION: At this point I am! The reason I won't be coming to the hospital until ten o'clock is because of the analysis (*psychoanalysis*), which will be four times a week. That is *enough!* That hour for four days a week is enough for me . . . plus what I have to do on my job (*angrily*), which is self-analysis. That is enough! I don't want any more!

CONSULTANT: I have the feeling that what is being presented by one of the participants in this group in regard to events outside the group also expresses something of what is going on inside this group here-and-now. Evidence for this is everyone being either late or absent yesterday, trying to find a schedule for this group which doesn't interfere with our other staff job activities, and so on. I think we are saying we aren't getting sufficient satisfaction from this group. What I feel is going on is a feeling of being let down . . . by the others in the group, by me. I mean, I came in with a microphone without much warning.[13]

PAULA: I mean, yeah, good God! How dare you upset anything anymore (*laughs*) in this whole precarious mess. (*pause*) I heard today that Lola (*her and Marion's supervisor*) had been telling Training (*training staff*) that they didn't need my services after all. (*to Marion*) One of us is going to go. (*She means, leave the Service.*)[14]

MARION: I don't think that either of us is going to go. Well, you see the pressure has shifted back to Training now.

296

	Doctor Klutchmire has assured her on the Admissions. I thought, Paula, that we had solved that . . . that she was just going to play with her ten slots and forget about this Service. (*She means, mind her own business.*)
PAULA:	Well, she has been under other pressures, too. But let her handle it!
MARION:	Well, *how* do you handle that, by the way?[15]
PAULA:	Do what?
MARION:	That *she* handles the pressures.
PAULA:	I told Doctor Modd and Doctor Shankle to tell her that they were not going to let me go. Which they did. (*happy laugh*)
MARION:	Yesterday she came over to see Doctor Klutchmire after that meeting we had, you know, and that she said, "You are the one that has to go!" I was the person she was talking to at that point. She wanted to see Doctor Klutchmire to get a little feeling about what is happening because I did make her feel guilty. And now she will be over Monday to see us both.
PAULA:	(*laughs*)
CONSULTANT:	It sounds like some of the resentment this group is expressing is because lack of support from others in the group—support that would make our life outside of the group easier and more comfortable. We seem to be making a preconceived notion that the purpose of this group is to relieve the pressures from outside the group. Traveling on this untested assumption, if we don't get the support we expect from the group for our extra-group concerns, the hell with the group![16]
TOM:	I don't even understand what is going on.[17]
MARION:	Well, she (*Lola*) is playing games with us.
TOM:	She is saying that one of the two of you has to go?
MARION:	Because she has to get a social worker for the Research Ward.
PAULA:	Yeah, in terms of hospital priorities . . . this Service has to lose a worker.
GRETA:	Has too many workers?

297

PAULA: I don't know. I was responding more to what you said before. I feel, in terms of my whole job structure, that I was really beginning to get comfortable and like I knew where I was going and things were working the way I wanted things to work. And I'm responding to being put in a particular corner. (*pause*) You know, I'm getting rather upset that everything is getting re-shuffled for the ninety-ninth time.[18]

GRETA: (*in a tense voice*) I'm quitting the group![19]

PAULA: This group?

GRETA: Yeah! (*to Marion*) What you're saying, Marion, really concerns me a lot. I'm thinking in terms of this group: You have been saying that you have been hiding this before. (*pause*) Somehow I feel it has been a long time in the making. I haven't been comfortable about your commitment to this group for quite some time. But I didn't know that you wanted to leave.

MARION: I knew you *hadn't* felt it. But I haven't recently felt . . . that, but maybe!

GRETA: I thought the last time we discussed changing all this, you didn't think that we should get into it. (*Apparently she means that Marion gave the impression to her of not wanting to explore the issue.*)

PAULA: I always feel that every time we start getting close, you threaten to leave. It was two weeks ago that we had the most meaningful interaction in terms of you.

MARION: Two weeks ago? Why just two weeks ago?

PAULA: (*laughs*) I'm feeling badly. I'm feeling that we reached a point where I was feeling even more satisfied about . . . well, I'll be personal, in terms of you and me . . . that it won't go on anymore.
(*pause*)

CONSULTANT: I think the participants are feeling frustrated at this point because they don't know what to do to keep everyone in the group—to keep them satisfied. They do what others seem to be asking for and then they find that they're not coming across the way they

298

thought they were, so the group falls in the bag of saying, "We have been here before. What is the point? What is the point of going on?"

(*long pause*)

GRETA: I have a lot of questions which just occurred to me. You know we just lost Ann (*one of the original group members who dropped out a week or two before*). I am wondering, I thought you (*to Marion*) wanted the supervision for your group. Are you quitting your group, too, or what?

MARION: The group will, I'm pretty sure, the group will have to end. (*pause*) And I had intended, intended it anyway—to end it in June or July. But (*pause*) I'm not doing that well in terms of getting good people (well motivated patients) to come in. So we only have three regular people that come. They're good, too. I mean, some of the people are more tentative than others. It got to the point, too, where I think they want to try something else. (She probably means the patients also want to stop therapy or try a different kind of therapy.) Yes, it was mutual. We can work this thing out. (*pause*) It seems to me Ann's leaving has some bearing on the situation here.[20]

GRETA: It seems like it would.

(*pause*)

CONSULTANT: It seems that when the group loses one of its charter members the other participants strongly call into question their own commitment to the group.

GRETA: What charter member?

MARION: There were six of us (*in the original sensitivity group*). (*laughs*) Of course, we went through this before.[21]

GRETA: (*laughs*)

(*pause*)

TOM: (*to Marion*) When did you plan to reveal your plans for your group (*to the present group*)?

MARION: No, it didn't come out all of a sudden.

TOM: It seems it came out only after someone asked you a question.

299

MARION: (*weakly*) I haven't been holding back. (*pause*) And it would have to come up. Yeah, I took the first opportunity I had. And I don't think I hold things back.

TOM: It seems to me it came out only as a result of something else. It didn't come out directly. You have made all sorts of decisions before you come to the group.[22]

MARION: Mm, hmm . . . except what Greta said was true that I have been . . . what . . . leaving and not leaving rather than face up to it.

GRETA: In a sense I feel with you. Like Paula said, I think you set yourself up and we go through a big hassle *and then you stay*. (*laughs*) I guess I don't feel like going through that again. (*pause*) And yet I almost feel you're going to feel that we let you down if we let you go. I sort of have two pulls—on a group level and my wanting to respond to you. I don't know which I should do.[23]

MARION: Yes, yes, I haven't solved the problem of huh . . . I don't know! Letting someone save me from the situation or something like that, and I guess that is what it is. And I know I haven't solved the problem. I was responding to what you said. I can hear that. (*pause*) But I still think in spite of all that, this (*pause*) leaving the group now sits well—pretty well, I will put it—with me (*pause*) than it has before. (*pause*) (*to Tom*) You're shaking your head.

TOM: No. It is the first time you indicated how you were feeling.

GRETA: I find it very hard to believe that all of a sudden you're so ready to drop the group.[24]

MARION: That is not all of the sudden, Greta.

GRETA: How come we haven't talked about it sooner?

TOM: You wanted to continue the group, I thought.

MARION: No, let me see. This is February. Well, in about March I had said in terms of six months, which was until June. No, I thought the group (*her therapy group*) should end at this point.

300

GRETA: That's not the point—whether the group should end or not!

MARION: No, I did talk about that before.

GRETA: Yeah, I remember that. That is not what I'm responding to. But somehow what I see you doing is asking for something that you are not really satisfied with—with Admissions downstairs.

MARION: Yes, I am now satisfied. I wasn't on Wednesday. On Wednesday I was told I had to go to some place else. But I am now.

PAULA: But two months ago you were almost one-hundred percent dissatisfied with having to do Admissions at all. And now you're saying you want to do Admissions one hundred percent.

MARION: Two months ago I was completely dissatisfied? I have always been dissatisfied with Doctor Klutchmire's tendency toward the old people. That is what I was dissatisfied with.

PAULA: Plus your office was being moved from one end to the other (*section of the building*), and what you could be doing in the community (*work with patients in the community*).

MARION: Yeah, and now guess what? I'm back in Admissions. So, perhaps it is a swing. Perhaps I am on a "pendulum."[25]

GRETA: I don't know if I'm projecting or not, but I would hate to work to six o'clock every night. For one thing, I'm not so sure you're really so happy about this.

MARION: I'm not. Well, that is, I have analysis. I want a job. I need the money. That is the way things are. (*pause*) You know I'm fortunate. Only psychiatric residents get permission to leave for therapy. I don't know anyone else who has an hour and a half leeway to get it.

CONSULTANT: I have the impression that the group seems content to discover dissatisfaction in one of the members and keep it there so that it doesn't have to deal with the dissatisfaction on a group-wide level. So the group is

301

just focusing on one person. (*pause*) I have the impression this group member is representative of a feeling shared by the other members of the group. (*long pause*)

PAULA: I'm in touch with the dissatisfaction, but I'm also in touch with feeling I do know what I want and I am up in the air in wondering if everything I want is going to be possible. But the reality is that I want to see that everything I want is . . . gets consideration along with the rest of the needs of the group.

CONSULTANT: It seems that the group is trying without much success to convince one of its members that her dissatisfactions don't have any reality because the group hasn't yet found out if the things the members want are possible or not in the group.

TOM: Pardon? Trying to convince one person what doesn't have any reality?

PAULA: I'm thinking exactly the opposite. The dissatisfactions have all kinds of reality. I am questioning (*pause*) the resolution of . . . the resolution of the dissatisfactions; that is what I'm questioning. (*pause*)

MARION: You do? You mean my leaving the group, or is there something else you question?

PAULA: What I was questioning right then was resolving this by saying, you know, that you are pleased by doing Admissions ninety percent of your time.

MARION: That is the job I want to do. There are other possibilities, but that is the job I want to do. (*long pause*)

GRETA: I don't know. I don't know about the group—but I'm trying to convince Marion to stay. You know, I feel rather uncomfortable about the things you're saying. As far . . . as the group goes, I don't know. I feel at a loss right now. (*pause*)

MARION: Why does it make you feel uncomfortable?

302

GRETA: Somehow I feel that you're . . . like Paula said, that this is pretty much on broad terms. Not only in terms of the group but in terms of your whole job . . . that a lot of things are happening to you that you should be uncomfortable about, *I think* (*pause*) and you're saying that they're not satisfying and that bothers me.

MARION: I'm not ever going to be totally satisfied. It is the best (*pause*) of what I can make of it . . . the situation.[26]

GRETA: I have the feeling that you have been feeling pressure from the group—not pressure that you want.

MARION: Yeah, I feel a pull back in this side (*gesturing toward Greta*). I feel I'm pulling against Tom and Paula. (*to Greta*) I don't feel I'm pulling against you. (*to Paula*) You're pulling this way. You're there and I'm here. You said something about what you want. (*impatiently*) I don't know what you want. What *do* you want?

PAULA: To stay in this Service, continue the group I have, get supervision of this group, explore some of the issues we have gotten into in sensitivity (*training*). (*long pause*)

MARION: So you want things to be the same? (*pause*)

PAULA: Well, you'll have to tell me what they were because apparently I saw them differently than you did.

MARION: (*not clear what her answer was*)

PAULA: I feel clear what I want in terms of the supervision end of it. I'm going to continue the group I have. In terms of the sensitivity group—more of it rather than less of it. I'm not one hundred percent clear of what we can get in this group, but I feel rather . . . especially when we had a couple of particularly good meetings where I felt we were getting somewhere deciding what we all wanted. I am saying I'm not totally clear what I want. I am clear I want to go on in the group—having felt very good about the sensitivity experience. (*pause*) I think as a group we were coming to terms with the issue of our consultant coming and how often. (*pause*)

303

And these are some of the real things to take a look at and work with.

GRETA: I'm beginning to feel myself beginning to pull back in the group. I am thinking about probably changing the times (when the group meets). It was a little more difficult to try than I realized to come up here (*for a group session*) yesterday. It bothered me more than I thought it would to have to mix up my Thursday schedule as well as my Monday schedule and added to this today (Friday). With you (*to Marion*) saying that you want to leave, (*pause*) some time ago I was feeling similar to you, in that I couldn't completely change my schedule and there was no point in having two sets of sensitivity groups and two sets of supervision, and then I had a very meaningful experience here in terms of the sensitivity part of it. I became much more involved than I had prior to that, and I decided that I wanted it. But now I am beginning to feel like that this would be the time to stop coming here. I'm grateful and, unlike you (*Paula*), I think I am beginning to wonder if it would not be better if I should decide not to come rather than if I fight for it. And *it had a lot to do* with other people leaving. I am sort of feeling "how long am I going to go on?"[27]

MARION: When you said, "other people leaving," are you talking about Ann and I, or just I?

GRETA: Both of you.(*pause*) I sort of feel that the meaningfulness of it (the group experience) has very much to do with the people.

MARION: Yes, but I thought our first group was meaningful, too.[28]

GRETA: No, I'm not saying it wasn't! But I thought more recently it got. . . (*Marion interrupts.*)

MARION: It got deeper, yeah!

PAULA: I agree with that. I feel differently in terms of where I feel *we four were at* . . . rather than Charley, Linda, or whomever.
(*pause*)

304

PAULA: In this group we four were at a certain point that was meaningful to me. (*pause*) What point was that (*answering her own question*)? Where we were working together, the things we started to talk about together and to go and start to say. At this point to continue the experience will mean bringing in new prople. (*The group in the past has brought in new members, who generally didn't stay very long.*) And starting at a new point is a different cup of tea, and I would get a very different feeling about it. (*pause*) But the way things are now it wouldn't bother me at all to bring new people into *this* group. (*long pause*)

GRETA: (*to Tom with a laugh*) We haven't heard from you. (*pause*)

TOM: I know. When we changed the time . . . I didn't like having to change the time. I had a group the same time. It was just that I didn't like having a thing a certain day and . . . I don't like to bounce back and forth (*change his schedule on alternate weeks*). (*pause*) I am living from day to day because I feel like we have been here before (*referring to people who dropped out or threatened to drop out of the group*), and we didn't get anywhere before.

MARION: The thing is that I am not the same person I was two months ago.

TOM: I'm not saying you *should* be.

MARION: Yeah.

TOM: I am saying that the changes that came about are perhaps what we went through together or something.[29]

MARION: Maybe it is just easier for me to do this (*drop out*) if you don't show up on Friday and we don't know where you are, because I think that affected me, too.

TOM: Well, I feel like shrugging my shoulders and looking for an excuse.

CONSULTANT: What the feeling in the group seems to be saying is that we are beginning to realize there is something to lose in the group, something to lose of ourselves, as well as the something we claim we can gain from the

305

group experience. It seems that this is what people in the group want to flee from . . . the possibility of loss of ourselves.

MARION: Fleeing from ourselves?

GRETA: I can't key on that at all!
(*pause*)

TOM: Well . . . well, I can see that if we were to invest all of ourselves in here and the same thing were to happen (*meaning that group members might still be dissatisfied*), we would be losing part of ourselves . . . Although if we continue we could probably be gaining something. So I can see that.

MARION: Sounds like you don't want to have to do any work.

TOM: No, I am not saying that!

MARION: You don't mind having to go through all that grief all the time?

PAULA: (*to Marion*) That irks me, too. I feel I will lose more of myself than you—that part of me I gave you two weeks ago.
(*pause*)

CONSULTANT: The group seems to be saying that the relationships that they have developed in this group, and all the feelings contained within, are a very important part of themselves. Rather than go on and have these parts of ourselves ruptured, we feel it would be better to forget the insult to the relationship, drop it, pretend it doesn't exist . . . perhaps hoping to keep the relationship suspended the way it is forever.

GRETA: Something you just said, Marion, a few minutes ago . . . something that happened here in the group did happen and affected your decision: You had said that Tom's not being here Friday. This strikes me as something that is important because it is something that happened here in the group. It is not outside forces.

MARION: I see what you mean. (*pause*) I don't know if I want to go through this business of being in analysis and the kinds of relationships I have to do in the group. Maybe

| | I am saying I don't have enough energy. But (*pause*) even in the therapy part I was telling you about, I had all kinds of tendencies for things to come out inappropriately to people in other relationships outside of therapy. This (*the process group*) would not have been an inappropriate place. I was sort of annoyed at myself. I think I want to have a better grip on these things, and it is threatening to me to do that here. I feel that I might have the same kinds of reactions as a result of this group, and it is very difficult here in the hospital (*meaning that she works here*). Do you know what I mean? |

GRETA: I think I *do*. I think I find it (*pause*) (*to Marion*) strange or rather upsetting . . . for some reason.

MARION: I don't know if I trust myself.

GRETA: (*quickly*) In this group?

MARION: Yeah, what I am trying to do . . . (*Paula cuts in.*)

PAULA: That is only one side of it; that is, what will I lose? I will lose whatever I get from each of you—from you, Marion; from you, Greta; from Tom; from each of you. The kind of things we have been doing together, you know, the reciprocal part of the things I give out. (*very long pause*)

GRETA: I feel sort of immobilized or something. We have to resolve something before next week. The way I feel, there is a lot of pressure to resolve what to do. I don't know what to do. I don't know if the rest of you feel that or not.[30]

TOM: I don't know if we want to do anything or not. It is much easier to put it in a bag and tie it all up.

GRETA: Yeah, I think it is much easier to have a new group or do something (*laughs*) closing it up.[31]

MARION: You're (*to Greta*) not getting much support I think.

PAULA: (*to Marion*) You consistently have presented the group with kind of something painful that hangs over us, and I keep wanting to say to you, "Hasn't there been something comforting, hasn't there been anything (*in the group*) to offset it?" Sure, I know it won't do anything

307

	to change your mind or anything. I can just keep trying to say that . . . but I feel very interested in wanting you to stay.
MARION:	The pain is (*pause*) I don't know if it *means more* . . . where it stands in the ultimate balance of things.
GRETA:	(*laughs*)
TOM:	(*asks Marion whether she wants to mend her ways*)
MARION:	Trying to change, Tom? No! Somehow I tend to look at the pessimistic side or something. I can shelve the comfort and remember the pain.
GRETA:	Part of the problem is that I don't know where you're at. Are you staying or leaving?
MARION:	I'm leaving.
GRETA:	Definitely? (*no answer; group laughs*)
TOM:	You say you are leaving. I could have believed that ten to twenty minutes ago, but it hasn't been sounding like that in the last few minutes.
GRETA:	That's it!
TOM:	That is why I can't do anything with it.
MARION:	What am I supposed to do with you all?
TOM:	It just doesn't sound to me like you're . . . if we asked you to stay and talk you would stay.
MARION:	No!
TOM:	No, it just doesn't add up right. It just doesn't feel right.
MARION:	(*sounding final*) I'm leaving. This is my last meeting.
TOM:	I still am surprised at you. I don't know how you can come in and someone says something and keys on you, and you say real quick that you're leaving and leave it at that.
MARION:	How would you like for me to leave it?
TOM:	It seems to me that you are just arbitrarily making it dramatic and taking off in the wilderness before someone can say something to make you stop and think and change your mind.
MARION:	That's probably warm.
	(*Tom and Greta don't accept Marion's evasiveness.*)
MARION:	(*excitedly*) O.K. It isn't the greatest decision that is

308

black or white. It isn't! I have feelings about leaving, but I just . . . I don't know what you want. I feel frustrated.

CONSULTANT: I have the impression that the frustration the group is experiencing has something to do with the way the group handled Ann last week.
(*pause*)

GRETA: That may be very true!

TOM: There could have been things operating in the group, but I don't see how we could have stopped her. I thought the group tried to stop her.

CONSULTANT: I wonder if the group has been sort of giving up on Marion because look what happened with Ann.

TOM: I don't think we gave up on Marion. What we were saying . . . no matter what we say . . . I mean, if she says, "I'm leaving no matter what you all say," what can we do?

GRETA: Just a minute ago I had a fantasy of seeing Marion getting up out of her chair and walking out.[32]

TOM: Why?

GRETA: Something that she said. I just had the vision of getting out of her chair and leaving. (*pause*) I feel you were very full of emotion . . . I don't know anger or what.

MARION: I don't know what you want me to say or do. (*pause*) You know, you talk about being immobilized, then you turn to me and ask me a question I don't know how to answer.

PAULA: I think I'm feeling we keep hearing people say, "I'm leaving," a week in advance. I think I'm finding it very discouraging as a person.

MARION: I don't follow what you mean.

PAULA: I keep hearing you say, "It is too much, or I just don't want to look at it right now, or I just want to get away from things." I'm feeling rather angry at this point. We have been trying to get across to people. It gets discouraging to me always to hear people say, "Stop me from feeling pain," because I feel the group has

309

been a very positive thing. I don't hear Ann or you saying that. I feel better about myself so that is why I am leaving, or that you came for something and you accomplished it . . . that there are things you want to do for yourself. Maybe you're saying it and I'm not hearing it. (*pause*) In a sense, you could have presented that you were chiseling out . . . so that is why you're leaving. But the way it came out was, "I can only stand so much. I can only stand four hours of analysis and I can't stand this, too."

MARION: Well, perhaps I'm still masochistic.
(*pause*)

PAULA: Well, I don't want to sit here and mope about it. I know I feel good about a lot of things that happened here in this group.

MARION: I know it is a shame I can't (*pause*) I can't make it sound positive. I always make it sound negative.
(*pause*)

TOM: I don't feel any urge to just turn my back and ignore you. But I see you as just this person who sits there, tossing out these flip comments. And if anyone says anything about how they're feeling, they get a flip answer back from you.

MARION: I don't think of them as flip.

TOM: But you're being very flip. What you have said today. (*pause*) It is just easier to ignore you than anything else. I don't know what it is but you're just not the same person I met last time (*in previous sessions*). I can't explain it.

GRETA: I think that can only be part of it because I'm not feeling that. I have a feeling that Marion has an awful lot of feelings and she is covering them up by saying, "I'm leaving . . . well, that's it!" But like several times I had a feeling that you (*Marion*) were really angry at me when I pressured you a little bit and . . . you are feeling a lot of pain today. And I guess you are feeling partially immobilized by not knowing how to deal with it because, if you decide to leave, I'm not sure you really want to get into it. Yet I *want* to resolve something.

MARION: But you want to resolve it for yourself, I think, Greta.

GRETA: Well, I suppose so, but I also want to see something resolved for you, too. Because of what happened to Ann, I thought that that was very meaningful for me and I thought for her, too, so I want to get beyond this. So I don't think your flip answers mean that you don't have any feelings about it. (*pause*) My feeling is that you are covering up an awful lot of the feelings that are there.

MARION: I don't think I did a very good job (*of explaining her feelings*).

(*very long pause*)

CONSULTANT: Well, let's stop and recapitulate what went on here today in the session. (*The consultant is indicating that the* formal *portion of the process group is over and is asking for a description and explanation of what happened in the session.*) (*long pause*) I had the feeling that quite a bit went on in here today in the group.

(*pause*)

GRETA: (*laughs*) I never know what to say after this (*in the* summary). I feel I have said it all (*in the session*).

CONSULTANT: I think that it is rather important for us to see the whole process, the whole forest. Too often we get caught up with little segments, the little trees. Therefore, we need to look at the whole process to understand what happened in this session.

PAULA: The microphone is one of those segments we get caught up in.

CONSULTANT: Was that one of the real concerns during the session—that little microphone?

PAULA: You mean, we started with talking about it? We started with little issues like "How come I didn't come yesterday?" and we end up with the whole thing. (*pause*) I think not coming is something for you to think about . . . a little smidgen of what to think about

311

. . . and what it means (*what are the important underlying issues*), but is fairly safe and fairly comfortable for me to deal with.

(*There is a heated encounter between Marion and Paula.*)

CONSULTANT: It appears that in the summary period we fall back in the same patterns and positions we were in during the session. Because, I guess, the feelings we had can't be turned off. I said, "Let's stop!" but our feelings aren't turned off that easily. We seem to have the same feelings that were generated in the session. And that brings up an important issue . . . something that you (*Greta*) mentioned: whether we should look at the individual or whether we should look at the group. In other words, as Greta put it: "There is a pull to look at what is happening in the group and the desire to relate to Marion." That is something that happens all the time. I think the fact that we saw this tells us something about this kind of process. This kind of process (*the perspective from which the consultant tries to encourage the group members to view their group experience*) is perhaps different from any other kind of group we have ever experienced. Certainly, it is not true of a therapy group which is concerned with individuals—our feelings and bringing in the past, or staff groups that are concerned with solutions to immediate problems and are not concerned with the process from which these problems are worked with. This group, then, is a very unique kind of experience for most of us, all of us. We are never really afforded the luxury of studying the process without strong pressure to find solutions to problematic situations. It is very important that we realize that understanding what happens in the life of a group, which we have the luxury to explore, is knowledge which can be applied to other groups also, where the opportunity for in-depth exploration is minimal.

GRETA: Part of the difficulty in looking at what happened is

312

that we are still very much emotionally involved in individuals, and I find it very difficult to think about a process and a totality.

CONSULTANT: Certainly, we are so caught up in a crisis and emergency, so that all we can think about is the immediate solution to the emergency. This doesn't insure much opportunity for learning. But, of course, necessity often supersedes study. Thus, if we don't detach a certain amount of our critical ego—our critical faculties—we are too emotionally invested to learn better solutions (by knowing more about the totality of the underlying conditions in the situation) to handle it next time. What I'm suggesting is that group experience needs to be intellectual as well as experiential.

PAULA: This touches on something that in a way happened in the group that met without you. Usually a sense of the process lurks behind my feelings. With you in here there is a certain perspective, a focus on process. We don't usually have this in our group when we meet without you. But last time we were able to comment about the process while it was happening and trying to resolve a situation with Tom, and it really felt exciting. (*pause*) What I was most aware of in terms of process was that a leaving involves both feeling positive and negative.

GRETA: There was some point at which I started to look at what was happening in an objective and intellectual way. I said to myself, we have to get together; we have to get together and decide something because Marion is going to leave. We need to determine the destiny of the rest of us in here.

CONSULTANT: I wonder if we can focus in on what Paula just said, which I think is a rather important phenomenon in dealing with feelings of separation and feelings of anger. On one level we don't like people to leave because of our feelings of loss and the disrupting and breaking of relationships. Therefore, we tried to keep

313

Marion in the group. But keeping Marion in the group meant that our feelings of anger—because we regarded her behavior as not completely open, "she always holds something painful over us," Paula said—became so overwhelming that it may have been too uncomfortable for us to keep her in the group, so that we tried to find subtle ways to push her out at the same time. That is, these motives were operating simultaneously. This gives a mixed message to Marion and to the rest of us. We seem to be trying to pull her back in the group while at the same time trying to push her out. As each of the people in the group may have been experiencing this conflict, taken in concert it becomes a rather overwhelming group mood. (*pause*) Is this something people felt during the session?

TOM: We were trying to push her out?

CONSULTANT: As well as pulling her back in. In fact, as I remember, Greta said, "Why is it that you don't leave?"

MARION: Yeah (*to Greta*) you were trying to make me leave. I was feeling that yeah, I'll leave. I'll be glad to.

PAULA: I was also feeling your (*Marion*) side of it . . . which was "O.K. You can kick me out if that is what you are feeling!" But it made you pretty angry.

MARION: My anger probably . . . (*Paula cuts in.*)

PAULA: I felt I made you feel uncomfortable.

CONSULTANT: You were going to say something, Marion?

MARION: Yes. I caught the anger and tried to push it away. As a result of the anger . . . What is the anger about, I wonder?

CONSULTANT: Does anyone have any ideas about this? I think we were talking about it during the session.

MARION: That I was saying that I would need you all?
(*pause*)

CONSULTANT: What I was feeling was that it concerned a feeling of loss. I think in many ways we were saying: "Suspend the relationship. Let's not challenge the relationship since it is at the point of rupture. It is already too taut—

314

it will break. Therefore, let us suspend it here . . . at this point. O.K., if you want to leave the group, O.K., fine, we will let you. This is the way it was with Ann. We still have a good relationship with Ann outside this group—nothing we really have to work on. So what if we didn't work out our feelings with her in the group? Why should we have to confront our real feelings about her? With her out of the group, we can maintain a 'good' relationship with her outside." But this is not profitable for us, is it? Nevertheless, we say the same thing to Marion: "Let's not get angry. You've been getting angry; we have been angry. It is better that you leave now. We will still have a 'good' relationship."

MARION: I think that is what I'm trying to say.

CONSULTANT: But can we really do this in life? I think we are trying to capture losses in our own past. I think we are saying to Marion, as we did to Ann: "Although I may never see you again, I will think about you until the end of time and with warm, positive feelings." It never worked like that in the past, but we still somehow try to redo our unpleasant separations from the past. This is in large part what the transference phenomena is all about, I think. We try to make the present situation into a situation from the past but without the old pain. We try to do away with the old pain . . . get rid of it.

MARION: That is what I tried to tell you when we were talking about my hostility. I couldn't come out with all that sweetness and light that everyone seemed to be asking for.

PAULA: But I seemed to be hung up on your either/or, too. No, I can't be one hundred percent good and comfortable, nor does it have to be quite as extreme as Ann's walking out. There are a lot of things that we are in need from you. I was trying to get across some of the very positive feelings. I don't know if I did. The very positive feelings I feel, and I felt very much the need to get them back.

315

	Not one hundred percent but something . . . and you didn't.
GRETA:	(*to Marion*) I don't know what you are saying. You mentioned sweetness and light. I don't know what you meant.
MARION:	Well, I guess I was reacting to . . . (*pause*) You were telling me how helpful I was and therefore my decision . . . Well, anyway, I don't know. I don't want to cause so much trouble, Greta, with my decision.
GRETA:	I didn't feel that way.
PAULA:	It would have meant a lot to us—now that I look at it—if it came out that way. I was feeling that the way you said it . . . what was coming out was something hostile, which was harder for both of us.
MARION:	Right! And because both of us were close to tears, I didn't try. I started out going to say everything was coming out negatively, but I didn't.
CONSULTANT:	I have a feeling that things are not finished. I would make a recommendation—and of course it is Marion's choice to reject it—that she meet with the leaderless group on Monday and come back on Friday and see at that point where we are. (*pause*) I think what has happened here is that we have gotten into things, and they still are not finished for any of us.
MARION:	Are you going to throw me out, Tom?
TOM:	I?
MARION:	You don't like this uncertainty, do you?
TOM:	What I think happened was that when we got into it with Marion and we said we have been here before.

EXPLANATORY NOTES

1. Tom has been the group member who is most likely to express doubts about the validity of sensitivity training. Until rather recently he was puzzled and a little upset by the consultant

316

and the other group members regarding behavior in the group in a different way from what common sense would dictate. Because he is the only male member of the group, Tom has borne pressures exerted by the others in the group to serve as a polarity of resistance (protection) against the consultant who sometimes exposes the females in the group to underlying "painful" material. Generally, Tom indirectly expresses his resistance role, such as in complaining about the consultant's cigar, the temperature of the room, the use of a microphone during this session, and so forth.

2. Until recently the group members have had considerable difficulty confronting the consultant and expressing dissatisfaction in a direct way. After the advent of alternate-week leaderless sessions, there has been improvement in this area. Nevertheless, the expression of hostility toward the consultant (Tom's remark about the consultant's chair) raised the anxiety of the group. Greta, one of the warmest and most outgoing members of the group, often serves as an integral polarity in the group, dissipating tension through laughter, smiles, and supportive remarks.

3. Paula is a most perceptive and psychologically sophisticated member of the group. She is the group member most apt to pick up the subtleties of the interpersonal strategies being enacted by herself and others in the group. She perhaps identifies more than any other group member with the consultant's focus on process and is, therefore, most self-critical and group-critical in the sense of "accepting" and elaborating on the consultant's interventions.

4. Marion is a charter member of the group. Until recently she has tried to keep the group discussion on an intellectual plane, discussing group phenomena and resisting confrontations of individuals in the group. After starting analysis about a year

317

before the present session, she seemed more comfortable discussing personal material. In recent sessions she has spontaneously brought up some painful experiences from her childhood that she felt related to her present group behavior. Although this kind of material is generally not discussed in a process group, the group accepted it as an expression of Marion's wanting to share something personal with the group. In terms of her role as a polarity, Marion has rather strong feelings of responsibility for what happens in the group and has striven to keep the group together by suggesting "rational" kinds of rules to set aside dissatisfaction. She serves in this capacity as a polarity for control and security in the group.

5. In recent weeks the group has been trying to persuade the consultant to become an active member of the group rather than a detached observer. Here Tom is probably expressing the group's discomfort about the consultant's relationship with the group. The group probably wants the consultant to assume a peer-like role so that they may be free to question his motives.

6. Here Paula is serving as the group's critical ego. She is suggesting that the group are trying to externalize their anxieties by regarding threats to the group as external rather than as forces operating among the group members. She is asking the group why they don't want to look at themselves.

7. As a polarity of control and security, Marion attempts to take leadership initiative in suggesting a "corrective" course of action, which she regards as external—the live microphone.

8. The others in the group seem to share Marion's discomfort, but they do not follow up Marion's suggestion. Greta's statement suggests that it may be because they regard the consultant as omniscient. Therefore, if he brought in the microphone he must have a good, sound reason for it. He need only tell the

318

group what his reasons are so that they, too, may understand. Implicit in this attitude is the dependency basic assumption (see Chapter 6). The burden for relieving the anxiety in the group, the participants seem to be saying, is that of the consultant because the members of the group don't understand what is going on and therefore can't be expected to remedy the situation.

9. Marion's bid for leadership having failed, she pushes Greta to take leadership.

10. Tom, Marion, and (probably to a lesser extent) Greta react with strong feelings to the expectation that they take responsibility for structuring the group experience. They seem to be saying: "To be in the present is not to know. We cannot adequately handle problems as they come up (in the here-and-now). We have to know beforehand what the problems will be in order to prepare for them."

11. Marion's disclosure of her frustrations and dissatisfactions with the group after the consultant confronted the group's resistance may indicate that the participants need "permission" from the consultant in order to open up.

12. The group is apparently uncomfortable because the consultant pointed to their dependent demands. They seize upon Marion's submission to authority as an opportunity to say, "You see, it is really Marion who is overly dependent—not the rest of us!" This phenomenon is discussed in the subsection on group pathology in Chapter 12.

13. The consultant's intervention at this point has at least three purposes: (1) He tries to prevent Marion from being the "scapegoat," because he believes all members are dissatisfied with the group. (2) He doesn't think the group is finished with him; there are still unresolved feelings, and he lets the group

319

know this. (3) He suggests that one can only go so far in finding fault with the group members, suggesting that the group has not yet explored what the members want from the group.

14. Paula is expressing some awareness that the group has transferred to the consultant its anger toward authorities outside the group. Perhaps it is even more important for group members to realize that they are no better able to resolve their conflicts in the process group than they have been with others outside the group.

15. Having failed to assume leadership and having failed to induce Greta to assert leadership, Marion now offers the crown of laurels to Paula. Although the group is discussing a job situation which appears to have no bearing on the present meeting, we assume that the group is actually dealing with intragroup tensions. Thus, if Paula is competent enough to handle a difficult supervisor outside the group, the hope may be that she is also able to show the other group members how to handle the present "authority" figure—the consultant.

16. Apparently Paula and Marion are competing for a job slot in their work situation. Neither seems to be aware of this, and to a large extent it may lie at the core of their angry exchanges in the group. The consultant could have interpreted this to the group, but in so doing, he would probably have frozen out the other group members. Therefore he chose to focus upon a more general and shared group concern. This is not to disregard Paula and Marion's conflict, but to consider it as representative of a general group issue.

17. Tom may be responding to the feeling that somehow the issue being discussed doesn't have enough significance for him to explain the strong feelings being generated in the group.

18. In trying to understand what is happening in the present group situation, the process group consultant often finds clues in the particular way feelings are expressed about events that occur outside the group. Participants usually feel more open about expressing their feelings about extra-group events than they do about current feelings. According to our theoretical assumption, the tensions currently experienced are similar to those experienced during the event being discussed. Therefore, extrapolating Paula's feelings about the job to the present group situation, we might infer that she is upset about Marion's leaving because that might mean reshuffling the group—bringing in new group members, breaking established relationships, and forming new ones.

19. Greta tells the group that she is quitting. Except for Paula's asking her which group she means, no one else seems to relate to this statement. Perhaps the others feel too overwhelmed with Marion's threat so that they selectively disregard Greta's threat.

20. It is important for group therapists to realize how they subtly collude with their patients. Marion's statements touch on this problem. Notice the parallel between what is happening in the group in which Marion is a therapist—she has only a few patients who attend sessions and their commitment is tentative —and Marion's own tentative commitment to the group in which she is a member.

21. Marion seems to represent the group members' feelings that their unresolved feelings about members who left the group prevents them from dealing with the reenactment of the threat of separation and loss.

22. The group has developed the norm that its members do not present the group with final decisions. Before making a final decision, a member is expected to present the situation and

321

several alternatives to the group. Tom is upbraiding Marion for having violated this norm.

23. Greta is expressing the pressures that bear upon group members to abide by group norms—in this instance, "Don't take a group member (Marion) seriously who plays games"—which clashes with their desire to respond to the needs of a member who is regarded as "deviant" by the others.

24. Greta is again expressing the group's unwillingness to admit that there are any real problems in the group. To do this the group needs to make Marion's dissatisfaction her problem rather than a symptom of group dissatisfaction.

25. Marion is apparently colluding with the group. They need to see her as being the problem rather than an expression of general group dissatisfaction. Marion feeds into this expectation by describing herself as moody.

26. Marion's statement suggests an important reason for the group's frustration with her. She tells the group that she is unhappy and suggests that she is unwilling to let the group help her with this.

27. Greta seems to realize that she shares Marion's concerns and that she has used Marion to avoid confronting her own feelings about the group.

28. Marion tries to dilute the intensity of her relationships with the others in the group in the hope, perhaps, that it will make it easier for them to let her go.

29. Tom is expressing the group's resentment that Marion has not recognised the group's benefit to her.

30. Greta is probably expressing the feelings of others in the group

as well as herself. This mood apparently developed as the group began to recognize that each of the members shared (at least in part) Marion's discontent and frustration. If all of the members were so affected, to whom could they go for help?

31. Tom's and Greta's remarks suggest that the group is in a flight-fight basic assumption. The fight with Marion led only to immobilization. Greta and Tom therefore suggest that flight is the best means of escape from the present threat to the group.

32. Tom and Greta have been subtly encouraging Marion to leave throughout the session. Here it is revealed in a wish-fulfilling fantasy.

References

1. Abrahamson, M. *Interpersonal Accommodation*. Princeton, N.J.: Van Nostrand, 1966.
2. Ansbacher, H. L. "The History of the Leaderless Group Discussion Technique." *Psychological Bulletin* 48: 383–391, 1951.
3. Ansbacher, H. L., and Ansbacher, R. R., eds. *The Individual Psychology of Alfred Adler*. New York: Basic Books, 1956.
4. Argyris, C. *Interpersonal Competence and Organizational Effectiveness*. Homewood, Ill.: Irwin, 1962.
5. Arieti, S. Quoted in J. Howard, "Inhibitions Thrown to the Gentle Winds." *Life* 65: 48–57, 1968.
6. Attneave, F. "Some Informational Aspects of Visual Perception." *Psychological Review* 61: 183–193, 1954.
7. Bach, G. *Intensive Group Psychotherapy*. New York: Ronald Press, 1954.
8. Bass, B. M. "Mood Changes During a Management Training Laboratory." *Journal of Applied Psychology* 46: 361–364, 1962a.

9. Bass, B. M. "Reactions to *Twelve Angry Men* as a Measure of Sensitivity Training." *Journal of Applied Psychology* 46: 120–124, 1962b.

10. Baumgartel, H., and Goldstein, J. W. "Need and Value Shifts in College Training Groups." *Journal of Applied Behavioral Science* 3: 87–101, 1967.

11. Bennis, W. G., Burke, R. L., Cutler, H., Harrington, H., and Hoffman, J. "Note on Some Problems of Measurement and Prediction in a Training Group." *Group Psychotherapy* 10: 328–341, 1957.

12. Berne, E. *The Structure and Dynamics of Organizations and Groups*. New York: Grove Press, 1963.

13. Berne, E. *Principles of Group Treatment*. New York: Oxford University Press, 1966.

14. Bettelheim, B. *The Empty Fortress*. New York: Free Press, 1967.

15. Bion, W. R. *Experience in Groups*. London: Tavistock Publications, 1961.

16. Blake, R. R. "Group Training Versus Group Therapy." *Group Psychotherapy* 10: 271–276, 1957.

17. Blanck, G. "Some Technical Implications of Ego Psychology." *International Journal of Psychoanalysis* 47: 6–13, 1966.

18. Blum, E. M., and Blum, R. H. *Alcoholism: Modern Psychological Approaches to Treatment*. San Francisco: Jossey-Bass, 1967.

19. Blumer, H. "Collective Behavior." In A. M. Lee, ed., *New Outlines of the Principles of Sociology*. New York: Barnes and Noble, 1951.

20. Bradford, L. P. "Introduction." *Journal of Social Issues* 4: 2–7, 1948.

21. Buchanan, P. C. "Evaluating the Effectiveness of Laboratory Training in Industry." In *Explorations in Human Relations Training and Research* (No. 1). Washington, D.C.: National Training Laboratories–National Education Association, 1965.

22. Burke, R. L., and Bennis, W. G. "Changes in Perception of Self and Others During Human Relations Training." *Human Relations* 14: 165–182, 1961.
23. Campbell, J. P., and Dunnette, M. "Effectiveness of T-Group Experience in Managerial Training and Development." *Psychological Bulletin* 70: 73–104, 1968.
24. Cantril, H. *The Psychology of Social Movements*. New York: Wiley, 1963.
25. Casteel, J. C. "The Rise of Interpersonal Groups." In J. C. Casteel, ed., *The Creative Role of the Interpersonal Group in the Church Today*. New York: Association Press, 1968.
26. Clark, J. V. "Toward a Theory and Practice of Religious Experiencing." In J. F. Bugental, ed., *Challenges of Humanistic Psychology*. New York: McGraw-Hill, 1967.
27. Clark, J. V., and Culbert, S. A. "Mutually Therapeutic Perception and Self-Awareness in a T-Group." *Journal of Applied Behavioral Science* 1: 180–194, 1965.
28. Cohen, R. A. "Anxiety." *Medical Annual of the District of Columbia* 19: 479–484, 541–542, 1950.
29. Corsini, R. *Methods of Group Psychotherapy*. Brookport, Ill.: William James Press, 1964.
30. Cottle, T. J. "Encounter in Color." *Psychology Today* 1 (No. 7): 22–27, 40–41, 1969.
31. Culbert, S. A. "Innovative Group Experiences." Paper presented at Mid-Atlantic Group Psychotherapy Meeting, Fall, 1968, at Sheraton-Park Hotel, Washington, D.C.
32. Eisenhower, D. *Look* 33: 14, 1969.
33. Elridge, S. *Fundaments of Sociology*, New York: Crowell, 1950.
34. "Encountertapes for Personal Growth Groups." Human Development Institute, Bell and Howell. Atlanta, Ga., 1968.
35. Enneis, J. "The Dynamics of Group and Action Processes in Therapy." *Group Psychotherapy* 4: 17–22, 1951.

36. Ezriel, H. "A Psycho-analytic Approach to Group Treatment." *British Journal of Medical Psychology* 23: 59–74, 1950.
37. Ezriel, H. "Notes on Psychoanalytic Group Therapy: II. Interpretations and Research." *Psychiatry* 15: 119–126, 1952.
38. Festinger, L. "A Theory of Social Comparison Processes." *Human Relations* 17: 117–140, 1954.
39. Festinger, L. *A Theory of Cognitive Dissonance.* Stanford, Calif.: Stanford University Press, 1957.
40. Festinger, L., Pepitone, A., and Newcombe, T. M. "Some Consequences of De-Individualization in a Group." *Journal of Abnormal and Social Psychology* 47: 382–389, 1952.
41. Fine, L. "Seminars in Group Processes." Brochure. Portland, Ore., 1969.
42. Fisher, S. "Body Attention Patterns and Personality Defenses." *Psychological Monographs* 80 (Nos. 9 and 617), 1966.
43. Foulkes, S. H., and Anthony, E. J. *Group Psychotherapy, The Psychoanalytic Approach.* Baltimore: Penguin Books, 1957.
44. Frank, J. D. "Theory in a Group Setting." In M. I. Stein, ed., *Contemporary Psychotherapy.* New York: Free Press, 1961.
45. Freud, A. *The Ego and the Mechanisms of Defense.* New York: International Universities Press, 1966.
46. Freud, S. *Group Psychology and the Analysis of the Ego.* New York: Liveright Publishing Company, 1921.
47. Fried, M. "Social Problems and Psychopathology." In *Urban America and the Planning of Mental Health Services* (Symposium No. 10, 403–446). Group for the Advancement of Psychiatry, New York, 1964.
48. Gage, N. L., and Exline, R. V. "Social Perception and Effectiveness in Discussion Groups." *Human Relations* 6: 381–396, 1953.
49. Gassner, S., Gold, J., and Snadowsky, A. M. "Changes in the Phenomenal Field as a Result of Human Re-

lations Training." *Journal of Psychology* 58: 33–41, 1964.

50. Gibb, J. R. "Review: Schutz's *Joy*." *Contemporary Psychology* 14: 199–201, 1969.

51. Glaser, A. "Making It: Gossip of the Literary Market Place." *The Washington Post*, March 2, 1969.

52. Goffman, E. *The Presentation of Self in Everyday Life*. Garden City, N.Y.: Doubleday, 1959.

53. Grater, H. "In a Leaderless Training Group." *Personnel and Guidance Journal*, 493–496, March, 1959.

54. Greening, T. C. "Sensitivity Training: Cult or Contribution?" *Personnel* 41: 18–25, 1964.

55. Haigh, G. V. "Psychotherapy as Interpersonal Encounter." In J. F. Bugental, ed., *Challenges of Humanistic Psychology*. New York: McGraw-Hill, 1967.

56. Hall, M. H. "A Conversation with Carl Rogers." *Psychology Today* 1 (No. 7): 18–20, 62–66, 1967.

57. Hare, A. P., Borgotta, E. F., and Bales, R. F. *Small Groups: Studies in Social Interaction*. New York: Knopf, 1955.

58. Harper, R. A. *Psychoanalysis and Psychotherapy, 36 Systems*. Englewood Cliffs, N.J.: Prentice-Hall, 1959.

59. Harrison, R. "Import of the Laboratory on Perceptions of Others by the Experimental Group." In C. Argyris, *Interpersonal Competence and Organizational Behavior*. Homewood, Ill.: Irwin, 1962.

60. Hartley, J. A. "A Semantic Differential Scale for Assessing Group Process Changes." *Journal of Clinical Psychology* 24: 74, 1968.

61. Heider, F. *The Psychology of Interpersonal Relations*. New York: Wiley, 1967.

62. Hobbs, N. "Group-Centered Psychotherapy." In C. R. Rogers, *Client-Centered Therapy*. Boston: Houghton Mifflin, 1951.

63. Hoffer, E. *The True Believer*. New York: New American Library, 1951.

64. Hollister, W. G. "The Risks of Freedom-Giving Group Leadership." *Mental Hygiene* 41: 238–244, 1957.

65. Hopkins, L. T. "What Is Group Process?" In C. G.

Kemp, ed., *Perspectives on the Group Process*. Boston: Houghton Mifflin, 1964.

66. House, R. J. "T-Group Education and Leadership Effectiveness: A Review of the Empirical Literature and a Critical Evaluation." *Personnel Psychology* 20: 1–32, 1967.

67. Howard, J. "Inhibitions Thrown to the Gentle Winds." *Life* 65: 48–57, 1968.

68. Jourard, S. M. *The Transparent Self*. Princeton, N.J.: Van Nostrand, 1964.

69. Kadis, A. L., Krasner, J. D., Winick, C., and Foulkes, S. H. *A Practicum of Group Psychotherapy*. New York: Harper and Row, 1963.

70. Kassajian, H. H. "Social Character and Sensitivity Training." *Journal of Applied Behavioral Science* 1: 433–440, 1965.

71. Kelly, G. A. *A Theory of Personality, The Psychology of Personal Constructs*. New York: Norton, 1963.

72. Kernan, J. P. "Laboratory Human Relations Training: Its Effect on the 'Personality' of Supervisory Engineers." *Dissertation Abstracts* 25 (1): 665–666, 1964.

73. Killian, L. M. "Social Movements." In R. L. Faris, ed., *Handbook of Modern Sociology*. Chicago: Rand McNally, 1964.

74. Krech, D., Crutchfield, R., and Ballachey, E. *Individual in Society, A Textbook of Social Psychology*. New York: McGraw-Hill, 1962.

75. Kris, E. "Ego Psychology and Interpretation in Psychoanalytic Therapy." *Psychoanalytic Quarterly* 20: 15–30, 1951.

76. Laing, R., Phillipson, H., and Lee, A. R. *Interpersonal Perception, A Theory and a Method of Research*. London: Tavistock Publications, 1966.

77. Laubach, E. E. "Elements of Group Behavior." In J. C. Casteel, ed., *The Creative Role of the Interpersonal Group in the Church Today*. New York: Association Press, 1968.

78. Lecky, P. *Self-Consistency, A Theory of Personality*. Garden City, N.Y.: Doubleday, 1968.
79. Lennard, H. L., and Bernstein, A. *The Anatomy of Psychotherapy: Systems of Communication and Expectation*. New York: Columbia University Press, 1960.
80. Lewin, K. *Field Theory in Social Science: Selected Theoretical Papers*. New York: Harper and Row, 1951.
81. Lippitt, R. "Dimensions of the Consultant's Job." *Journal of Social Issues* 15: 5–12, 1959.
82. Lippitt, R., Watson, J., and Westley, B. *Dynamics of Planned Change*. New York: Harcourt, Brace and World, 1958.
83. Locke, N. *Group Psychoanalysis*. New York: New York University Press, 1961.
84. Lohman, K., Zenger, J. H., and Weschler, I. R. "Some Perceptual Changes During Sensitivity Training." *Journal of Educational Research* 53: 28–31, 1959.
85. Luchins, A. S. *Group Therapy, A Guide*. New York: Random House, 1967.
86. Lurie, L. "Innovative Group Experiences." Paper presented at Mid-Atlantic Group Psychotherapy Meeting, Fall, 1968, at Sheraton-Park Hotel, Washington, D.C.
87. McCann, D. L. "Sensitivity Training—A Unique Experience." *The Asclepian*, bi-monthly publication of the University of Maryland School of Medicine, College Park, Md.
88. McNair, M. P. "What Price Human Relations?" *Harvard Business Review*, 15–27, March–April, 1957.
89. Mann, J. "Group Therapy with Adults." *American Journal of Orthopsychiatry* 23: 332–337, 1953.
90. Massarik, F., and Carlson, G. Cited in M. D. Dunnette, "Personnel Management." *Annual Review of Psychology* 13: 285–314, 1962.
91. Meerloo, J. A. "Mental Contagion." *American Journal of Psychotherapy* 13: 66–82, 1959.

92. Miller, M. Mimeographed. Washington, D.C., 1968.
93. Moreno, J. L. "Psychodrama and Group Psycho-therapy." Paper read at the American Psychiatric Association Meeting, May, 1946, at Chicago, Ill.
94. Moreno, J. L. *Who Shall Survive?* Washington, D.C.: Nervous and Mental Diseases Publication, 1953.
95. Mouton, J. "Training for Decision-Making in Groups in a University Laboratory." *Group Psychotherapy* 10: 342–345, 1957.
96. Mouton, J., and Blake, R. R. "University Training in Human Relations Skills." *Group Psychotherapy* 14: 140–153, 1961.
97. Mullan, H., and Rosenbaum, M. *Group Psychotherapy, Therapy and Practice.* New York: Free Press, 1962.
98. National Training Laboratories Institute. "News and Reports" 2 (No. 2), Washington, D.C., April, 1968.
99. Odiorne, G. "The Trouble with Sensitivity Training." *Training Directors Journal,* 9–20, October, 1963.
100. Orizon Institute. Brochure. White Oaks, Maryland, 1969.
101. Oshry, B. I., and Harrison, R. "Transfer from Here-and-Now—to There-and-Then: Changes in Organizational Problem Diagnosis Stemming from T-Group Training." *Journal of Applied Behavioral Science* 2: 185–198, 1966.
102. Parloff, M. B. "Advances in Analytic Group Psycho-therapy." In J. Marmor, ed., *Frontiers of Psychoanalysis.* New York: Basic Books, 1967.
103. Parsons, T. "General Theory in Sociology." In R. K. Merton, L. Broom, and L. S. Cottrell, eds., *Sociology Today, Volume 1: Problems and Prospects.* New York: Harper and Row, 1959.
104. Powell, J. W. *Education for Maturity: An Empirical Essay on Adult Group Study.* New York: Hermitage House, 1949.
105. Reid, C. "Preaching and Small Groups." In J. C. Casteel, ed., *The Role of the Interpersonal Group in the Church Today.* New York: Association Press, 1968.

106. Rice, A. K. *Learning for Leadership*. London: Tavistock Publications, 1966.
107. Rogers, C. R. "The Process of the Basic Encounter Group." In J. F. Bugental, ed., *Challenges of Humanistic Psychology*. New York: McGraw-Hill, 1967.
108. Ruesch, J., and Bateson, G. *Communication, The Social Matrix of Psychiatry*. New York: Norton, 1951.
109. *San Francisco Chronicle*. August 29, 1968.
110. Sata, L. S., and Derbyshire, R. C. "Group Process, T-Groups and Sensitivity Training: A Demonstration of the Living Laboratory." Mimeographed. College Park, Md.: Psychiatric Institute, University of Maryland, 1967.
111. Schecter, D. E. "The Integration of Group Therapy with Individual Psychoanalysis." *Psychiatry* 22: 267–276, 1959.
112. Schutz, W. D. *Joy: Expanding Human Awareness*. New York: Grove Press, 1967.
113. Schutz, W. D., and Allen, V. L. "The Effects of a T-Group Laboratory on Interpersonal Behavior." *Journal of Applied Behavioral Science* 2: 265–286, 1966.
114. Shapiro, R. "Innovative Group Experience." Paper presented at Mid-Atlantic Group Psychotherapy Meeting, Fall, 1968, at Sheraton-Park Hotel, Washington, D.C.
115. Shostrom, E. "Group Therapy: Let the Buyer Beware." *Psychology Today* 2 (No. 12): 36–40, 1969.
116. Slavson, S. R. *A Textbook in Analytic Group Psychotherapy*. New York: International Universities Press, 1964.
117. Smith, P. B. "Attitude Changes Associated with Training in Human Relations." *British Journal of Social and Clinical Psychology* 2: 104–112, 1964.
118. Spotnitz, H. *The Couch and the Circle*. New York: Knopf, 1961.
119. Stanton, A. H., and Schwartz, M. S. *The Mental Hospital*. New York: Basic Books, 1954.

120. Stock, D. A. "A Survey of Research on T-Groups." In L. P. Bradford, J. R. Gibb, and K. D. Benne, eds., *T-Group Theory and Laboratory Method*. New York: Wiley, 1964.

121. Stock, D. A., and Thelen, H. A. "Emotional Dynamics and Group Culture." In M. Rosenbaum and M. Berger, eds., *Group Psychotherapy and Group Function*. New York: Basic Books, 1963.

122. Stoller, F. H. "The Long Weekend." *Psychology Today* 1 (No. 7): 28–33, 1967.

123. Sullivan, H. S. *The Interpersonal Theory of Psychiatry*. New York: Norton, 1953.

124. Tavistock Institute of Human Relations, Washington School of Psychiatry. Brochure. Washington, D.C., 1968.

125. Taylor, F. K. *The Analysis of Therapeutic Groups*. London: Oxford University Press, 1961.

126. Thelen, H. A. *Dynamics of Groups at Work*. Chicago: University of Chicago Press, 1954.

127. Thomas, H. F. "An Existential Attitude in Working with Individuals and Groups." In J. F. Bugental, ed., *Challenges of Humanistic Psychology*. New York: McGraw-Hill, 1967.

128. Tirnauer, L. "Innovative Group Experiences." Paper presented at Mid-Atlantic Group Psychotherapy Meeting, Fall, 1968, at Sheraton-Park Hotel, Washington, D.C.

129. Tirnauer, L. "Encounter Group Workshops." Brochure. Washington, D.C., 1969.

130. UMALE. Anderson Research Foundation. Brochure. Los Angeles, Calif., 1968.

131. Van Dellen, T. R. In a syndicated column on medical problems. *New York Daily News*, 1967.

132. Watts, A. W. *Psychotherapy: East and West*. New York: Ballantine Books, 1961.

133. Whitaker, D. S., and Lieberman, M. A. *Psychotherapy Through Group Process*. New York: Atherton Press, 1964.

134. Wolf, A., and Schwartz, E. K. *Psychoanalysis in Groups*. New York: Grune and Stratton, 1962

Index

Behavior
  choice within the group, 208
  conceptualizing, 197–200
  deviant, 229
  goal-directed, 201
  interpreting to the group, 149–150
  motivation, 206
  of participants outside the group,
    163–164
  overdetermined participant, 175
  passive-aggressive participant, 199
Bennis, W. G., 284
Berne, Eric, 134, 178, 216, 217
Bernstein, A., 64
Berzon, Betty, 57
Bettelheim, B., 229
Bion
  W. R., 38, 40, 76, 99–100, 106–115,
    116, 183, 199, 206, 233, 288
  method, 38–41, 99–101
Blake, R. R., 32, 104
Blanck, G., 185
Blum, E. M., and R. H., 24
Blumer, H., 28
Body language, 42
Boring, Edwin, 198
Bradford, L. P., 98
Buchanan, P. C., 282
Burke, R. L., 284

Campbell, J. P., 282, 284, 285
Cantril, H., 29
Carlson, G., 285
Casteel, J. C., 22, 24, 33–34, 97
Catharsis, use of, 102–104
Clark, J. V., 80, 284
The Clouds (Aristophanes), 102
Cognitive system, 209
Cohen, R. A., 246
Consultant, the, 35–36, 39, 40–41, 44,
  45, 48, 51, 64, 67, 69, 70, 82–87,
  91–92, 106, 113–114, 127, 153, 173–
  195

as participant, 182
as role-model, 153
counter-transference and, 193–195
directive, 188–189
function of, 172, 183, 200
interpretation, 185
intervention of, 183
non-directive, 189–190
responsibilities of, 188
techniques of, 164–165
see also Behavior; Group; Techniques
Corsini, R., 37
Cottle, Tom, 71–72
Crutchfield, R., 201
Culbert, Sam, 40, 284

Demonstration
  see Techniques, demonstration
Dependency groups, 113–114
Depersonalization, 243
Derbyshire, R. C., 282
Dewey, John, 96
Director
  see Consultant
Discomfort
  see Group, discomfort, function of
Discussion groups, 56
Divorcees Anonymous, 24
Drama, therapeutic use of, 102–103
Dunnett, M., 282, 284, 285

Ego, surrender to the group
  see Group, ego-surrender to
Eisenhower, D. 25
Eliot, T. S., 21
Elridge, S., 28
Encounter
  groups, 42, 45–48, 50, 53, 54, 71,
    203, 210–211
  Tapes, 57
Enneis, J., 168

336

Esalen
approach, 53–55
Association, 279
Institute, 54–55
Evergreen Institute, 42
Exline, R. V., 284
Experience in Groups (Bion), 110–115
Ezriel, Henry, 35, 115–116, 250

Fear, participant
of exploitation, 258–259
of injury, 258–259
Festinger, L., 130, 140, 238
Fight-flight, 109
Fine, L., 45
Fisher, S., 241
Foulkes, S. H., 125, 152, 187, 224, 249
Frank, J. D., 178
French, Thomas, 116
Freud
Anna, 191
Sigmund, 106–107, 239
Fried, Marc, 23

Gage, N. L., 284
Gassner, S., 284
German Military Psychology Corps, 100
Gestalt groups, 42, 44–45, 53, 81, 131
Gibb, J. R., 53–54
Gibran, Kahil, 228
Glaser, A., 53
Goffman, E., 125
Goldstein, J. W., 285
Grater, H., 284
Greening, T. C., 87, 88–89
G-responses, 249
Group
alienation, 263–264
anger, 229
assumptions, basic, 113–115
attention, participants' need for, 220

behavior, Bion's interpretation of, 11
collusion, 233–235
competition, 267–268
consensual validation, 242–244
dependency, 123, 252–253
discomfort, function of, 187
dynamics movement, 97
ego-surrender to, 237
entity, 177, 179–180
estrangement, 263–264
first meeting of, 110–111
flight from confrontation, 265–266
forces, 112
frustration, 158–159
guilt, 255
hostility, 256–257
leader
see Consultant
leadership, 231–232
mentality, 238–239
Bion's concept of, 112
mood, 250
narcissism, 253–255
pairing, 257–258
participants as separate individuals, 178
pathology, 228–230
polarity, 232
process, 108–109, 223–224
role-playing, 161–163, 202–203
silence, 246–248
size, 181
subgroups, 177
tasks, 144–146
tension, 35, 116–118
themes, 251–252
types of
see Groups, types of
Groups, types of
application, 69, 170–172
basic encounter, 48–49
dependency, 113–114

337

James, William, 96
Jourard, S. M., 166

Kadis, A. L., 249
Kassajian, H. H., 285
Kelly, G. A., 105, 208
Kennedy, John F., 41
Kernan, J. P., 285
Khrushchev, Nikita, 41
Killian, Lewis M., 287
Klein, M., 106–107
Krasner, J. D., 249
Krech, D., 201
Kries, Ernest, 87

Laing, R., 205
Laubach, E. E., 224
Leader, group
  see Consultant
Leaderless groups, 56–58, 71
Lecky, P., 206
Lennard, H. L., 64
Lewin, Kurt, 93, 97–98, 131
Lieberman, M. A., 116–118, 250, 251
Lippitt, Ronald, 98, 104, 262
Locke, N., 178
Lohman, K., 284
Luchins, A. S., 42
Lurie, Leon, 44, 45

Mann, J., 123
Marathon groups, 42, 43–44, 45
Masochism, 217–218
Masserik, F., 285
Mayo, Elton, 97
McCann, D. L., 61
McLuhan, Marshall, 33
McNair, M. P., 93–94
Meerloo, J. A., 241, 243, 244
Metacommunication, 211

Methods
  see Groups, types of; Sensitivity
    Training Groups; Techniques
Milieu, 102
  therapy, 102–104
Miller, Michael, 43, 102, 103
Moreno, J. L., 26, 41, 42, 90, 100, 103–104
Mouton, Jane S., 55
Mullan, H., 274

Narcissism, 218–220
National Training Laboratories
  see Institute of Applied Behavioral
    Research
Neurotics Anonymous, 24
Newcombe, T. M., 238
Nonverbal signals
  see Participant, nonverbal signals

Odiorne, G., 93
Orizon Institute, 55
Oshry, B. I., 284

Pairing in the group, 257–258
Parloff, M. B., 178, 179, 180, 239
Parsimony, 176
Parsons, T., 119, 199
Participant
  anger, 229
  core attitudes, 208, 209, 210
  criteria for, 273–275
  dependency, 108
  discomfort, function of, 187
  disturbed, the, 270
  fear
    of exploitation, 258–259
    of injury, 258–259
  interpersonal
    accommodation, 23, 132–141
    transference, 204–205